George Dobson

Russia's Railway Advance into Central Asia

George Dobson

Russia's Railway Advance into Central Asia

ISBN/EAN: 9783741118135

Manufactured in Europe, USA, Canada, Australia, Japa

Cover: Foto ©Andreas Hilbeck / pixelio.de

Manufactured and distributed by brebook publishing software (www.brebook.com)

George Dobson

Russia's Railway Advance into Central Asia

RUSSIA'S RAILWAY ADVANCE

INTO

CENTRAL ASIA

*NOTES OF A JOURNEY FROM ST. PETERSBURG
TO SAMARKAND*

BY

GEORGE DOBSON,

AUTHOR OF THE LETTERS IN THE "TIMES" ON "THE CENTRAL ASIAN RAILWAY."

ILLUSTRATED.

LONDON
W. H. ALLEN & CO., 13, WATERLOO PLACE
AND AT CALCUTTA

1890

PREFACE.

THE present volume is the outcome of a journey from St. Petersburg to Samarkand in the spring of 1888, on the occasion of the opening of railway communication with the ancient city of Tamerlane, and of a series of letters published in the *Times* in the autumn of the same year, giving the first English description of the Central Asian Railway. I have been encouraged to return to the subject in the form of a separate publication by the advice of many readers of my letters, and by the use made of them by other authors. Not more than eight of the following fifteen chapters appeared in the *Times*, and these have been so completely rewritten, altered and amplified, that they contain a large amount of fresh, and, I hope, interesting information. The remaining seven chapters are entirely new, and bring the account of the Transcaspian province down to the present time.

Preface.

While I have certainly not neglected the political side of the subject and the question of Anglo-Russian relations, I have not written from the exclusively political point of view. It has always seemed to me that prejudice and confusion of ideas about Russia are due in a very great measure to this purely political treatment.

An impartial book of a general character, such, for instance, as Schuyler's "Turkistan," which in my opinion has not been superseded by any subsequent work, may be more useful in helping Englishmen to draw their own political conclusions than many of the writings of professional politicians and journalists. This merit, at least, I hope, I may claim for the results of my own humble efforts.

Such information as I have been able to obtain is from purely Russian and mostly new sources. My best thanks are due to many friends in Russia and the Transcaspian,—to General Annenkoff, Colonel Alikhanoff, Prince Gagarine, Dr. Heyfelder, Mr. Rodzevitch and others, who have kindly furnished me with maps, photographs, and information, and otherwise given their assistance.

I believe I have been able to follow a somewhat new line of interest connecting St. Petersburg with Samarkand, Moscow with India, and the Cossacks with the Turkomans, as links in the chain which binds Russia to Central Asia, and has naturally drawn her onward in that direction. The chapter on trade also offers a new aspect of the subject, which has hitherto been overlooked.

I should feel sorry if Russian friends attributed anything I may have written to malice or Russophobia. My attachment to their country, and the rule of impartiality which I have always endeavoured to apply to my journalistic duties, ought to be sufficient proof against any such assumption. It would be equally unjust if English readers concluded from my residence in Russia that I have become in the least indifferent to the danger involved in Russia's railway advance into Central Asia.

G. DOBSON.

ST. PETERSBURG,
April, 1890.

CONTENTS.

CHAPTER I.

INTRODUCTORY.

PAGE

Hasty completion and opening of the Central Asian Railway—The first locomotive whistle heard in Samarkand—Climax to the Russian tide of conquest—General Annenkoff's triumph—International inauguration of the railway—Foreign guests—First Englishman to enter Samarkand by railway—Difficulties of obtaining permission — Opposition to Annenkoff's desire to throw open the railway to the general public—Invitation to Professor Vambéry cancelled by the Diplomatists—Objections to foreigners, especially Englishmen—Excursions to the Afghan frontier forbidden—Authorization required to visit the railway—Authorities to be applied to—Favours to Frenchmen—Permission granted to few Englishmen—Many applicants refused—Russia's imitation of the ostrich in the Transcaspian Sands—What she is probably afraid of—Asiatic suspicion of character—Russia conquers in Asia by affinity of character as well as by force of arms—Author's application for permission—Necessity for approval of the Governor-General of Turkistan—His semi-independent jurisdiction—Strange multiplicity of authorities concerned in granting permission—Telegram to General Rosenbach—Starting without permission—The most direct routes to the Transcaspian—Projected railways to the Caspian and Persian frontier 1

x   *Contents.*

CHAPTER II.
MOSCOW AND INDIA.

Railway travelling beyond Moscow—Finger-posts pointing to the East—Moscow's connection with the object of my journey—Comparisons between St. Petersburg and Moscow—Nondescript character of Moscow—Its commercial influence—It sets the business fashion — St. Petersburg: Russia's European disguise — Moscow : the heart of Russia, and the mainstay of relations with the East and the Central Asian Railway—Prominent commercial importance now given to the Russian railway advance—Englishmen first endeavour to reach India overland through Moscow —Voyage of Richard Chancellor—Journey of Anthony Jenkinson — Sir John Merrick's negotiations for a transit through Muscovy to India—We incite the Muscovites to independent efforts towards India—Peter the Great—Jonas Hanway—Napoleon—England's abortive attempts to arrest Russia's movements —More reasonable policy—Useless criticism of new Afghan boundary—The danger lies in the inherent faults of Asiatic rule in Afghanistan—Russia's complaints of Abdurahman Khan misconstrued—England has no control over Afghan Ameer—Baron Jomini's suggestion of a permanent frontier Commission—Would not the Russians step into Afghan Turkistan as they walked into Kuldja?—Justifiable opinion that England will never fight over Afghanistan—Dangers and uncertainties of North-Eastern frontier—Probable repetition of troubles of 1885 if this part neglected—Russian explorers already at work . . 23

CHAPTER III.
THE COSSACKS.

The most remarkable phenomenon of the Slavonic race—Numbers and territories of the Cossacks—Dress and

Contents. xi

PAGE

equipment—Railways through the Cossack provinces
—Historical interest and character of the Cossack
steppes—Cossack aversion to trees—Reafforestation
—Herodotus on the absence of wood—Coal-fields of
the Don—Their output—Successful competition of
English coal—Coal, wood, and petroleum fuel on
Russian railways—Novotcherkask, the modern Cossack capital—Starotcherkask, the ancient capital—
Cossack regalia and charters—English sword of
honour presented to a Cossack Ataman—The Cossack
in Europe—Cossack colonizers abroad—The Cossack
in Asia—Cossacks selected to attack India—Important extension of Cossack territory—Cossack dislike
to trade—Cossack administration—Cossack organization on the Don out of date—Ineffectual attempts to
level the Cossacks with the Russians—Turkoman
Cossacks—Cossacks of the Kooban and Terek—
Resemblances between Cossacks and Circassians—
Russia glides imperceptibly into Asia—No sharp distinctions—A Russian on his experiences in Central
Asia—Easy fraternization between Russians and
Asiatics—The Cossack an instrument of *rapprochement*—Cossacks and Circassians merge into Turkomans—Colonel Alikhanoff, remarkable specimen of
Russian and Asiatic combined—Absorption of Kalmucks and Kirghiz by Cossack cavalry—Russia's
power of assimilation and coalescence—Carlyle's
opinion—Vladikavkaz—Pretentiousness of Russian
names—Amiability of Russian railway travellers—
Annenkoff's invitations and guests. 48

CHAPTER IV.

THROUGH THE CAUCASUS TO THE CASPIAN.

Sharp interchanges of climate and temperature—Snow-
slips and accidents—Rapid posting with a Russian

xii *Contents.*

PAGE

Consul—Lermontoff's dispute between Elburz and Kazbek—False alarm—The Georgian military road—The gorge and pass of Dariel—The Terek—Parting of the waters—Desolate scenery of the northern slopes—Primitive dwellings—The Ossetins—"Mountain of tongues"—Ruined towers and castles—Tamara, the Cleopatra of the Caucasus—Kazbek—English climbers—Descent into the valley of the Aragua—Beauty of the Transcaucasus—Boast of the Georgians—Towers of refuge—Game—The Koora—Illusory notion of the Caucasus being a weak spot in Russia's armour—Similar idea of Armenian frontier—English and Russian influence among the Turkish Armenians—Russia's use of the religious element in conquering the Caucasus—England's contrary policy of assisting the Mohammedans—English mistake in this connection during Crimean War—Overdrawn reports of disaffection during Afghan frontier crisis—English hopes of utilizing it, and awkward habit of giving warning—Similar reports of English sympathies among the coast population of Finland—Simply a question of compulsory military service—How settled—Overrated separatist tendencies of "Young Georgia"—The Tsar's visit—Loyalty of the Caucasus—Highway robbery and brigandage—A Circassian Dick Turpin—Circassians running amuck—Unbridled temper of the natives—Insignificant religious antagonism—The Russian's faculty of identifying himself with the Asiatic—Conversation with General Zelennoi—Departure from Tiflis—Valley of the Koora—Resemblances between the Apsheron peninsula and the Transcaspian—Russified Persians—Arrival at Baku—Taken in charge by the police—Delayed for want of a steamer—Interview with the Governor Baku—The Transcaspian Railway flooded—Baku fair—Start for Oozoon Ada—Foreigners and ¦English steamers on the Caspian—Poles in the Transcaspian—Their grievances—A Polish rebel . . . . [75

CHAPTER V.

OOZOON ADA AND KRASNAVODSK.

Arrival at Oozoon Ada — Wretched Aspect—Delay—Floods—Interrupted communication—Description of town—Buildings and population—Shipping firms—Sand storms—Silting up of harbour—Inundations—No fresh water—Description of seaboard—Labyrinth of salt lagoons—Long Island—Dardja peninsula—Ancient channels and delta of the Amu Darya—Proposed restoration of old bed of the Oxus, now practically useless except for irrigation — General Glookhofsky's project and opinion—Dangerous proximity of railway to the Persian frontier—Necessity of supplementary communication by water — Oozoon Ada versus Krasnavodsk — Commission on — The question shelved—Reasons for—Transference of railway terminus unnecessary —Effect of proposed branch line to Krasnavodsk—Arrival of train from Askabad—No first-class carriages—Extent of rolling stock—Special accommodation for Mohammedans . . 109

CHAPTER VI.

OOZOON ADA TO GEOK TEPÉ.

Departure from Oozoon Ada — Howling wilderness—Desolation—Persian *hamals*—Railway dam—Blood-red water—Kizil-Soo—Michailofsk : the original terminus—Bala Ishem—The Balkans—The Kuren and Kopet Dag mountains : lifeless appearance and Turkoman avoidance of—Fertility of their Persian slopes—Insignificant valleys and streams on Russian side—Rise of Tedjent and Murghab—The mountains relieve the sight, and supply the water—Failure of wells—Memorial of Skobeleff's march—Gradients—The salt steppe—Mirages—Ninety per cent. of desert—Fast and movable sands—"White earth," or *loess*—Proposed colonization and irrigation—Expected results—Old channels of the Oxus crossed by the railway—Former bottom of the sea—Naphtha Dag and petroleum supply—Kazandjik: the first freshwater source—Delays and damage caused by floods—Insufficiency of culverts—Easy construction of the line—Difficulties of the sand—Cuttings—Part of road re-made twenty times—Materials lost in the sand—Speed and cheapness of construction — Competition between General Annenkoff and the Minister of Communications—Effects of floods—Troubles and pastimes of Annenkoff's guests—Kizil Arvat: beginning of the Akhal Tekke oasis—Population—Fountains—Bami—Junction with the Atrek—Character of the oases—Turkoman *obas*—Towers of refuge—Salt, sand, and grass steppes—Saxaoul—Discomforts of the railway—Military control—Turkoman platelayers—Turkoman dress—Cossack justice—Persian navvies and porters—Russian tenderness for the Tekkes and dislike of the Persians—Persia and the Yomud and Goklan Turkomans—Russia claims them—Treatment of Persians—Official monopoly of railway accommodation—Fellow-passengers 128

CHAPTER VII.

GEOK TEPÉ TO MERV.

Arrival at Geok Tepé—The fortress—Disease—Removal of the Russian settlement—Siege and slaughter—Burning the dead—Skobeleff the "Split Beard"—Unjust criticism of Skobeleff—Dr. Heyfelder's opinion of—Author's acquaintance with Skobeleff—His typical Russian character—A great leader of men—His cruelty at Geok Tepé explained—Difference between his mode of warfare and the English method—Killing of women inexcusable—Mr. Marvin on the subject—

Contents.

PAGE

Remains of the Siege—Alleged neglect of the Turkomans to use their water supply against the Russians—Their chivalrous bravery—Osman Pasha's mistake repeated at the Turkoman Plevna—Arrival at Askabad—Akhal Tekke oasis—Giaours—Ak-soo—Artik—Luftobad—Its retention by Persia disapproved of by Skobeleff—Dooshak—Nearest point to the Afghan frontier—Future junction of Russian and Indian railways—Refusal to permit Englishmen to go to Kelat—Tedjent river and oasis—Sarakhs and Zulficar—Population and administration — Fever—Tigers, boars, lizards, and tortoises—Losing sight of the mountains—Camels—Their proposed introduction into Russia—Depilation of—Present style of caravan progression—Arrival at Merv—Delay—Merv station—Garden irrigation—No Native town—Russian town—Floods and draining—Koushut Khan Kala—Forced growth of business—Turkomans in the hands of Jews and Armenians—Attempt to bathe in the Murghab—The "Penjdeh sore"—Filters—A wash in a bath-house . 156

CHAPTER VIII.

MERV TO SAMARKAND.

Departure from Merv—Bairam Ali—Ruins of four cities—Woman's influence in the destruction of ancient, and capture of modern, Merv—Transcaspian Sahara—Abomination of desolation—General Tchernaieff's attacks and General Annenkoff's success—Moving sands—Intense heat—Refreshments—Improvised restaurant of trucks—The stations—Protection of rails from the sand—Saxaul and its uses—Wooden palisades—Wells—Abrupt termination and vagaries of the sand—Oasis of Chardjui—Russian Chardjui—Cutting in two of the railway bridge—Further detention—Night drill of Russian troops—Colonel Alikhanoff—A nice opening of the railway!—Reasons for cutting the bridge—It

Contents.

PAGE

breaks down—Description and cost of the bridges—Uncertain navigability of the Amu Darya—Its rapid current—M. Charikoff's voyage to Kerki—Dinner to Alikhanoff and the author—Farabia—Train of house-trucks—Repair of the bridge—My hut on wheels—The start over the river—Reception by the Bek of Chardjui—The festival-train—More sand—Kara Kul—A Bokharan bombardier—Arrival at Bokhara—Our reception by Generals Rosenbach and Annenkoff—Lunch—Bokharan guests refrain — Re-departure—Station of Bokhara—Valleys of Miankul and the Zerafshan—The "devil's wain"—Astonishment of Bokharans — Katta-Kurgan — Turkistan frontier — Arrival at Samarkand—Construction and condition of the railway—Annenkoff's reward—Cost and rapid building of the line—Defects :. culverts and weakness of the bridges—Important significance of the railway—General Prjevalsky's opinion 176

CHAPTER IX.

SAMARKAND.

Arrival at Samarkand, "the Face of the Earth"—Inauguration festivities—The station and the town—Situation of the city—Zarafshan River and Siob Canal—Gold-strewing—Russian town—Fortress and citadel—Coronation stone—Execution block—Contrast of Russian and native quarters—Russian and native art—Deterioration of native talent—Clumsy attempts at restoration—Military club and amusements—Orthodox temple—Site of Russian town—Native town and its ruins—Principal mosques and colleges—The shepherd saint—Mausoleum of Shah Zindeh—Legend concerning Kazim-ben-Abbas—His tomb—Mohammedan votaries—Bibi Khanum College — Slanting minarets—Tamerlane's tomb—Kala Afrosiab—Oldest

Contents. xvii

irrigation canal in the world—Valley of the Siob aryk —Primitive mills—Tomb of a giant prophet—Alikhanoff in the mosques—Jews and Hindoos—Population. 203

CHAPTER X.

SAMARKAND TO BOKHARA.

Departure from Samarkand—Our Anglo-French Embassy —Impressions on a Russian railway through foreign territory—Russia's careful absorption of Bokhara— Numbers and particulars of Russian and native troops— Russia holds the key of Bokhara's existence—Quarrels over water, and their consequences—Water police— Water as a measure of wealth and position—Schemes and difficulties of irrigation—Valley of the Zarafshan— The "fire devil"—Origin of the name of Samarkand —Russo-Bokharan frontier—Resemblance and difference between the two conquests under Alexander of Macedon and Alexander of Russia—Kerminé—The "Father of Bokhara"—Arrival at the station of Bokhara—Bad accommodation—We retain our housecar—Journey to the capital—Native carts—Electricity in Ameer's palace—"Shaitan feringhee"—Contempt for Europeans—Gates and walls of the city—Difficulties of progression—Conolly's fate—An Englishman photographs the Ameer's lunatics — Russian Embassy—Influence and abilities of M. Charikoff and his secretary — Native women—Various races and their dress—Jews—Persian shiites—Bokharan sunnites, Orthodox Russians and Russian Tartars— Arrival at Embassy—The *dostarkhan*—Ablutions— Doctor Heyfelder—A Russian ambulance—Disease and rate of mortality—Hospitality of the Ameer and Russian Embassy—Ameer's presents—Ambassador's establishment 226

xviii   *Contents.*

CHAPTER XI.

THE CITY OF BOKHARA.

Stay in the capital—Civilities of the Russian Embassy—
Inadvisability of going about unattended—Necessity
of a guide—Ameer's chamber of horrors—Visit to the
prison—Its inmates and filthy interior—The sheep-
tick dungeon and black hole—Conolly's subterranean
cell now closed—Manner of feeding prisoners—
Kalian minaret : a place of execution ; ascent of by
an Englishman—Ameer's palace and clocks—Official
visit to the Ameer's Minister of Commerce—Our procession through the streets—Bokharan guard of honour
—Reception by the Minister—More sweetmeats—
Pilaff and Tea—Conversation on trade—Diplomatic
answers—Inspection of the guard of honour—Objections to making presents—The reshta worm—Dr.
Heyfelder's experiments—Spurious Bokharan postage
stamps—Russian and native transmission of correspondence—Ameer's absence from the Railway inauguration—Opening of the line to Bokhara, and
invasion of the capital by Russians and Turkomans—
Assassination of the Divan Begi—*Lex talionis*, and
torture of the assassin—Ameer's executioners—Originality and population of the city   251

CHAPTER XII.

BOKHARA TO MERV.

Departure from Bokhara—Breakdown of the Amu Darya
bridge—Descent into a barge—Boundary between
Iran and Turan—Hardships of Russian Expeditions
—Difficulties and dangers abolished by the Railway
—Peter the Great's instructions—Expeditions under
Tcherkasky and Bucholtz—Peter's efforts to open up
roads to India—His apocryphal testament—Perofsky's
failure—Successes of Kaufmann and Tchernaieff—

Contents. xix

Peter the Great's dream realized—Speed and method of constructing the Railway — Comparisons with American construction—The Railway's receipts and traffic—Arrival at Merv — Welcomed by Colonel Alikhanoff — The Governor's house — Turkoman carpets—Alikhanoff's escort—Bathing—Snakes in the Murghab—Origin of the river's name—Alikhanoff's trophies—Relics of the disastrous English retreat on the Koushk—A Turkoman Khan's opinion of the English, Russians, and Afghans—Introduced to the Khans of Merv—Alikhanoff and his Turkoman subordinates 275

CHAPTER XIII.

MERV AND THE TURKOMANS.

Russian Merv—Chardjui—Mr. Marvin on personal aspect of the situation — Alikhanoff's importance, career, origin, and appearance—His swordmanship in play and earnest—He reminds me of Skobeleff—Wardenship of the Marches—Reception of Salors—Alielis—Yomuds—Contrast between Alikhanoff and Komaroff — Alikhanoff as magistrate — Turkoman militia — Alikhanoff's satellites—Turkomanland, a place of exile—Exiles and adventurers—Afghans—Circassians banished to the Transcaspian—Banquet by Yellow Khan—Native dining and smoking — The "earth pipe"—The Khan takes strong drink—Mahommedan tricks to save appearances—Tekke women—Female acts of belligerency — Photographing the harem—Alikhanoff's tutelage of Turkomans—Departure from Merv—Extent of territory and population—Foreign elements in the majority—Administration—Elders and greybeards—Justice—Native punishment—Authority of the Khans—Fiscal, commercial, and agricultural figures—Imports and exports — Religion, customs, and immorality—Military importance of Turkomania,

xx   *Contents.*

PAGE

and commercial aspect of Bokhara—Former opinions concerning the Turkomans—Mr. Veniukoff and Mr. Palgrave—Neglect of Turkomans by England, Turkey, and Persia—Russia's policy towards the Cossacks—Persian Cossacks—The Turkomans became marauders from necessity—Turkoman character—Hardships in the Kara Kum—Water difficulties—Underground reservoirs and water-caverns—Origin and development of the Tekkes—Comparisons with the Cossacks—Turkoman *aul* and Cossack *sietch*—Prisoners—Hadji Baba—Tekkes and Cossacks as slave-owners and raiders—Cossack Ataman and Turkoman Khan—Turkoman *aiaman* and Cossack *nabieg*—Dissimilarities—The Cossack link—Reasons for not enrolling the Turkomans as Cossacks—Calmuck Cossacks—Proposed Cossack colonies — Natural Turkoman-Cossack organization—Mahommedan militia in the Caucasus—History of the Tekkes for 300 years—Their conquest of the Akhal oasis—The Jews of Nookhoor—Turkomans as Russian troops—Skobeleff's opinion—Intrigues and denunciations—Askabad —Meeting with General Komaroff—Return to Baku .   291

CHAPTER XIV.

THE RAILWAY AND TRADE.

British alarms at the commercial success of the Railway — Exaggerations and contradictions — Facts overlooked—Brilliant future—Big talk—Increased traffic not all increase of trade—Tapping the old land routes —Falling off of Asiatic business at Nijni—Baku fair —Mr. Ivanoff's opinion—Political and commercial centre of gravity—General Tchernaieff's desert tract through the Ust Urt—Inconvenience of military railway management—Annenkoff's eye to business—His personal supervision of the line—Mistaken notion of the recency of Russia's conquest of the Bokharan

Contents. xxi

PAGE

market—Reversal of business methods—Opinions of
Messieurs Grigorieff and Petrofsky—Indian tea trade
—Russian and Persian figures—Indian testimony—
Bad effect of Abdurahman's attitude towards England
—Interruption of trade by Afghan troubles—English
muslins—Russian and British trade in Khorassan—
English cottons at Tabriz—Turban cloths—Former
blunders of British merchants—Russian sugar monopoly—Overturn of Bokharan trade—Messieurs Petrofsky, Krestofsky, and Heyfelder on — Will the
increase last?—Speculation and loss—Bad wares—
Mr. F. Law on Russian speculation in Persia—A
German's enterprize in Afghanistan—Export of sheep's
gut for sausages—Bokharan sheep in Russia—A *coup*
in sugar—Russian statistics, how obtained—Russian
and Bokharan trade with Afghanistan—Figures for
1887 and 1888—Apparent superiority of Anglo-Indian
trade—Figures for 1889—Deductions from—Balance
of trade on the side of Afghanistan—India's participation in the overplus—Latest figures—Exports into
Afghanistan conveyed by natives—Decline of Orenburg—Central Asian cotton—Cotton cultivation on
the Murghab 365

CHAPTER XV.

CONCLUSION.

History of the Railway — Technical details — General
Annenkoff, Prince Khilkoff, and Colonel Shebanoff—
Cost of construction—Traffic receipts—Financial suc-
cess—Proposed extension to Tashkent and Omsk—
Effect of more direct extension to Orenburg—Isola-
tion of Transcaspian line—Proposed lines to the
Caspian and the Transcaucasus — Vladikavkaz-
Petrofsk—Necessity of direct railway communication
with the Caspian—Inconveniences of the Volga and
Georgian Road—Proposals for joining the railways

xxii   *Contents.*

PAGE

of the Cis- and Trans-caucasus—Projected lines of
Vladikavkaz-Petrofsk and Tsaritsin-Petrofsk—General
Annenkoff on the strategical importance of his Railway against India—Incorrect notion of the centre of gravity having been shifted—Importance of Turkistan in Afghan frontier affairs—New independent administration in the Transcaspian—Personal changes—Retirement of General Komaroff — Alikhanoff—General Kouropatkin—Appointment of M. Sessar to Bokhara—His opinion of Abdurahman — Military train service—Strategical position of Merv station—Proposal to refill old bed of Oxus from Chardjui—Station of Bokhara—Steam navigation on the Amu Daria—Projected canal—Kara Koul wine—Dimissal of the Khans of Merv 403

Appendix   . 437

LIST OF ILLUSTRATIONS.

1. Arrival of the First Train at the Station of Samarkand . . . . . . *Frontispiece.*
   PAGE
2. Tiflis 78
3. Georgian Military Road at Ananoor . . 88
4. General View of the Station of Geok Tepé . . 158
5. Ruined Mosque near Askabad . . . 166
6. Railway Bridge across the Amu Daria . . 188
7. The Tomb of Tamerlane . . 220
8. A Street in Bokhara . . . 254
9. Turkomans drinking Yellow Tea . . 326
10. Tekke Turkoman Ploughing . . 334

MAPS.

1. Existing and Projected Railways between Europe and Asia 22
2. Central Asian Railway in relation to the Afghan Frontier 38
3. The Russian Central Asian Railway . . . 110

RUSSIA'S RAILWAY ADVANCE

INTO

CENTRAL ASIA.

CHAPTER I.

INTRODUCTORY.

Hasty completion and opening of the Central Asian Railway — The first locomotive whistle heard in Samarkand — Climax to the Russian tide of conquest — General Annenkoff's triumph — International inauguration of the railway — Foreign guests — First Englishman to enter Samarkand by railway — Difficulties of obtaining permission — Opposition to Annenkoff's desire to throw open the railway to the general public — Invitation to Professor Vambéry cancelled by the Diplomatists — Objections to foreigners, especially Englishmen — Excursions to the Afghan frontier forbidden — Authorization required to visit the railway — Authorities to be applied to — Favours to Frenchmen — Permission granted to few Englishmen — Many applicants refused — Russia's imitation of the ostrich in the Transcaspian Sands —

Russia's Railway Advance.

What she is probably afraid of—Asiatic suspicion of character—Russia conquers in Asia by affinity of character as well as by force of arms—Author's application for permission—Necessity for approval of the Governor - General of Turkistan — His semi-independent jurisdiction — Strange multiplicity of authorities concerned in granting permission—Telegram to General Rosenbach—Starting without permission—The most direct routes to the Transcaspian —Projected railways to the Caspian and Persian frontier.

SHORTLY before the fifth anniversary of the coronation of the present Tsar, the 27th of May, 1888, General Annenkoff determined, with his characteristic energy, that the final section of the Central Asian Railway to Samarkand should be rapidly completed, and officially opened for traffic on that auspicious day. It seemed hardly possible to finish all the remaining work by so early a date, but the "Russian Lesseps" was equal to the task, and the last verst or two of rails were laid down with such headlong precipitancy, that there was not enough time to secure all the bolts and fastenings before the whistle of the first locomotive was heard by the astonished natives, echoing through the crumbling ruins of Samarkand. In the meantime the indefatigable constructor issued a number of invitations to attend the fêtes in cele-

Introductory.

bration of this great achievement, which was to unite the world of Western Europe with the very heart of Central Asia.

It was no ordinary feat to have forged this iron link through hitherto all but impassable deserts between the silence and conservatism of the venerable city and tomb of the great Asiatic Conqueror, and the restlessness and resistless advance of modern European life and civilization. There could scarcely have been a more fitting climax to that tide of conquest, which, after the lapse of many generations had reversed its direction, and flowing back from West to East, had reached, a little more than twenty years before, the ancient capital of Sogdiana. The civilization of the West was now to set its seal upon that which had been secured to it by force of arms, and that promoter and carrier of civilization—the railway—was to render easy of access one of the most renowned cities of the ancient world. In achieving this important result, General Annenkoff had triumphed not only over natural obstacles, but also over Russian inertia and official opposition; and his success had been so signal and instructive that, in the opinion of a French traveller, expressed before the

Russia's Railway Advance.

Geographical Society of Paris, the construction of a similar railway through the Great Sahara was now only a question of time.

As soon as it became known that General Annenkoff intended to give to the inauguration of the railway the character of an international, and not exclusively Russian event, I felt an ardent desire to join the fortunate party of foreign tourists, who had been invited to make this fascinating trip, and if possible to be one of the first Englishmen to travel by railway to Samarkand. I had long entertained a wish to make a closer acquaintance with the remarkable enterprise by which Russia, in spite of her backwardness in general, and the proverbial slowness and unprofitableness of her railway construction, had at last succeeded in surprising and interesting the world ; and here was a splendid opportunity of judging for myself how far the adverse criticisms of the work had been justified by the facts. In my eagerness to make this excursion I must, I fear, confess to having been animated with a somewhat similar spirit to that which must have possessed the eccentric Briton who is reported to have offered a large sum of money for the privilege of being the first passenger through the new St. Gothard tunnel ; but there

Introductory.

was no necessity for offering any premium in this case, as General Annenkoff, with an excusable pride in the offspring of his energy and perseverance, was only too willing to convey the first foreign visitors without even payment of the ordinary fare. Eventually, after some little difficulty, I was successful in performing the journey, and subsequently I learned from General Annenkoff that I had been the first Englishman to traverse the whole extent of the railway. Several fellow-countrymen had previously passed over parts of the unfinished line, but none before me had accomplished the entire railway journey to Samarkand.

The first question that arose was, should I be permitted to go? As an Englishman, and a keen observer of Russia's movements towards India, I was not without certain misgivings that political suspicion might be roused in the mind of some bureaucrat whose consent was necessary, and that difficulties would then be thrown in my way. The railway was a military one and under the control of the Minister for War; and although it was now to be opened to the public, this did not necessarily mean that unrestricted freedom of travelling over it was to be enjoyed by Englishmen and other foreigners indiscriminately. Even General Annenkoff's invitations were not all approved of in St. Petersburg, and I believe that the General is still at variance with the Diplomatic authorities on this point. He has always been most anxious to advertise his railway, and attract every possible kind of passenger, irrespective of nationality; for he fully appreciates the value of the receipts to be derived from foreign travellers, as well as from European and Asiatic commerce; but the Foreign Office and the Ministry of War, as might be expected, regard the matter from quite a different point of view.

One of General Annenkoff's invitations was intended for Professor Vambéry, the "false Dervish," who worked his dangerous and tedious way through the deserts now conquered by the railway, at a time when the bare idea of such an undertaking would have been scouted with derision. Nobody could have appreciated better than the celebrated Hungarian Orientalist the wonderful transformation which the Russians have already produced, and are still effecting, in those inhospitable regions; and had General Annenkoff been permitted to extend his hospitality to the learned Professor, the latter might perhaps have been induced to modify his well-

Introductory. 7

known bias against Russia. A generous endorsement of the invitation by the Russian diplomatists might have helped to turn a bitter foe into a useful friend, but the St. Petersburg Foreign Office thought differently, and would not agree to the proposal.

Nothing perhaps could better demonstrate the uncertainty and instability of affairs on the new frontier delimited by Colonels Ridgway and Kulberg, from the Russian point of view, than the jealousy with which the Transcaspian region is still guarded from the " evil eye " of Englishmen, and from the scrutiny of all foreigners who are suspected of not being the friends and admirers of Russia. Even foreigners, who are known to be friendly to Russia, are not expected to abuse their privilege of travelling over the Transcaspian railway by visiting any parts of the Afghan or Persian frontiers from the Russian side. This, at least, must be inferred from the report, that a reprimand had been administered to Colonel Alikhanoff for having assisted several Frenchmen to visit Penjdeh and Zulficar. In my case the authorities seemed anxious that I should not stray too far from any of the places along the line of railway; and some months later another Englishman, who started to cross the

Persian frontier in the direction of Meshed, was peremptorily requested to return to Askabad.* As soon as there is the least danger or spurt of revolt by some Asiatic adventurer or pretender, or the slightest movement of Afghan or Turkoman tribes near the border, the presence of Englishmen is sure to be unconditionally prohibited, as was shown in the case of a person highly recommended from London, whose request was refused on account of the commotion which followed the flight of Ishak Khan into Bokhara, and the appearance of Abdurahman Khan at Mazar-i-Sherif. Now that this perturbation among the frontier population has subsided, General Annenkoff maintains that everybody can go over the railway without any difficulty, though I doubt very much that the special permission hitherto required by the General's superiors could be dispensed with. This authorization will, no doubt, always depend to a great extent on circumstances and persons; but I am inclined to think that the restriction on foreign intrusion will be severely enforced from time to time, until that happy period when the Afghan Buffer shall be superseded by contiguous fron-

* One or two Englishmen have since been permitted, as a favour, to go this way to Meshed.

Introductory. 9

tiers, and the railways on both sides brought into junction.

The grounds on which permission to visit the railway is granted or refused, and the particular authorities who are entitled to decide the question, are very difficult to define. Matters of this kind are often likely to be decided more by the momentary influences of persons in power, than by any settled rules or regulations. In Russia there is little solidarity among Ministers and officials, and when a question has to be submitted to the decision of several of these "High Excellencies," an applicant may often have to relinquish all hope of obtaining a decided answer one way or the other. The authorities, whose concurrent approval appears to be necessary at present, are the Minister for War, the Governors-General of Turkistan and Transcaspia, M. de Giers, and the head of the Asiatic department, M. Zinovieff, but other dignitaries might at any moment claim to have a say in the matter.

Hitherto Frenchmen have been the most favoured guests over this railway, and the number of books in which they have recorded their impressions seemed to call for some independent English description, such as I hope to be able to give in the following pages. Common hatred of Germany, and sentimental coquetry between the two nations, have brought our Parisian friends into such fashionable repute among the Russians, that this in itself is almost enough to enable them to go where others are not admitted, or, if admitted at all, not altogether without reluctance. It happens also that General Annenkoff is connected by marriage with a well-known French family, and this will further explain why the guests at the festivities at Samarkand were mostly all Frenchmen. General Annenkoff is, in fact, the most popular Russian in France. A few Englishmen before and since have been permitted to visit the railway and its districts, but many applicants have met with refusal.

Considering the number of French books, already referred to, in which the railway has been fully described, it seems unaccountable that the Russians should continue to screen this consummation of their conquest with an exclusiveness almost Chinese. Besides published accounts, several British and Indian military and diplomatic officers have passed over the railway, and have, of course, reported on the subject to their respective departments; so

Introductory.

that everything about it must be known in the only quarters where the Russians might reasonably fear the consequences of such knowledge; in spite of which they seem to cherish the notion that their new territory is still a *terra incognita* to everybody but themselves, and act as if the allegiance of their new Turkoman subjects were liable to be undermined by the British tourist. There is perhaps just a dash of reason in their possible fear that a second Captain Burnaby, or another O'Donovan, possibly a British Ashinoff, might strike off from the railway to some vulnerable or disaffected corner of the Afghan or Persian frontiers, and, in certain propitious circumstances, excite the natives against Russian rule. I remember that when the Russian army stood round Constantinople in 1878, and the threatening British Fleet was lying anchored off the Princes' Islands, it was reported, rightly or wrongly, in the society of Pera, that some adventurous spirit among the temporary Turkophile colony of British subjects had suddenly disappeared into the Rhodope Mountains, and that the outbreak in the Russian rear was greatly assisted by this individual's encouragement. Perhaps the Russians are afraid of something similar occurring on their Transcaspian frontier. I am persuaded, however, that there is also a more general reason for this Russian imitation of the ostrich in the sands of the Transcaspian, and that is the natural distrustfulness of the Russian character—an element which seems to be ingrained by political education, or rather political suppression, which in Russia almost amounts to the same thing. The Russians naturally are only somewhat less suspicious of strangers than the Asiatics, whom they so easily conquer and assimilate. This is no imputation on the Russian character, as we find many eminent Russians, who have turned their attention towards the East, openly declaring that the similarity between the Russian and the Oriental constitutes one of their greatest natural advantages. In reality, Russia triumphs in her Asiatic provinces quite as much by affinity of character as by force of arms, and no one can properly understand Russia in Europe until he has seen Russia in Asia.

Regarding my own case in obtaining permission to visit Merv and Samarkand, I must observe that several months previously, when I wished to go over the new railway as far as it was then ready, General Annenkoff felt so sure

Introductory.

of my being met with a refusal, that he strongly advised me not to think of making an application; besides which, I received other verbal testimony of the feeling that then existed against allowing me to inspect the movements of Russia beyond the Caspian.

Notwithstanding these ill-omened prophecies and dissuasions, I was determined to try my luck with the select few who had been invited to assist at the inauguration of the Bokharan branch of the Transcaspian railway, or, at least, to follow closely on their heels. There was this much in my favour, that I was well known to the Russian authorities, whose record of me was, so to speak, a fairly clean one, extending over many years of residence in Russia as the representative of a great English newspaper, which nevertheless did not exempt me from what, I was told, were the usual formalities. These began with the intercession of the British Embassy, in the form of a prompt note from Sir Robert Morier to M. de Giers, which at once elicited the kind offices of M. Zinovieff at the head of the Asiatic Department, and that gentleman took the next step by submitting my name to the Minister for War. The War Minister in his turn then declared that he must first communicate with General Rosenbach at Tashkent or Samarkand.

It struck me as very strange that the War Minister should have to telegraph to his subordinate, the Governor-General of Turkistan, General Rosenbach, in order to procure the latter's consent to my journey through the much guarded Transcaspian, which is not even within the bounds of his jurisdiction.* Yet the approval of General Rosenbach was represented to me as absolutely necessary. In vain I observed that it was the Transcaspian that had hitherto been so jealously closed against foreigners, and not Turkistan, which includes Samarkand. Therefore, if General Rosenbach's consent was necessary for my visit to Samarkand, why was General Komaroff not also applied to for permission to visit Askabad and Merv? Apart from this, I was well aware that General-

* The question has since been seriously raised in St. Petersburg of detaching the Transcaspian province from the administration of the Caucasus under Prince Dondoukoff-Korsakoff, and of uniting it with the Government of Turkistan; but this change has not yet been effected, and there was no thought of it at the time I refer to, especially as a commission on this very subject had just decided that the province should either remain as it was, subject to the Caucasus, or be separated into an independent province under General Komaroff alone.

Introductory.

Adjutant Rosenbach was the chief in authority over the last section of the railway between the Amu-Daria and the Zerafshan, as this part of the line runs through the territory of Bokhara, which has always been politically under the control of the Governor-General at Tashkent. But I had previously been under the impression that the exclusively military rule and semi-independence of the Turkistan General-Governorship, which in the earlier times of Russian extension in Central Asia had been brought forward to excuse the unexpected movements of Kaufmann and others, had been all but abolished by the new civil organization of that province, after it had been superseded by the Transcaspian place of arms. By this reform, as I had understood it, the Turkistan province was considered to have completed the work of its almost irresponsible Governors-General in pushing forward frontiers so vainly imagined by England to be stationary or impassable, and while ceding this onerous function to its younger and more vigorous neighbour, the Transcaspian province under General Komaroff, it was gradually to fall into the ranks of the other Imperial provinces and become more dependent upon the central authorities in St. Petersburg. I had also formed the idea, that even the political supervision of Bokhara by the Governor-General of Turkistan, had now been changed by the appointment of a Diplomatic resident at the Ameer's capital, under the immediate direction of the Foreign Office on the Neva. The natural deduction from all this was, that the permission of the powers in St. Petersburg would be quite sufficient for my journey, unless it were a question of referring to General Komaroff of the Transcaspian, whose name, however, was not even mentioned. I soon found that I was altogether mistaken. Here was evidently another case of that complicated multiplicity of authorities, often in conflict with each other, which is a characteristic feature in the bureaucratic system of Russia. It was very clear that there had been no real introduction of the changes which I had heard so much about, and General Rosenbach seemed to be as independently powerful under the Emperor as ever had been any of his predecessors. Now that a Russian military railway cuts off the wedge formed by Bokhara between Turkistan and Transcaspia, he is more than ever the Yarim Padshah (half Emperor) or viceroy of the Ameer's country. Hence his consent was indispensable, although, as I was at once informed,

Introductory. 17

the higher authorities in St. Petersburg had not the least objection.

Accordingly a telegram was sent to General Rosenbach, and I had to wait for a reply. After waiting several days for the answer, I got tired of delay; and as time was getting short, I took the bull by the horns, and started off without any permission at all. There could be no doubt, I was assured, that it would eventually be granted, but the form had to be gone through all the same. This may appear to have been a bold and rather rash proceeding on my part; but while I could plainly see that there was no intention of forbidding me outright, there seemed to be a very strong desire that I should not go. I therefore started by the night train from Petersburg to Moscow without any kind of pass or document, and only armed with a verbal promise from the Asiatic Department, which was faithfully kept, that my permission should be telegraphed to me on the way as soon as it arrived.

The necessity, as long as it exists, of obtaining this authorization is the only reason that need take the traveller through St. Petersburg and Moscow on his way to Central Asia, unless he wishes to visit these places *en route*. The most direct road from London to the Transcaspian lies through Berlin, Odessa, Batoum, Tiflis, and Baku. Another way, which is presumably much longer, may be chosen *viâ* Constantinople, either by sea, or overland by the new Oriental express train from Paris. From St. Petersburg there are several ways of reaching the Caspian, all passing through the most interesting and picturesque parts of European Russia. One is by boat down the Volga, from Nijni Novgorod or Tsaritsin to Astrakhan, and thence into the Caspian; a second by railway to Baku, with a break in the railway communication of 135 miles over the Dariel Pass of the Caucasus between Vladikavkaz and Tiflis, which has to be traversed with post-horses; and a third by rail through the Crimea to Sevastopol, and thence by sea to either Novorosisk or Batoum. I selected the second route, as appearing, according to Russian maps, to be the most direct of the three. The Crimean route seemed one of the longest, and I naturally considered that quicker means of locomotion must necessarily be offered by the direct railways than by the steamboats on the Volga or the Black Sea. It seems, however, that a quicker passage can often be made on the river, in spite of triple the dis-

Introductory.

tance by water, as compared with the short voyage across the Caspian from the railway terminus at Baku. This does not say very much for the speed of Russian railways; but apart from the snail's pace of the trains beyond Moscow, the advantage in point of time of the water way from the railway terminus on the Volga down stream into the Caspian, is probably due to the unfortunate break between the Cis- and Trans-Caucasian railways.

The mountain road between these two railways can be traversed at the quickest in twenty hours, without stopping, except for a few minutes at each post station for change of horses. General Annenkoff, who does everything faster than anybody else in Russia, has done it in eighteen hours; but "His Energy" (Energeetchestvo), as he is called, instead of "His Excellency," travels with an escort of Cossacks like a Grand Duke, and brooks no delay. Ordinary mortals are often delayed here in the winter by the snow in the Pass, when navigation on the ice-bound Volga is impossible. On the other hand, the Volga route is available in spring, when the mountain road between the two railways is often rendered impassable for days together by the swollen torrents and floods.

Russia's communications in these parts will never be complete until the great Caucasian range is pierced by railway to Tiflis, or turned by a flank movement in railway construction from Vladikavkaz to the port of Petrofsk. The continuation of the Vladikavkaz line by 160 miles to the Caspian port of Petrofsk could be easily extended along the shore to Baku, another 227 miles, and so on to the Persian frontier, thus avoiding the mountains altogether.

The inhabitants of Tiflis, who feel themselves isolated by the main range of the Caucasus from the great centres and railway routes of Central Russia, are very anxious to have a railway through the mountains direct from Vladikavkaz; but as such a gigantic piece of work would cost at least forty millions of roubles, and necessitate the construction of sixty miles of railroad at a height of 3,000 feet, it is not likely to be undertaken for some time to come. For these reasons the flank movement has already been decided upon, and the Vladikavkaz and Petrofsk line will probably be the next important railway built in Russia. This will be easily continued round the Caspian to Derbent, Baku, and the Persian frontier, as the Caspian

Introductory.

littoral is not so steep and rugged as the coast of the Black Sea at the other end of the Caucasian range.

Another and more direct line is also being discussed, which would run from Tsaritsin on the Volga straight to Petrofsk, without touching the line from Rostoff to Vladikavkaz, thus providing a much shorter route from Moscow to the Caspian than the prolongation of the Vladikavkaz line. Either of these two lines would greatly shorten communication between the Russian central provinces and the Transcaspian, and would be of enormous commercial importance, not only for trade with Central Asia, but also with Persia. The approach of the Vladikavkaz-Petrofsk, or Tsaritsin-Petrofsk railway to the Persian frontier will, it is considered, increase the necessity of a Persian railway through Resht to Teheran; and when uninterrupted railway communication is once established between Moscow and the Persian capital, the Muscovite merchants and manufacturers hope to compete still more successfully than ever with their British rivals. They are quite aware that their railway advance on Persia would probably force on the realization of the projected English railway from the Persian Gulf to Ispahan, or the proposed German line through Asia Minor; but, according to their computation, which I have never been able to verify, because they omit to mention the starting point of the calculation, even in that case the lines referred to would give them the advantage of less railway communication by 400 miles as compared with their British and German competitors, irrespective of the sea voyage from London to Bender Bushir, and from Hamburg to Scutari. In any case, the necessity of linking the Transcaucasus and the Caspian to the rest of Russia by the construction of one or more of the railways described, has now become a matter of vital importance. Until this is done, the Transcaspian railway will remain isolated, and incapable of developing the full measure of its capacities.

CHAPTER II.

MOSCOW AND INDIA.

Railway travelling beyond Moscow—Finger-posts pointing to the East — Moscow's connection with the object of my journey — Comparisons between St. Petersburg and Moscow—Nondescript character of Moscow — Its commercial influence — It sets the business fashion—St. Petersburg : Russia's European disguise—Moscow : the heart of Russia, and the mainstay of relations with the East and the Central Asian Railway—Prominent commercial importance now given to the Russian railway advance—Englishmen first endeavour to reach India overland through Moscow—Voyage of Richard Chancellor—Journey of Anthony Jenkinson—Sir John Merrick's negotiations for a transit through Muscovy to India—We incite the Muscovites to independent efforts towards India—Peter the Great—Jonas Hanway—Napoleon—England's abortive attempts to arrest Russia's movements—More reasonable policy—Useless criticism of new Afghan Boundary—The danger lies in the inherent faults of Asiatic rule in Afghanistan—Russia's complaints of Abdurahman Khan misconstrued—England has no control over Afghan Ameer—Baron Jomini's suggestion of a permanent frontier Commission—Would not the Russians step into Afghan Turkistan as they walked into Kuldja?—Justifiable opinion that England will never fight over Afghanistan—Dangers and uncertainties of North-Eastern frontier — Probable repetition of troubles of 1885 if this part neglected—Russian explorers already at work.

ALTHOUGH I started from St. Petersburg, I felt that my long journey through Russia was really to begin at Moscow, where I expected to receive the necessary permission to proceed; besides which, the night express to Moscow is so much superior in speed to most of the trains beyond, that as a rule the failings of real Russian travelling begin to impress one only after leaving the old capital. The 403 miles to Moscow are traversed in fifteen hours, at the rate of about thirty miles an hour; whereas when I subsequently calculated the rate of progress over 1,652 miles from St. Petersburg to the foot of the Caucasus, including the comparatively rapid train to Moscow, and going as fast as all the other trains would convey me, I found that the average speed altogether had barely exceeded fifteen miles an hour. This slow locomotion is aggravated by the long and frequent stoppages, ostensibly for refreshment, which literally eat up the time on Russian railways; and although perhaps

Moscow and India. 25

necessary in a country of such vast and dreary distances, are none the less annoying to the traveller in a hurry to reach his destination.

It is not my intention, however, to hurry on towards the Transcaspian in this description without pausing occasionally on the way to read the more prominent finger-posts pointing to the East, and to notice the principal factors in Russia's advances into Central Asia, as they present themselves along the route. These, after leaving Moscow, are the Cossacks and the Caucasus; the first having been the principal pioneers and leaders, and the second the chief basis of Russia's Eastward march; but first and foremost in interest connecting it with the object of my journey naturally comes Moscow.

The foreign visitor to the metropolis on the Neva is generally told that in order to see Russia proper he must leave polyglot and cosmopolitan St. Petersburg, and go on to Moscow; and certainly, if he cares to see the Eastern face of this Janus-like Empire, he cannot do better than follow this advice. The city of St. Petersburg, which is the Westward face of the Russian two-headed eagle, and which has been aptly designated by a native writer as one huge department for the transaction of the official business of the Empire, has nothing about it distinctively and exclusively Russian ; whereas Moscow exhibits just as much of Asia as enters into the very blood and fibre of the Russian people. To put it broadly, the one has always been genuinely Russian, while the other was originally made to be something of a sham, to suit the taste and impress the minds of Western Europe.

Moscow has probably been described oftener than St. Petersburg, though never to the extent which its importance and originality deserve. Field-Marshal von Moltke, in his letters, said that it reminded him of such incongruous places as Bagdad, Buda-Pest, and Palermo. Nearly everything in it suggests the East, and yet not the real East. This peculiar nondescript character of the city no doubt startles the stranger from the East, almost as much as it does the European from the West. If the latter is astonished by the unique and grotesque architecture in and around the Kremlin, the other must experience a shock to his Oriental instinct for beauty of form and harmony of colour when he beholds the lack of symmetry and ugly combinations of glaring colours of the old Muscovite stronghold.

Most accounts of Moscow tell us of its

marvellous old Kremlin, or citadel, its multitude of churches, and its semi-oriental character; but little if anything has ever been said of its great commercial importance, and the general influence which it exercises throughout the country. It exhibits far more of the real stir and bustle of commercial life than St. Petersburg; and the Eastern merchants, who constantly appear upon its Bourse, are never seen among the crowd of Germans, interspersed with a few Russians, and still fewer English, upon the Exchange on the banks of the Neva. Moscow, with a million more inhabitants in its province than is contained in the larger government of St. Petersburg, is, without doubt, the great commercial centre and the heart of Russia, where all national movements, including the invasions of the East, have been chiefly inspired and nourished. East, west and south of it, lie stretched out in profusion nearly all the natural, and unfortunately much neglected, riches of the country; and if any proof be wanting of the commercial advantage of Moscow over St. Petersburg, even in the trade between the Baltic and the central provinces, it will be found in the fact that St. Petersburg is now being discarded in favour of the more direct and convenient routes between

Moscow and Libau, Riga and other Western ports.*

Moscow also sets the fashion in business manners and methods for the whole of the Russian interior, leaving European ways of business to those who prefer them at the ports of the Neva, Baltic, and Black Sea, where foreigners predominate. The old Muscovite merchant, with long hair and top boots, who opens negotiations with his "all lowest salaam" or "very special bow," still holds his own round the Kremlin; and although many of the younger generation are clad in European tailoring, and strike their bargains over champagne instead of tea, they are by no means radically changed by these adoptions. Moscow, and especially commercial and manufacturing Moscow, is a real power in the State. Its merchant princes, led by the late M. Katkoff, gained for the present Minister of Finance his appointment from the

---

* Novve Vremya says, that for the last ten years, thanks to the competition of railways with the Volga, a great part of the cereals which ought to be exported through St. Petersburg are now sent direct to the ports of the Baltic, where the export trade has made enormous progress; while the grain trade of St. Petersburg, although not materially diminished, has not increased for many years past.

Moscow and India. 29

Tsar ; and they now exert a powerful and often decisive voice in the commercial policy of the Empire. Nor have the political pretensions of the ancient capital been ignored in the "Muscovite policy" of the present reign.

The Nicholas railway to Moscow is the only one of the railways radiating from St. Petersburg which leads directly into genuine, Slavonic, and "holy" Russia. All the other lines run into those annexed provinces of the Baltic, Finland, and Poland, inhabited by foreign-bred and heterodox peoples, whose Russification is being carried out at the present moment with greater severity than at any previous time. The northern city of barracks and palaces, standing guard, as it were, over these heterogeneous elements, is the purely European disguise which Peter the Great forced Russia to assume for the purpose of imposing the power of his enormous Empire upon the Western nations, and of serving as an inlet for as much of European culture as Russia required for her civilizing mission in the East ; and these are services which the Muscovite Chauvinists might make some allowance for in their unmitigated condemnation of the "Palmyra of the North." But Moscow, "the city of churches, the golden-domed, myriadbelled, white-stoned, emerald-roofed, and thousand-towered," has always been, and still remains, the typical picture and centre of Russia, and the mainstay of those relations with the East, which have thus far culminated in the railway to Samarkand.

The relation between the Central Asian Railway and the Moscow district is now far more important than that which existed between the caravans and the Moscow merchants, when their only means of transport were the camels of the nomad of the desert. In and around Moscow are still to be found the principal men who maintain the trade with Central Asia, and contribute most to the commercial employment of the Central Asian Railway. All questions of through tariffs, freights, and facilities pertaining to railway traffic with Central Asia, have a direct bearing upon Moscow as the centre of the Empire, while St. Petersburg in this connection is almost completely ignored.

The new railway has thus already become closely associated in Russia with the development of Central Asian trade, and nothing more is now heard, at least not in public, of the military purposes for which it was originally begun. In fact, the importance attached to its commercial prospects almost causes one to forget that the strategical demands, which are apparently satisfied for the present, and not the commercial considerations from which so much is now expected, were the primary reasons for its rapid construction. The commercial significance of the line came into prominence only when, contrary to expectation, its extension was carried north-east through Merv into rich and flourishing Bokhara, instead of being turned off south near Sarakhs in a purely strategical and unprofitable deflection towards Herat. This proposed branch in the direction of the so-called "Key of India," the Russians have told us, could be made in a couple of months, whenever rendered necessary by the approach of another crisis like the fight on the Koushk. Had the work of frontier delimitation gone on smoothly, the railway would probably not have reached the Oxus down to the present day; for it certainly is a fact that in consequence of the "woeful incident" at Dash-Kepri, the main line was extended to the Amu-Daria with extraordinary celerity; and there can be little doubt that any further serious misunderstanding between England and Russia about Afghanistan would set General Annenkoff's railway battalions at work again on the American system with redoubled energy. In happy default of this contingency, the Russians, with General Annenkoff and his friends, have decided to regard the railway solely as an instrument for increased commercial activity between Russia and Central Asia. From this point of view they will even argue that their advance into Central Asia, whether by railway or otherwise, has never been dictated by any unworthier motives than those of commerical cupidity and security for commercial relations, such as those which first led England to India. This, it may be admitted, is fairly true as far as it applies to the time before Peter the Great; but we know well enough that another and powerful incentive has since actuated Russia in planning expeditions against India, and that is the desire of revenge for English opposition in Europe, and especially at Constantinople. "Be our friends in Europe," say the Russians, in effect, "and leave Turkey to us; otherwise we will worry and attack you in India whenever we get the opportunity."

It is a curious and noteworthy fact in regard to Russia's improvement of her advance towards India, by means of the Central Asian Railway, that England endeavoured to contract com-

Moscow and India.

mercial relations with India in much the same direction, *via* Moscow, and with the aid of the Muscovites, long before her commercial intercourse had been established with the East Indies by the sea route round the Cape. As will be seen, it was not the apocryphal testament of Peter the Great that gave the first impulse to the Russian hankering after India.

The commencement of commercial dealings with Moscow through Archangel, effected by Sir Hugh Willoughby and Richard Chancellor in 1554, some fifty years before the establishment of the first British factory at Ahmednuggur, was no doubt made in the hope of eventually getting overland as far as India. This much is clearly indicated by Russian authors, who state that the English merchants then settled in old Muscovy were not satisfied with Russian markets, and the exclusive privileges granted to them by the Tsar, but were always talking of the wealth of India, and bewitching the Russian imagination with prospects of the gain that would accrue to both parties if the Muscovites would only assist the English in getting there through Central Asia. At last, in 1558, Anthony Jenkinson obtained special passports from the " Great Lord Tsar of Muscovy," enabling him to penetrate

D

into Central Asia, and after great difficulties and dangers he got as far as Bokhara. The idea of a transit trade to India *viâ* Moscovy was not, however, abandoned; and finally, in 1614, official negotiations were opened on the subject by Sir John Merrick, a commercial ambassador from King James to the Tsar Michael Feodorovitch, the first of the Romanoffs. Sir John Merrick's proposal was to find new trade routes to India and Persia by way of the Volga and the Obi; in realizing which scheme, the Russians were to give their authority and assistance in return for England's mediation between the Tsar and the King of Sweden, and the payment of £20,000 into the Tsar's exhausted exchequer. This proposal, which was several times renewed down to 1620, failed to elicit the least favour from the conservative Boyars and merchants of Moscow, who, in spite of the allurements held out by Merrick as to the golden results of a joint trade with India, were persistent and successful in persuading the Tsar to withhold his consent. "The English," said the Muscovite oppositionists, "are a strong and rich people, and our Russians can never get on with them in anything."

Irrespective of this particular project of

Moscow and India.

Anglo-Russian trade with India, the privileges then accorded to British commerce in Russia were strongly opposed by the Moscow merchants, until at last, when a pretext arose in the establishment of the English Commonwealth, and the decapitation of Charles the First,—events which greatly disgusted the Muscovite autocrat,—this commercial grievance was quickly remedied by the Tsar's abolition of all privileges to foreigners, and the expulsion of the British traders from every part of Muscovy except the part of Archangel.*

As soon as the English merchants of the seventeenth century had gone from Moscow, the Russians made several attempts to form a connection with India on their own account. Not that this was by any means the commencement of their efforts in that direction; for the first Russian ambassador to India, a merchant named Nikitin, was sent from Moscow in the fifteenth century, just two hundred years earlier; but the

* The mercantile community of Moscow at the present day are closely imitating their ancestors of two-and-a-half centuries ago by protesting against the temporary immunities recently granted to Captain Wiggins and the "Phœnix Merchant Adventurers of Newcastle-on-Tyne," in their attempts to trade with Siberia through the mouths of the rivers Obi and Yenissei.

Tsar Alexis Michailovitch, who expelled the British merchants from Moscow, had learnt so much from them about the riches of India that he was afterwards induced to despatch four separate embassies to the Great Mogul in the course of a few years. When Peter the Great arrived on the scene, that illustrious pioneer of Russian development was also led to interest himself in the matter by what he heard about India during his stay in England and Holland and on returning to Russia he naturally initiated fresh efforts to reach the tempting goal.

Some years later, in the reign of George the Second, there was another spurt of English commercial enterprise into Central Asia towards India *viâ* the Caspian Sea, which was the subject of some diplomatic discussion with the Russian Government. The principal personage in this revival was Jonas Hanway, whose celebrated journey, like the former expedition of Anthony Jenkinson, seems to have led to no practical or lasting result; and thenceforward England found it more convenient to confine the development of her means of communication with India to the element on which she reigned supreme.

The last foreigner who entertained the

Moscow and India.

notion of reaching India through Moscow (not as a merchant, but as a conqueror) was Napoleon the First; and his direct march upon the old Russian capital shows that he was fully aware of the greater importance of that city for the object of his invasion, as compared with the new residence of the Tsars on the Neva.

After the encouragement and incitement thus unconsciously given to the Russians in their aspirations towards India, it is not surprising that they soon began to make giant strides in the direction of the coveted land; and the consequence of these movements was that we subsequently entered upon a long period of abortive attempts to keep Russia at a respectful distance from our Indian frontiers by periodical and useless alarms and protests, often thereby exposing our own weakness, which unfortunately also tended to stimulate the advance of our rival rather than to check it.

This unreasonable policy has now been happily superseded by a more rational and practical view of the whole question. If we once helped to lure the Russians on towards India, and then provoked them to advance by frequent fits of "Mervousness," they have now roused us in our turn to do something more than make verbal protests and empty threats. We have at last set about organizing our own "scientific frontier," and the buffer frontier of Russia and Afghanistan has been conjointly defined on the North-West.

And yet we are told by the critics that this part of the Russo-Afghan frontier, for various reasons, cannot be regarded as permanently established. Russia, they say, as well as England, seeks a scientific frontier; and as the delimited boundary, according to Sir West Ridgeway, runs for the most part through a sandy, treeless, and waterless desert, it cannot be considered by Russia as a satisfactory or durable line of demarcation. No one can deny that the frontier, like most things, has its inherent defects; but in depreciating or condemning it, are we not inviting Russia to seek a better one for herself, and a worse one for us? Are we not encouraging her to advance still nearer towards India? Although perhaps a bad frontier, it suits us well enough as long as Russia continues to respect it. All we have to do is to prepare to protect it with something more than mere words and threats in the event of Russia being led to violate her engagements; and there is certainly no necessity for us, of all people in the world, to lead her on to do so.

It is not, however, the imperfections of this part of the frontier which need give any cause of fear that the Russians will ever wish to overstep it; the source of possible trouble is rather to be found in the inseparable faults of Asiatic rule on the opposite side. During the recent suppression of rebellion in Afghan Turkistan, and the subsequent "Bloody Assizes" held in that region by Abdurahman Khan for the purpose of punishing the accomplices of Ishaak Khan, and while the Russians were raising something like an alarm in consequence, most English writers and speakers on the subject seemed to think that every possible cause of complaint on the part of the Russians was removed by the authentic contradiction of the alleged hostile intentions of Abdurahman against Russia. This was simply begging the question, as nobody in Russia seriously believed for a moment in the hostile intentions or proceedings which rumour attributed to Abdurahman Khan. To have done so would have been to convict the Ameer of sheer madness. What many competent Russians feared (and this fear was shared at one moment by Englishmen officially interested in the matter), was that the effects of the Ameer's punitive expedition, so close to the Russian borders, were liable to prove dangerous to the peace and tranquillity of the Bokharan Uzbegs and others, whose relatives by blood and race were being tortured and executed by hundreds on the opposite side of the Oxus. The extent of the panic on the frontiers may be estimated by the fact that no less than 3,000 families of these Afghan Uzbegs, including the Khan of Kunduz, fled across the river into Bokhara, besides which another crowd of refugees accompanied Ishaak Khan over the Russian part of the frontier. Trade, too, was completely suspended. This abnormal state of things was the true cause of alarm; but whether it was justifiable or not is a question that can be argued *ad infinitum*. One might say that the Russian Government ought to have been more thankful than alarmed at the acquisition of so many new subjects and vassal *protegees*. Of course the mere movement of Afghan troops towards the frontiers would induce the Russians to take extra precautions on their side, just as they have so often done to the alarm of Europe, for the same reason, on the frontiers of

Austria and Germany. Consequently General Krestiane's battalion at Kerki was reinforced on this occasion by three others. Another disquieting symptom at the time was the Russian belief, which had been confirmed, to a great extent, by English opinion, and very much strengthened by the refusal of the Ameer to receive the Durand mission, that the English in India had no influence or control whatever over the Afghan Ameer and his doings,—that in fact he had become far too strong for us. It was of no use therefore, argued the Russians, to rely upon the power of the English to prevent the possible occurrence of serious difficulties and annoyances on the frontier. England, it is plain, has no direct control over Abdurahman Khan, and knowing this well enough, the Russians will not put up with anything on his part which they may consider injurious or troublesome to themselves simply out of regard for English assurances that he, the Ameer, has no hostile intentions.

When we see how Russia preserves her own frontier interests by watching over them on the spot, it is difficult to appreciate the British protectorate over the Afghan frontier without a similar practical kind of control. The late Baron Jomini remarked to me, soon after the unfortunate incidents of 1885, that England's old plan of carrying on frontier affairs in Central Asia would no longer work; that England and Russia could not continue as before to keep apart and insist upon having no direct frontier relations. There must, he observed, be frequent border difficulties in the future; and the best way to prevent them from becoming acute and endangering the friendliness between the two nations would be to keep permanent commissioners on, or near, the Afghan frontier itself. England had joined with the Powers in establishing an International Commission for regulating the Danube. Why could she not help to maintain a Commission to superintend the frontier affairs of Afghanistan? This would be the only way to obviate the ever-recurring scares and anxieties, which are always liable to end in some hasty action of the Russian military authorities before diplomacy in London, St. Petersburg or Calcutta can interfere.

It is certainly very fortunate that Abdurahman was able to quell the insurrection, and to purge the disaffected districts as promptly and as well as he seems to have done it, though his success, it appears, was due more to good luck than to superiority. And there is no

Moscow and India. 43

doubt that the despatch of General Rosenbach, Governor-General of Turkistan, with the Tsar's special orders from St. Petersburg, where he happened to be staying on leave, was sufficient to arrest any little adventure by which General Komaroff or Colonel Alikhanoff may have contemplated taking advantage of the situation.

Let us, however, suppose that the Ameer, Abdurahman, had not been able to pacify his Turkistan province, or that any of the mortal diseases from which he suffers had proved fatal in the midst of the work, and the country had been thrown into a protracted state of anarchy, with perhaps more than one pretender struggling for the throne. What would the Russians be likely to do in such a case, if their side of the frontier were seriously disturbed, or, to follow the reasoning of the Russophobe, if they chose to consider it to be so, merely for the purpose of a pretext, and the English arbiters of the fate of Afghanistan were powerless and conspicuous by their absence? Is it not well within the bounds of probability, nay even of certainty, that they would then feel themselves called upon to step into Afghan Turkistan to restore order, as they entered under similar circumstances into Chinese Kuldja? All the Chinese power did not suffice to keep the Kuldja frontier quiet enough to satisfy the Russians, who at last walked into the province, and took the work of pacification into their own hands. This hypothesis may be easily dismissed on the assumption that any such action would be an immediate *casus belli* with England; but we cannot be surprised if the Russians should think the contrary when they learn from English politicians that in pledging ourselves to the present Ameer of Afghanistan to defend the integrity of his dominions we added the important qualification : "to such extent, and in such manner as may appear to the British Government necessary." This important reservation naturally leads to the interpretation that, while not being in a position to take Afghanistan herself, England is determined to keep Russia out of it by all means in her power, short, however, of going to war; and when once convinced that England will never go to this length for the sake of territory north of the Hindu Kush, Russia is not likely to fear the consequences of any possible action on her part such as I have imagined.

But the North-Western Boundary defined by the Anglo-Russian Commission, and referred to

Moscow and India. 45

in the above remarks, is not the whole of the Russo-Afghan frontier. There are still the Northern and North-Eastern confines of Afghanistan verging upon Chinese Kashgar, comprising several petty Khanates semi-independent, or loosely connected with Afghanistan, or Bokhara, where no Boundary Commission has ever been at work, and where no exact information has yet been gathered by either Government. Although Russia may have tacitly acquiesced in some of the acts by which Abdurahman has already made good his pretensions on these parts of his frontiers, she might at any time declare that she never agreed to them officially, as long as they have not been made the subject of a formal understanding. For the benefit of those who may not be versed in Afghan frontier intricacies, I may mention that the part of the undefined Russo-Afghan frontier to which I am now referring is bordered by the disputed main stream or streams of the Upper Oxus, and the contested Khanates of Shugnan, Vakhan, &c. The misunderstanding arose through the utter ignorance of the country upon which the first Anglo-Russian agreement of 1873 as to this region of the frontier was based, and which is a clear proof that no lasting confidence in that part of the Ameer's boundaries with Russia can be felt until a joint Commission has gained the necessary knowledge on the spot for the conclusion of an agreement, that cannot afterwards be repudiated on the plea of ignorance.

Several years ago Russia protested against the Afghan occupation of Shugnan, one of the small Khanates above alluded to; and if the protest was not pressed home, nor the affair treated like the Afghan trespass on the left bank of the Koushk, it was only because the Russians were not near enough to the spot, and not prepared to back up their contention. This, I believe, is the only time Russia has followed the example of England, and made a protest in Central Asian affairs without being able to take action in support of it. If we wait to define the rest of the boundary until the Central Asian Railway has perhaps been pushed forward in other directions as well as towards Tashkent, and the Russians have crept up to the Northern parts of the Afghan frontier as close as they now are on the boundary of the North-West, we may easily have a repetition of the disagreeable experiences of 1885. Russian politico-scientific explorers like Prejevalsky are already busy in that region. It will be remembered that the year before last the well-known traveller, Grombtchefsky, with his escort of Cossacks, boasted of having taken prisoners two Afghan sentinels in order to elude the Afghan troops sent to intercept his progress towards Kundjut. This traveller was recently again on Afghan territory, making his way through districts where Abdurahman Khan is at present, or was very lately, making war on the semi-independent rulers of one of the above-mentioned Northern Khanates. And last year another Russian explorer, Captain Pokotilo, asserted that the Eastern frontier of Bokhara extended beyond the stream of the Upper Amu Daria or Pianja, which, I believe, is not the opinion of political geographers in England or India.

CHAPTER III.

THE COSSACKS.

The most remarkable phenomenon of the Slavonic race —Numbers and territories of the Cossacks—Dress and equipment—Railways through the Cossack provinces — Historical interest and character of the Cossack steppes—Cossack aversion to trees—Reafforestation—Herodotus on the absence of wood— Coal-fields of the Don—Their output—Successful competition of English coal—Coal, wood, and petroleum, fuel on Russian railways—Novotcherkask, the modern Cossack capital—Starotcherkask, the ancient capital — Cossack regalia and charters — English sword of honour presented to a Cossack Ataman— The Cossack in Europe—Cossack colonizers abroad —The Cossack in Asia—Cossacks selected to attack India—Important extension of Cossack territory— Cossack dislike to trade—Cossack administration— Cossack organization on the Don out of date—Ineffectual attempts to level the Cossacks with the Russians—Turkoman Cossacks — Cossacks of the Kooban and Terek—Resemblances between Cossacks and Circassians—Russia glides imperceptibly into Asia—No sharp distinctions—A Russian on his experiences in Central Asia—Easy fraternization between Russians and Asiatics—The Cossack an in-

The Cossacks. 49

strument of *rapprochement*—Cossacks and Circassians merge into Turkomans—Colonel Alikhanoff, remarkable specimen of Russian and Asiatic combined—Absorption of Kalmucks and Kirghiz by Cossack cavalry—Russia's power of assimilation and coalescence—Carlyle's opinion—Vladikavkaz—Pretentiousness of Russian names — Amiability of Russian railway travellers—Annenkoff's invitations and guests.

HAVING thus briefly traced some of the more salient points in our relations with Russia concerning India, I now pass on to notice another potent factor in Russia's Eastward progress, which appeared about half way on my journey between Moscow and the Caucasus. I refer to the Cossacks of the Don, the Kooban, and the Terek, named after the three rivers which run through their respective settlements.

The military territories of these descendents of that strange confraternity which Baron Haxthausen called the most remarkable phenomenon of the whole Slav race, now cover about 3,000 square miles of steppe land on the Don, between Voroneje and the Sea of Azoff, 1,700 more on the Kooban, between that Sea and the North-Western Caucasus, and another 1,100 square miles on the Terek and Sunja, towards the North-Eastern slopes of the mountains.

E

These three divisions of Cossack militia, although forming separate administrative units, are subject to the same kind of organization, and only differ in the minor details of dress and equipment. The principal weapon, for instance, of the Cossacks of the Don is the pennonless lance, which is never carried either by those of the Kooban or the Terek, whilst both the latter have adopted the long-skirted uniform and large piercing dagger of the neighbouring Circassian. There are nine other Cossack fraternities and colonies guarding the extensive frontiers of Asiatic Russia from Kamchatka and the Pacific Ocean to the Caucasus and the Black Sea, but none of them are as important, or as strong in numbers, as the three sections through which my journey led me on this occasion. In fact, these three large bodies of Cossack horsemen, next to the extinct Republic of the Zaporagians of the Dnieper, destroyed by Catherine the Second, may claim to have been the progenitors of all the other communities of these famous troops. The Cossacks of the Don, who now supply the largest force of Russian irregular troops, constitute a third of the whole Cossack population, and the latter is estimated at about

The Cossacks.

one forty-fourth of the entire population of the Empire.

The continuous line of railway from Moscow, which runs for 1,240 miles to the foot of the Caucasus, and passes through these three military provinces, belongs to four different companies, called after their principal stations. These are Moscow-Riazan, Riazan-Kozloff, Kozloff-Voroneje-Rostoff, and Rostoff-Vladikavkaz ; and there are only two changes of trains, one at Voroneje and the other at Rostoff, along the whole of this distance. At Voroneje I was fortunate in receiving at last my passport for the Transcaspian from the Director of the Asiatic Department of the Foreign Office, Privy Councillor Zinovieff, who had kindly sent a telegram on the subject to the care of the station-master. A few hours after leaving this town, I entered the boundaries of the Cossacks of the Don at the small station of Chertkova, named after a former Ataman-in-Chief.

Here begin those vast and treeless plains, the southern counterparts of the great northern tundras, and once the camping ground of many races of men from the depths of Asia, whose traces are still visible in the innumerable *Kurgani*—those sepulchral monuments, " where urns of mighty chiefs lie hid," which break the monotony of the landscape in all directions. Of late years these ancient tumuli have yielded many valuable additions to the relics of the past; though in some of them the modern archæologist has found himself forestalled by previous visitors, who, like the dead they seem to have plundered, have long since mingled their bones with the dust. Quite recently, for instance, a Russian antiquarian, while excavating an entrance into one of these barrows, discovered the remains of a human skeleton, with its arms still hugging a large vase, which was evidently being carried off when the robber must have been suddenly buried alive. Nor are the remains of antiquity in this district all of the sepulchral kind, for those who care to search below the surface. The late Mr. John Hughes, the founder of the immense iron and steel works of the New Russia Company, on the southern part of these wavy steppes, used to be able to trace the passage of the first workers in metals over this country right away from the Caucasus, and finally through Spain into Wales and Cornwall.

Eventually succeeding to the nomadic hordes, migratory tribes, and ancient colonists, who once trod this historical ground, came those

The Cossacks.

bands of outlaws and freebooters, flying from Muscovite as well as Tartar tyranny, who, after serving as moss-troopers and borderers between Russia and Tartardom, gradually settled down into the Cossacks of to-day.

The broad steppes now inhabited by this singular population of born soldiers, are not all as desolate or as unlovely as many persons may imagine. The preconceived idea, which is often entertained of their flat and barren character, is not confirmed on actual acquaintance, at least not as far as regards the country of the Don, which takes the form of undulating downs, covered in spring, before the sun has scorched the ground, with the richest and most luxuriant vegetation. Tall and feathery grasses wave in the breeze, and fragrant herbs scent the air; while the lark revels in this turfy paradise in such large numbers that his loud and ceaseless song has well been called the music of the Russian steppes. The scenery, it is true, is almost destitute of tree or bush, and the heat is often most intense. Only the moving shadow of a passing cloud can give relief from the powerful glare of the midsummer sun. Such is the favourite home of the freedom-loving Cossack, who has always had a strange aversion to trees, because they obstruct his wide view across the open country. When constant watch had to be kept against the stealthy approach of the Mongol enemy, and no intercepting object was safely to be tolerated, the absence of forest, which is now so much deplored, was then, no doubt, a considerable advantage; whereas at the present day this want of timber is felt to be a serious and ever-increasing inconvenience. A beginning has, therefore, been made at reafforestation, if such a term can be properly used in relation to a region which, although a matter of some dispute, is described by Herodotus as unwooded even in his time. Young plantations are now flourishing at many places along the railway, thus screening it from the drifting snow; but the greater part of the track is still so much exposed, that large numbers of wooden battens have to be spread out in winter against the terrific snowstorms which sweep across these unsheltered plains.

At the station of Alexander-Grooshevsk, the only town in the military territory of the Don possessing municipal government, the traveller gets a good glimpse at the anthracite coal-fields, with their numerous pits, producing some half a million tons of coal a year. Altogether the

The Cossacks. 55

annual out-put of the Don and Donets coal mines, which has increased far beyond the carrying capacity of the railways, and would further increase with a better demand, is about a million and a half of tons, including bituminous and anthracite; in spite of which, and the proximity of the Black and Azoff Seas, English sea-freighted coal is still able to compete successfully with Russian coal at all the South Russian ports. A great deal of the local coal is used on the railways between Kozloff and the Caucasus, this being the coal-burning section of the Russian lines. To the north of the Kozloff locomotives are still fed with wood, the blazing sparks of which, issuing in showers from the wide-mouthed funnels, are very liable to set fire to the dry wooden cabins of the peasantry; while on the lines of the Transcaucasus and Transcaspian the residue of petroleum is now the only fuel in use.

About twenty miles farther on, the train stops at Novocherkask, the modern military capital of the Cossacks of the Don. This is a neat and clean-looking town, situated on a considerable elevation or ridge, which was selected as its site by a former Ataman, Count Platoff, whose monument, surrounded by Turkish cannon, now adorns the principal square. Another monument will shortly be erected here to the great Cossack chieftain, Yermak Timofaivitch, the conqueror of Siberia.

At the foot of this city-crowned ridge, and bordering the railway line, flows a tributary of the Don, called the Aksai, which at once reminds one of Asia, for the name is, no doubt, a modification of the Turko-Tartar Ak-soo, or white water, so frequently repeated in the names of rivers and localities all through Central Asia. From the height of Novo or New Cherkask, one can discern the old capital of the Cossacks, or Stary-Cherkask, now little more than a village, far off over the plain, which here begins to develop its absolute flatness. The situation of the old town is as low and unhealthy as that of the new one is high and salubrious. In spring the entire plain between the two towns is generally inundated by the overflow of the river; when the ancient town is half-submerged, and looks in the distance like a sea-girt island. This spring-tide flood once deceived a careless French author to such an extent that he wrote of Novo-cherkask as a town on the borders of the Azoff Sea. There is nothing of interest at Stary-cherkask, except the chains and fetters that once shackled the limbs of the Cossack rebel

The Cossacks. 57

Stenka-Razin. Everything that remains of Cossack autonomy and all that pertains to the separate military corporation of the Cossacks under the Minister for War, has been transferred to New Cherkask, where may be seen the empty symbols of their former independence, pompously styled the Cossack regalia, as well as the written evidences of their present subjection. The chief insignia of authority are a gilt truncheon, or baton, from the Empress Catherine, a long wooden staff, metal-tipped at both ends, from Peter the Great, and the principal mace—half sceptre and half war-club—called the *Boolava*, presented by the same monarch, and always handed to each successive Heir-Apparent on his assumption of the Chief Atamanship of all the Cossacks. These baubles, together with the sword of Alexander the First, the Cossack uniform of Alexander the Second, and a number of standards and Tartar horse-tails, are always religiously carried in procession on all great occasions. In the room where most of these relics and trophies are displayed, are also exhibited in glass cases fourteen charters, in which all the later Tsars have repeatedly confirmed the attenuated rights and privileges of the Cossacks, and in so doing have expressed their sentiments in curious variations of tone and language, according as the gallant Cossacks have been in favour, or under a cloud. The most complimentary and generous of these documents is signed by Alexander the First, and was given on the conclusion of the patriotic war for the expulsion of the French. This is beautifully engrossed upon vellum, and ornamented with excellent miniature paintings of Cossack warfare. The coldest and curtest of the whole series is from the imperious and haughty Nicholas, written upon a sheet of common ministerial note-paper. To an Englishman, the most interesting object in this collection is a handsome English sword of honour, from which the jewels it once contained have been extracted by the family of the late recipient. The following inscription on the blade explains its presence in this out-of-the-way spot :—" A Common Council, holden in the chambers of the Guildhall of the City of London on Wednesday, the eighth day of June, 1814, resolved unanimously that a sword of the value of 200 guineas be presented to the Hetman*

---

* It is strange that Englishmen continue to write Hetman instead of Ataman. The two words may be of the same Scandinavian origin and meaning; but Hetman was the title of the elected chief, or headman of the

The Cossacks.

Count Platoff, in testimony of the high sense this Court entertains of the consummate skill, brilliant talents, and undaunted bravery displayed by him during the protracted conflicts in which he has been engaged for securing the liberties, the repose, and the happiness of Europe."

At the time this sword was presented, just after the Cossacks had made their first appearance on the boulevards of Paris, and before their place in popular imagination had been usurped by the Uhlans of Prussia, the wild-looking denizens of the Don were almost as much feared on the continent of Europe as they have always been in Russian Asia down to the present day. Since that time Europe has scarcely increased its knowledge of these peculiar troops ; and the recent disastrous escapade of the Cossack adventurer Ashinoff, whose colonizing bubble on the coast of the Red Sea was ignominiously burst by the guns of the French Admiral Olry, did not exhibit the best traits of the Cossack character. It is a curious fact in this connection,

Little Russian and Ukraine Cossacks under the Poles, and has not been used in Russia since the time of Mazeppa, or rather, of Count Razoumofsky, the favourite of the Empress Elizabeth.

that the only other Russian who ever attempted to establish a Russian colony abroad, the late Mr. Miklukho Maclay, was of mixed Cossack and Scotch descent.

But if Europe has in any way forgotten the exploits of the Cossacks, all parts of Russian Asia, on the contrary, and some parts that are not yet Russian, are constantly making their closer acquaintance. The Cossack has been appropriately chosen to typify the Russian advance into Central Asia, and is often referred to as destined to confront the Sepoy on the heights of the Hindoo Kush. It must be remembered that in the old days the Cossacks were more than once selected to attack or threaten India. When the arrangement with Napoleon for a joint raid across the Indus fell through, and the Cossacks were ordered to make the campaign alone, the eccentric Emperor Paul wrote to their Ataman, Count Orloff:—"All the riches of India shall be yours for this expedition"; but happily a violent change of reign nipped this ambitious scheme in the bud.

My journey through the Cossack country happened to coincide with an important extension of the Cossack military rule over certain neighbouring territory at the mouth of the

The Cossacks. 61

"silent Don" and round the shores of the Azoff Sea, about which there was much discussion and disagreement among my fellow-passengers in the train. This territorial aggrandizement of the Cossacks of the Don entailed the inclusion of the two important commercial towns of Rostoff and Taganrog, which had hitherto remained outside the Cossack jurisdiction. The change had been decided upon by a special commission, under the presidency of the Governor of Koursk, after the visit of the Tsar and the Heir-Apparent as the new Ataman-in-Chief in 1887; but it did not appear to please either the Cossacks, or the trading populations of the towns newly annexed.

The Cossacks were afraid that the secret design of the Government was to weaken their separate organization by mixing them up with a population used to other methods of administration, which, to a certain extent, the latter were still permitted to retain, while the large business communities of Rostoff and Taganrog considered that the Cossack *régime* would be a serious check upon the progress of their rapidly-increasing trade and the satisfactory working of their civil institutions.

The Cossacks have always been averse to

trade from the earliest times, when their military commonwealth recognized no other occupation than war and plunder. Every Cossack being born to arms, he is only likely to attain the object of his ambition, as embodied in the proverb that "the Cossack who knows how to wait becomes an Ataman," if he devotes himself entirely to the traditional calling of his caste. The small extent, therefore, to which these inveterate warriors are interested in trade may be seen by the fact that although the province of the Don alone maintains about 58,000 fighting men, and can muster as many as 128,000 on an emergency, it can only show 440 Cossacks engaged in business, as compared with 11,000 other traders not belonging to the Cossack community.

The administration of the Don province is still a purely military one, with its own police and body of local Atamen; the whole being controlled by the *locum tenens* of the Imperial Ataman-in-Chief, assisted by a military council, and subject to the Minister for War. Such an organization, it is admitted even by Cossacks themselves, is altogether out of date in its present situation. The Cossacks have always been the pioneers of Russian power, and the

The Cossacks.

guardians and extenders of Russia's Eastern frontiers. In this capacity their proper place has always been on or near these frontiers, and when the frontiers are moved forward the Cossacks should all be moved forward with them. Now that Russia's limits have widened out hundreds of miles farther East, this antiquated system of military colonies on the Don has no longer any *raison d'être*. Its only utility seems to be in the advantages which it affords as a depôt for the supply of a comparatively inexpensive light cavalry to the armies of the West, as well as of the Eastern confines of the Empire. But this does not compensate for the detrimental influence which the sole rule of the Ataman and Minister of War is calculated to exercise on the development of a region peculiarly destined for material progress. The Government has more than once tried the thin edge of the wedge against Cossack separatism by attempting to establish the ordinary civil institutions of the rest of the Empire, beginning with the Zemstvo, but the gallant spearmen of the Don have always strenuously opposed its introduction. They simply abstained from electing any members to form these territorial assemblies, and continued to discuss all local affairs in their ancient *kroug* or circles. It is, therefore, not at all unlikely that their suspicions may have some foundation in regard to the cunning way in which they are now to be gradually assimilated administratively to the rest of the population around them by an apparently flattering extension of territory. Out of a population of a million and three-quarters, before this extension, there were already some 700,000 non-Cossack colonists and Little Russian peasants; so that with the additions now made the extraneous population of the province will probably equal that of the Cossacks. The municipal councils and mayoralty of the newly-incorporated towns are continued under the Minister for War instead of the Home Office, but the Zemstvo assemblies have been temporarily suspended. There are several other alleged reasons which may have induced the Government to make this change, such, for instance, as the isolated position of Rostoff and Taganrog in relation to their former administrative centre at Ekaterinoslav, in which province they were reckoned, and the supposed appearance of a large number of pernicious and dangerous persons, who could be better dealt with under the Cossack Government.

The Cossacks.

But this last consideration is not worth much in view of the fact that the Cossack region, which originally recruited its population among the malcontents of Russia, is still a notorious refuge for passportless vagrants and Siberian runaways. Even Nihilists have issued from the Cossack ranks during the last three years.* The central Government, however, has now established an office of *gendarmerie* at Novocherkask, and this branch of the political police will no doubt soon see into the matter. In any case, the change above described has been made in spite of Cossack obstinacy and commercial dissatisfaction, and both Cossacks and those with whom they are now mixed up will have to be content to be gradually amalgamated into the shape required by the supreme Government in St. Petersburg. The same manipulation and treatment undoubtedly awaits the Cossack Turkomans of the Transcaspian, who are simply a reproduction in the main of the Cossacks of the Don and the Dnieper. Transformation and Russification are the resistless fate of all the

* The fact of the minor state of siege having been proclaimed this year (1890) in the Don Cossack village of Kasperofka, shows that something is still seriously wrong.

heterogeneous tribes and races whom Russia folds in her wide embrace.

Soon after passing the busy town of Rostoff and crossing the ancient Tanais, the railway leaves the Cossack territory of the Don, and enters that of the Kooban and the Terek. Here the steppe assumes its proper appearance, and becomes a perfectly level prairie, extending 2,800 square miles between the Caspian and Black Seas, right away to the mountains of the Caucasus. It supports a population of 650,000 Cossacks, and 160,000 other persons, who are not of the Cossack fraternity. The greater part of the land appeared to be waste or pasture, but there were unmistakable evidences of cultivation, as well as of inadequate means of railway transport in the enormous quantities of grain piled up in sacks on all the goods platforms, and spoiling from the effects of rain, and the want of proper shelter.

The orthodox Cossacks of the Kooban and Terek are often confounded with the Mohammedan Circassians of the Caucasus, owing to identity of dress and other resemblances, in which, contrary to the general rule, the conquerors have imitated the conquered. A couple of squadrons of the Kooban Cossacks, who

The Cossacks. 67

always serve as the Tsar's body guard at St. Petersburg, and ride at the head of all processions, are frequently miscalled Circassians. Generations of close contact, and a certain amount of admixture with the Circassian mountaineers, have fully exercised the Russian talent of imitating their next-door neighbours. It is indeed difficult, in this Empire of the Tsars, to say exactly in every case where the European Russians end and the Russian Asiatics begin. There are no sharp distinctions : no absolute ethnological boundaries. In the Russian provinces of the Baltic and the Vistula, among populations long subject to the higher civilization of Western Europe, there are deep-rooted differences of race as well as religion, which can never be obliterated by the severest measures of official Russification ; but in the Eastern provinces of her Empire, Russia glides gradually and imperceptibly into Asia, and there finds a much readier acceptance of her influence and culture. The Russian takes as kindly to the manners and customs of Central Asia as the Asiatic in Russian uniform quickly feels himself at home in Russian society. A well-known Russian, who once held an important office in Turkistan, has publicly described how congenially he passed his time among the natives, often wearing their costume, and squatting all day long in their fruit gardens and orchards, cloying himself with the inevitable sweetmeats, and talking gossip. He felt, as he says, that the time thus spent, although wasted from the European point of view, was in perfect harmony with his Russian nature, and he was often constrained to ask himself whether he was not an Asiatic as well as a Russian. The subject races of Russia in the East are not kept at arm's-length. As soon as they become the subjects of the great White Tsar, after undergoing once for all the customary process of merciless castigation, recommended by Skobeleff, whose policy was simply cruel only to be kind, the Russians readily fraternize with them, and both parties soon arrive at a mutual understanding. In this *rapprochement* the Cossacks undoubtedly play a very important part. They may be said to merge imperceptibly into the Circassians of the Caucasus, just as the Caucasian tribes merge into the Turkomans round and across the Caspian Sea. The latter have only to tack the cartridge cases on to the breasts of their long-skirted tunics, and they are

The Cossacks.

at once as much Cossacks as any of the latter who have been for generations under Russian rule. The Turkoman Khans, under their Russo-Caucasian chief, Colonel Alikhanoff, who is himself a remarkable specimen of the combination of Russian and Asiatic, have already adopted quite naturally the Cossack-Circassian uniform, and in these days of "clothes-philosophy" this is not an unimportant detail. Their style of riding, high saddles, short stirrups and restive steeds, are also much the same as we see on the Don or in the Caucasus, and if they were mixed up with Kooban Cossacks and Caucasian militia, it would not be easy to pick them out from among the rest. Even the broad-visaged and bandy-legged Calmuck and Kirghiz are beginning to lose their distinctiveness in the all-absorbing Cossack cavalry. Such is Russia's power of assimilation and coalescence in the East. Thus, with the aid of this faculty, and not alone by force of arms, "are the Russians drilling under much obloquy," as Carlyle puts it, "an immense semi-barbarous half-world from Finland to Kamchatka into rule, subordination, civilization, really in an old Roman fashion, speaking no word about it, and quietly hearing all manner of vituperative able editors speak."*

I reached the end of my unbroken railway journey of four days and nights at Vladikavkaz, the head-quarters of the Terek Ataman, and a military Cossack settlement established at the entrance to the Dariel Pass, for the purpose, as its name implies, of controlling the communications through the Caucasus. The appellation of this place was continually getting mixed up in my mind with another similarly-sounding name of the chief Russian port on the Pacific coast; and this led me to reflect upon the remarkable pretentiousness of certain Russian names. We have a notable triplet of them in Vladikavkaz, Vladivostok, and Vladimir, meaning respectively

---

* Asiatic nations are fast adopting the Russian system of Cossack troops. Persia has for some time had her own Cossacks, such as they are ; and Japan is about to act upon the advice of a commission of officers lately sent to investigate the military organization on the Don, and to introduce Japanese Cossacks at Yeddo. In 1880 the entire Cossack population of Russia of both sexes, exclusive of non-military colonists and the clergy, numbered 2,150,837. At present it must be quite 2,500,000. Out of this number 160,000 are standing troops. Their territorial divisions are the Don, Kooban, Terek, Astrakhan, Ural, Orenburg, Siberian, Semiretchinsk, Transbaikal, and Amoor Cossacks.

The Cossacks. 71

command of the Caucasus, mastery over the East, and ruler of the world. The two last seem to breathe that lust of universal Empire which fills the dreams of Russian soldiers and politicians. Vladikavkaz was legitimately and appropriately so named after Russia had conquered the Caucasus, and thus secured for herself an indispensable base of future advances in Central Asia; but in naming Vladivostok she has gone far ahead of the consummation towards which her aspirations and subtle policy are always supposed to tend. As for Vladimir, which is now a common Christian name, and the title of a Russian province, it contains the prophecy of what many Russians modestly consider the ultimate destiny of their country.

As far as Vladikavkaz I had been ninety-two hours in trains, and I now had before me a journey of 132 miles by road across the mountains in order to reach the railway of the Transcaucasus. The tedium of this long railway journey had thus far been greatly relieved by the conversation and information of many interesting fellow-passengers, for the Russians, as a rule, are very sociable travellers. It would, indeed, be strange in a country of such vast distances, where railway travellers are often thrown together in one compartment for three or four days at a stretch, if they all hid themselves behind newspapers and never uttered a word to each other. In fact, it would be difficult to find a newspaper in the provinces beyond Moscow capable of engrossing attention to this extent.* The Russian traveller prefers to talk, and is quite uneasy and miserable until he finds somebody who will reciprocate. He has no craving for railway literature, even on the longest journeys. His favourite pastimes are talking and smoking, or card-playing. Nothing is more rare in Russian trains than the reading of books or newspapers, but a provoking inquisitiveness takes its place, and induces the Russian to seize upon every opportunity of plying his fellow-passengers with questions until he has perfectly satisfied himself as to their business and destination. In my case the first example of this characteristic trait was afforded by a Moscow merchant, who was the first to inform me, rather to my surprise, how little personal interest was being taken among the class to which he belonged in the important

---

* There are only 668 newspapers and periodical publications in the whole Russian Empire in Europe and Asia, less than a sixth of the number published in the United Kingdom.

railway event on the other side of the Caspian. In spite of the emphasis put upon the commercial importance and prospects of Russia's first great railway in Asia, none of the celebrated merchants of St. Petersburg and Moscow were to be present at the *fêtes* in Samarkand—not even those who have become famous for their semi-political caravan trade with the Asiatic border countries. Certain committees of the Exchanges in the two capitals had been invited, but apparently none of the members had accepted the invitation. The idea of making merry over the opening of the railway was apparently no business whatever of the Government, and the invitations were entirely the private concern of Generals Annenkoff and Rosenbach. As it turned out, the guests who, with great difficulty, eventually found their way to the Samarkand terminus of the Transcaspian Railway formed, with one or two exceptions, a kind of family party of General Annenkoff's. The General's two daughters, his niece, Princess Galitzin, and his brother-in-law, Comte de Vogüé, a well-known French writer on Russia, with half a dozen friends from Paris—these, with the Vice-President of the Imperial Geographical Society and the Mayor of Baku, comprised the distinguished visitors from Russia and abroad. This company also included a couple of representatives of the French Press, one of whom was also a delegate of the French Ministry of Commerce. In pursuit of this interesting party I hurried on through the Caucasus to Baku.

CHAPTER IV.

THROUGH THE CAUCASUS TO THE CASPIAN.

Sharp interchanges of climate and temperature—Snowslips and accidents—Rapid posting with a Russian Consul—Lermontoff's dispute between Elburz and Kazbek—False alarm—The Georgian military road —The gorge and pass of Dariel—The Terek—Parting of the waters—Desolate scenery of the northern slopes—Primitive dwellings—The Ossetins—"Mountain of tongues"—Ruined towers and castles— Tamara, the Cleopatra of the Caucasus—Kazbek— English climbers—Descent into the valley of the Aragua—Beauty of the Transcaucasus—Boast of the Georgians—Towers of refuge—Game—The Koora —Illusory notion of the Caucasus being a weak spot in Russia's armour—Similar idea of Armenian frontier—English and Russian influence among the Turkish Armenians—Russia's use of the religious element in conquering the Caucasus— England's contrary policy of assisting the Mohammedans— English mistake in this connection during Crimean War— Overdrawn reports of disaffection during Afghan frontier crisis—English hopes of utilizing it, and awkward habit of giving warning—Similar reports of English sympathies among the coast population of Finland—Simply a question of compulsory military service—How settled—Overrated separatist tendencies of "Young Georgia"—The Tsar's visit—Loyalty of the Caucasus—Highway robbery and brigandage—A Circassian Dick Turpin—Circassians running amuck—Unbridled temper of the natives—Insignificant religious antagonism—The Russian's faculty of identifying himself with the Asiatic—Conversation with General Zelennoi—Departure from Tiflis—Valley of the Koora—Resemblances between the Apsheron peninsula and the Transcaspian—Russified Persians—Arrival at Baku—Taken in charge by the police—Delayed for want of a steamer—Interview with the Governor of Baku—The Transcaspian Railway flooded—Baku fair—Start for Oozoon Ada—Foreigners and English steamers on the Caspian—Poles in the Transcaspian—Their grievances—A Polish rebel.

IF any traveller wishes a short and sharp experience of almost all the climates and temperatures of Europe and Asia without crossing frontiers, or enduring the vexations of Customhouse formalities, he has only to pass from European into Asiatic Russia in the early, or latter, part of the year. The Colossus of the North, its head crowned with snows, and its feet strewn with flowers, is richer in diversity of climate, as well as in race and language, than probably any other continuous Empire. Going south-east from St. Petersburg, the tourist may encounter a variety of change in this respect that is very remarkable. He may be confronted,

Through the Caucasus to the Caspian. 77

as it were, with the glow of a sun that scorches and almost blisters his face, while a cold wintry wind blows up from behind, rendering a thick overcoat a positive necessity. He will probably pass through the opposite extremes of heat and cold more than once in the course of a few days.

When I left St. Petersburg the fag-end of an unusually severe winter was still lingering on in the capital on the Neva. Not a green bud had yet appeared on the naked boughs, which had hardly yet lost their encrustation of snow, and even heavy furs were still being worn by the majority of the inhabitants. Near Moscow the verdure of spring began to make its appearance, and past Voroneje, the beginning of the steppes, quite a midsummer heat supervened. Everything graduated into summer as the train advanced. The heat increased by degrees as the foot of the Caucasus was approached, and, on mounting across the grand range crowned by Kazbek and Elbruz, the writer and his companion were again plunged into the depths of winter. It was so cold that a travelling rug over a top-coat was not enough to keep us warm. Closely-packed snow stood piled up in thick-set massive walls at the side of the mountain road, and showed a most dangerous inclination to topple over and descend in avalanches on the slightest thaw. In such a case the unwary passenger would inevitably be buried alive or hurled hundreds of feet down into the gorge below. Even the slightest movement of subsidence in these ugly snow-packs would frighten the horses and imperil the traveller's life. The fall of a loose stone or piece of rock from the overhanging cliffs nearly precipitated a diligence over the fatal edge a little time before ; so that when I passed along this part of the road, Cossack sentinels were stationed at the more dangerous points to prevent, if possible, the recurrence of accidents of this kind ; although even these agile troopers, who are equally at home in the mountains and on their native plains, are not always able to escape the peril from which they are expected to guard others. A few years ago a whole squadron were completely buried or swept off into the yawning abyss of the narrow valley beneath. One of the higher mountains bears the name of "The Major's Wife," in commemoration of an officer's spouse, who was so completely lost by one of these terrific snow-slips, that no traces were ever found of her remains or those of her servants.

Then came the steep zigzag descent into the lovely valley of the Transcaucasus, watered by the river Aragua. The reckless, but skilful, manner in which our *yemstchik* whipped his post-horses down this narrow winding pathway, carved out of the perpendicular sides of mountains 8,000 feet high, taking the abrupt turnings and curves with a whirl round that nearly overbalanced the carriage, was enough to take one's breath away. Ordinary tourists do not, as a rule, travel here at this pace, which I must state was entirely due to the fact that I was journeying in the company of the Russian Consul at Van, in Asia Minor, and that our progress was very much accelerated by the extra pressure of a special *podorojnaya*, or posting certificate, and the never-failing inducement of copious gifts of backsheesh. Mr. Kolyoobakin was going on a visit to his home in Tiflis, and, like myself, was anxious to lose no time. We therefore travelled all night, and did the 200 versts from Vladikavkaz to Tiflis in twenty hours. A pleasanter and more appropriate companion than this gentleman it would have been impossible to find. His mind was well stored with the lore and history of the Caucasus; and when we left Vladikavkaz, in the dusk of the evening, and were already in sight of the white-capped giants of the Russian Alps, he recited to me the beautiful lines of Lermontoff's poem on the great dispute between Elburz and Kazbek. No guide could have given me a better introduction to the Caucasus; and as I listened to the verses wherein the snow-capped Elburz tells the hoary-headed Kazbek, guarding the decrepit and drowsy Orient, to look at the martial hosts advancing out of the northern mists, I felt that here was a poetical miniature of Russia's conquering advance into the East.

Soon after we had entered the gorge of the mountains from Vladikavkaz a little scare, which turned out to be a false alarm, discovered to me that night travelling in the Caucasus, even over the well-guarded Georgian road, is not free from occasional troubles, other than snowslips and carriage accidents. Near this part there are several villages of the Ingoosh tribe, who are reputed to be all robbers to a man. Some years ago their repeated crimes induced the military Governor to hang up such a large number of them to posts along the Vladikavkaz-Petrofsk road, that the ghastly operation lasted nearly three days. They have often robbed the mail, which is now strongly guarded here with an escort of Cossacks, and have been known to waylay solitary travellers after nightfall. As we trotted along, the horse-bells jingling, and the darkness gradually increasing with the narrowness of the defile, the accustomed eye of our driver discerned several men at long distances apart lurking in the rock hollows along the side of the road. Then a solitary Circassian rode by ahead of us, whereupon the *yemstchik*, or driver, turned round to observe that it "looked rather queer," and then set his team agoing *ventre-à-terre*. In order to be ready for any emergency, we unpacked a shot-gun and a bulldog revolver, but the night mail soon came galloping up behind us with half a dozen light troopers armed to the teeth, and we felt safe enough in this company until out of all danger past the next post-house.[*] As we descended into the valley from the cold region above, the weather again became intensely hot, and continued to get more so on the way across the Caspian until we reached the torrid heat and burning sands of Turkomania. The dominating feeling, how-

[*] Four highwaymen are now awaiting trial at Tiflis, for an armed attack on the post team on this road near Ananoor, 8th August, 1889. They were successfully repulsed, and only shot dead one of the post-horses.

ever, in all this rapid transformation of climate and temperature, though certainly not rapid railway travelling, was the novelty of going by rail to Bokhara, the noble and the ancient city of Tamerlane.

The Georgian military road, at which I have thus taken a glance in connection with the curious interchanges of climate and weather during my journey from the fens of Finland to the sands of the Transcaspian, is a piece of work that well deserves a more extended notice. It is probably the finest Imperial highway in the whole of Russia, the next best being the Vorontzoff road in the Crimea. What it actually cost to make, and still costs to keep in repair, would be a question like that put to the Emperor Nicholas in regard to the expense of building and renovating the Isaac Cathedral in St. Petersburg, and which that frankly-speaking monarch answered by saying, that only the Almighty and the architect could possibly tell. When the Emperor Alexander the Second went over it, he said that he had expected to see golden mile-posts erected all the way to account for the enormous expenditure. The first part of the road runs with a gradual ascent through the gorge of Dariel, and along the sides of the river Terek, beneath the beetling brows of the rocks and mountains that guard both sides of the defile. Several small iron bridges lead the winding road across from one side of the river to the other. The scenery is grand, but stern and wild. Bare stony cliffs, and granite rocks, suspended over the traveller's head in many places, and dull brown mountain sides with scanty vegetation, enclose and overshadow the narrow roadway and foaming river as far as Mount Kazbek. Here the valley of the Terek begins to open out, and the road ascends rapidly towards the Krestovaya mountain, as it is called, at a height of 7,698 feet above the sea. Between Kazbek, through Kobi, and the highest point, where a cross marks a disused turn in the road, and gives the name of Krestovaya to the summit of the pass, there is a difference of 2,158 feet over a distance of about seventeen miles. The steep rise to the top of the pass from Kobi is the most dangerous part of the road. Avalanches frequently slide down the sides of the mountains in the spring, and not only fill up the deep ravine cut out by the noisy, frothy Terek, but hurl their masses of ice and snow against the opposite mountain wall, and scoop out tons of earth and stone. A couple of road sheds, or tunnels, with slanting roofs have now been built on this part for the sheltered passage of travellers during the dangerous seasons, and an Ossetinian stone hut and refuge on the very summit of the pass, which is the highest dwelling in all the Caucasus, has been provided with a bell for giving warning when the road is to be avoided altogether. Here is the watershed of the rivers Terek and Aragua, the first flowing down the northern, and the other down the southern, side of the range. On this plateau at the parting of the waters, and before they separate to rush in headlong fury down opposite sides of the pass, the meandering streams become almost still and stagnant; while all around among the higher mountains rise into fuller view the "silent pinnacles of aged snow." All along the northern ascent the scenery is desolate, and only imposing by the enormous masses of stratified granite and stone piled up thousands of feet on both sides of the defile. The different mountain-tribes inhabiting the district, whose wretched flat-roofed and square-built hovels of loose stones, with open fronts, are seen perched up on the topmost crags, among the eagles and vultures, are still as primitive and uncivilized as when they were first driven up into these lonely heights thousands of years ago, by the Mongolian nomads, who took possession of the lower regions and plains. North of the pass the road leads through Ossetia, or the country of the Ossetins, whose language has been considered by some philologists as possessing an affinity with the German. But the bewildering babel of languages in the Caucasus, or "Mountain of tongues," as it was anciently called, is still a baffling study for European professors. It was once reckoned by Arabian writers that, with the dialects and divisions of the various distinct languages, they numbered some 300 or more. Pliny speaks of 130 interpreters having been necessary to transact business with these numerous linguistical groups at Dioscura, the present region of Abkhazia. Even at the present day a goodly number would be necessary to communicate properly with the more isolated mountaineers away from the main thoroughfares, where Russian is not yet the common medium of intercourse.

A number of ruined castles and towers are passed all along the road as far as Tiflis, and most of them have their legendary history.

They are nearly all situated at great heights above the valley, and their dilapidated walls and round towers are scarcely distinguishable from the dull, dirty colour of the surrounding mountains. After passing the Dariel fort, a square piece of loop-holed walling, buttressed with projecting towers at the corners, which formerly commanded the defile, but is now used as a barracks, the first object of interest is the so-called castle of Tamara, the celebrated Queen of Georgia. In Lermontoff's poem and Rubenstein's opera of "The Demon" there is a Princess Tamara, who resists all the temptations and blandishments of Satan; but the historical Tamara, as described by local tradition, was herself a kind of female demon. "Beautiful as an angel, and deceitful and cruel as the devil," this Cleopatra of the Caucasus appears to have been in the habit of enticing every handsome man who passed through the valley into her castle, and after a night of music and revelry his mangled remains were generally found on the morrow, cast down the precipice below. It is curious how dominant over all other historical personages is the name of this heroine throughout the Caucasus. Like the innumerable relics of Peter the Great in Russia, and of Alexander of Macedon in Central Asia, everything in the Caucasus not to be otherwise accounted for is at once attributed to Tamara. On one of the rugged spurs of Mount Kazbek, and visible as well as attainable on horseback from the post station, is an ancient church and monastery of the Trinity, said to contain certain sacred objects brought from Palestine by the Holy Nina, who was the female Baptist of the Georgians. A cross made of vine stems, which she is said to have carried, is still preserved in one of the churches at Tiflis. High above all is seen the white capped Kazbek, with its eight glaciers; and from the station at this point the start is generally made by extremely rare parties of climbers. The first to reach the top, 16,500 feet, was an Englishman named Parrot, nearly eighty years ago; and Mr. Freshfield has lately opened a fresh phase of interest in the region by the account of his new experiences. English mountain explorers now make their appearance every year, and unfortunately two of them have already lost their lives on the Koshtan tau, a mountain 1,200 feet higher than Kazbek.

If all is wild and desolate north of the pass on the Georgian road, on the southern side, as the wonderful zigzag descent is made into the valley of the Aragua, the scene becomes one of striking beauty. Here all the mountain sides are thickly wooded with oak, plane, chestnut, wild fruit-trees, and, in fact, every possible variety of tree and bush. The descent is very abrupt, and cleverly contrived by a series of winding galleries cut out on the face of the steep cliffs in front of the post station of Mlet. Once down in the glen watered by the crystal stream of the Aragua, which is seen descending like a silver streak down the mountain side, the road lies pretty level through a flourishing valley as far as the station of Ananoor, where a much smaller rise of ten versts takes place over the pass of the same name by a *détour* away from the bed of the Aragua, which is met again past the station of Dooshet. The whole of this part of the way passes through the country of the Christian Georgians, who, unlike the other mountaineers, were never conquered by the Russians, as they proudly declare, but voluntarily placed themselves under Russian protection. Their stone-built villages are scattered all over the mountain slopes, sometimes at altitudes that seem almost inaccessible, and

GEORGIAN MILITARY ROAD AT ANANOOR.

their cattle graze in the most marvellous manner over the sides of steep mountains that appear impossible places for any animal to keep its foothold. You never see a hamlet without the ruins of its tower of defence, which was an indispensable structure in the midst of or near every cluster of stone hovels before the Russians established their rule. It is probable, however, that these towers were more for refuge than defence, like those on the Turkoman plains of the Transcaspian. They rarely have doors, and were generally entered from underground. The valley hereabouts is reputed to be swarming with game of all kinds, from the wild mountain goat and the bear down to the large indigenous pheasant and the partridge; but it is remarkable that the traveller sees hardly a sign of animal life as he passes along through this beautiful country. The birds, says Russian writers, are afraid of the mountains, and the quadrupeds are no doubt only driven down into the valley by the cold and the snow in winter. The road strikes across the Poti Batoum and Tiflis Railway at the unpronounceable station of Mtskhet, at the confluence of the Aragua with the Koora, and the latter river pours its muddy stream into the clear current of the Aragua and runs through the city of Tiflis, which lies deep down between the mountains fifteen miles farther off.

But the beauty of the Southern Caucasus did not make me forget that this country was not only admitted to be a great military base and depôt for Russian operations in Central Asia, but was also regarded as a weak spot in Russia's armour, that could easily be turned to account by her European enemies. It has often been a favourite theme with the British Press that the alleged discontent of the inhabitants of the Caucasus was serious enough to be utilized against Russia in the event of war. A similar idea has prevailed about the Armenian frontier; but as the Armenians are much worse treated by the Turks, and as Russia has on her side the Armenian Catolicos, and thus holds the keys of the Armenian Church, she is much more powerful among the Turkish Armenians, when she chooses, than we can ever hope to be. We listen to their complaints, but get nothing done for them, in spite of our protectorate over Asia Minor. The religious element has always been Russia's strongest lever for either aggressive or defensive purposes. Without its help, the Caucasus would hardly have been conquered so soon and so completely as it was. Had the Georgians not been the one Christian people in the heart of the mountains who required Russia's support, or afforded her a pretext for giving it, against their Mohammedan persecutors, it would probably have made all the difference in Russia's subsequent operations. A strict attention to this matter gave Russia her first foothold in the country. England, on the contrary, in view of strengthening the allegiance of her Mahommedan subjects in India, has always refused to play on this string. Our policy has generally been to take sides with the Mussulmans against the Christians, even when we have had the chance of assisting both parties without offending either of them. Such appears to have been our blind neglect of opportunities during the Crimean war in ignoring the feelings of the most important people in the Caucasus. Had English, instead of Turkish, troops then entered the Trans-caucasus, we should have had the sympathy, and perhaps more than the sympathy, of the Christian tribes of Georgia on our side. Since that time conditions have greatly changed, and the future is not likely to offer another opportunity ; but the belief that the Caucasus must always be a flaw in Russia's panoply is still entertained.

At the time of the Afghan frontier crisis and the "unfortunate incident" on the Koushk, a notion was spread in London that the Caucasus had been declared to be a hotbed of sedition by the Russian authorities themselves, and that the chance of an inevitable brush with the legions of the Tsar was a good opportunity to consider the feasibility of taking advantage of such a state of things. Of course, the very act of loudly proclaiming any such hostile intention with the customary frankness of the British Press was quite enough to turn the tables upon ourselves, and defeat our own ends from the very beginning. Russia's rapidity of advance and, to a great extent also, her success in Central Asia and the Transcaspian, has been not untruly ascribed to the open discussion of Russia's weak points by the British Press and Parliament. There is no ill wind that does not bring good to somebody; and there can scarcely be any doubt that in the East the Russians have profited not a little by our frankly expressed fears and intentions. As it was in the Transcaspian, so it may be in the Caucasus; and who knows to what extent the changes already made in this mountainous region, and the reforms still contemplated in the near future, have been engendered or hastened on by the characteristic and straightforward British habit of giving due warning when and where we intend to strike in defence of British interests? The same thing was attempted during the Tsar's State visit to Finland in 1885 by the report sent to a London paper, and inspired by a small section of the Swedish element, that in the event of a war about the Afghan boundary, a British fleet might depend upon the sympathy and aid of the coast population of the Finnish Gulf.

The origin of the discovery of a vulnerable place in the Caucasus was a series of reports made by the different governors and military commanders of the Caucasian provinces on the subject of the introduction of the general principle of compulsory military service. These reports were merely unfavourable to the embodiment of the Mahommedan mountaineers as regular troops together with the Christians, and pointed out the tendency there would be to insubordination and other evils if such a step were taken without any preliminary measures for the purpose of smoothing the way. Somehow a garbled summary of these documents, which had been hawked about St. Petersburg as news many months before, found its way to Paris and thence to London, and a way of checking Russia in her encroachments towards India was thought to have been found out. As a matter of fact, it was only a question of temporizing with the mountain-tribes, and of allowing the last expiring embers of Schamyl's fanaticism to die out. At first a project of forming two separate armies, one of Christian infantry and the other of Mussulman cavalry, was put before the Government; but eventually the Mahommedan population were exempted for several years to come from service in its obligatory form in return for the payment of a small tax, or enrolled as Cossack militia according to their option, while a beginning was made with the Christian natives by the successful drafting into the common army of several thousand men for the first time in 1887.

While on my way over the steppe towards the Caucasus, I was accompanied a short part of the journey by an ex-governor of one of the Caucasian towns, who took occasion to talk, without any inducement on my part, about the aspirations and supposed dangerous proclivities of "Young Georgia," which, he said, were nothing but a mild species of agitation for home rule. They had, however, been exaggerated in St. Petersburg into a revolutionary movement for the separation of the Caucasus, and even into an affinitive "circle" with the "Nihilistic" groups of the rest of the Empire, which the *Moscow Gazette* maintains are equally active in working for the independence of Siberia, Poland, and Finland, as well as of the Caucasus. My fellow-traveller explained the matter as regards the Caucasus by declaring that the so-called movement was little else than a schoolboy ebullition, which had been overrated by certain local officials for the purpose of justifying measures calculated to show their own zeal and ingenuity, and of attracting the attention of the central authorities in their favour. In any case, there was no greater discontent in the Caucasus than in most other parts of Russia. And certainly, if outside appearances go for anything, I should infer from the success of the Imperial State visit to the Caucasus last year, which I was able to witness on my return from Samarkand, that the Great White Tsar has no more loyal and devoted subjects in the whole of his dominions. At the same time, of course, the military and other precautions which were taken on that occasion for guarding the Imperial person, are indication enough that the Caucasus was considered just as likely to be the arena of Nihilist exploits as any other part of the Empire. Of brigandage and highway robbery there is plenty on the roads less frequented, and not so well protected as the military route through Georgia. One of the most notorious brigands and outlaws, who has long been the scourge and terror of the districts near the Turkish frontier, and always manages to escape over the other side when hard pressed, is said to have been led into his present wild mode of existence by the arrest and exile of some of the members of his family. This man, Kerim by name, has become the Dick Turpin and Claude Duval of the Caucasus, and the stories of his exploits in robbing Russian travellers, always killing them on the slightest resistance, and in eluding the pursuit of the troops frequently moved against him, are already a part of the folk-lore of the country. Some time ago an entire regiment was sent to seize him in the mountains, where he had suddenly made his appearance. A cordon of several miles was gradually drawn in close around his hiding-place, and at last a storm of bullets were aimed at the supposed Kerim high up on the slope. The bullet-riddled figure, however, turned out to be nothing but the long shaggy felt mantle (*boorka*) and lambs'-wool cap of the robber chief stuck upon a pole. The owner, with his followers, had again escaped in the most marvellous manner. There is little doubt that he enjoys the sympathy and assistance of the natives of the border districts where he lurks, else his capture would have been effected long ago.* There are also frequent cases of Circassians running amuck among the Russians in such an extraordinary manner as might seem to indicate a strong feeling of hatred not yet entirely extinguished by the blessings of Russian rule. A few months ago an incident of this tragic character occurred at one of the railway stations. The mere touch of a Russian gendarme in order to prevent one of these ferocious individuals from entering a car in which he could not, for some reason or other, be admitted was enough provocation for the offended Circassian to whip out his long *kinjal* and stab every Russian within reach. He killed the gendarme with one thrust, and then rushed

---

* This robber chief is now at Teheran, where the Shah's Government promises the Russians he shall be kept. He escaped some months ago, wounded, over the Turkish frontier, and thence fled into Persia.

into the waiting-room and buffet, slashing all the time at everybody in his way. Three persons were killed outright, and half-a-dozen others mortally or seriously wounded. As soon as his revenge was satisfied the frenzied ruffian took to his heels; but when he found a Cossack close at his back he turned about and fought like a madman until cut down and almost hacked to pieces. Such incidents, however, are due more to the savage instincts and unbridled temper of the people than to any serious political disaffection. So fiery and excitable are the natives, that at the club in Tiflis all scabbards have to be emptied at the doors before the military members are allowed to enter. It is true that during the last campaign in Turkey one or two regiments of Mahommedan cavalry showed signs of insubordination, owing to contact with kindred Circassians in the service of the Turks; but this was an insignificant flicker of religious fanaticism in peculiar and exceptional circumstances. In the long run, whatever little religious antagonism may still lie dormant among the Mahommedan mountaineers, they cannot resist the remarkable faculty displayed by the Russians of identifying themselves with the Asiatic peoples whom they conquer.

On arriving at Tiflis rather late in the evening, I found that General Zelennoi, the appointed Commissioner with General Lumsden on the Afghan frontier in 1884, had been apprised of my coming by telegraph from St. Petersburg. I chanced to meet the General in the supper-room of the hotel attentively conning *The Times*. He at present holds the post of chief over the Asiatic Department of the General Staff at Tiflis, and when good luck threw me in his way within an hour after my arrival, he was taking a little relaxation from a hard day's work of examining officers in Oriental studies. Tired as I was, I could not resist the attraction of a long conversation with such an interesting personage, and we sat up and discussed the late difficulties of the Afghan frontier and things in general until far into the small hours of the morning. The old topic of the reasons why he did not meet General Lumsden on the frontier was again reviewed, and I must confess that he made out a very good case to show that his contention for a settlement of the chief frontier points before starting, was eventually admitted in the work of his successor, Colonel Kulberg, in conjunction with Sir West Ridgeway, and completely justified afterwards by the transfer of the negotiations about Khoja Saleh from the Oxus to St. Petersburg. This, he assured me, was the only reason why he had never started for the Afghan frontier. In any case, had he gone there to meet Sir Peter Lumsden at the proper time, the Russian fight with the Afghans at Dash Kepri, which put an end to both Generals as Afghan Boundary Commissioners, would probably never have taken place.

I left Tiflis the next day by train for Baku, in order to catch a boat, which the agent of the Caucasus and Mercury Steamship Company had twice assured me was to start on the day following for Oozoon Ada. Knowing the uncertainty of Russian information in general, I took the precaution before quitting Tiflis of paying a second visit to the Company's office, where I received an absolute confirmation of the assurance that a boat was to start on the day named with one of the directors on board; so that I felt sure this time of not being delayed at Baku.

The single-line railway to the city of "Eternal Fires" and spouting petroleum runs through a low, flat country, leaving the snow-clad peaks of the Caucasus far to the north, and following the valley of the river Koora, which flows between very low banks, bordered by extensive tracts of marshy land, causing a great deal of damage to the railway at high water, and teeming with water-fowl of every description. The last bit of country traversed by the line over the Apsheron peninsula resembles in many respects the district of the railway in the Transcaspian. The same sandy flats, dried-up salt marshes destitute of all vegetation, and the same bare brown or buff-coloured hills, common to the greater part of the Caspian shores, give a dismal aspect to the landscape long before you catch sight of the tall well-derricks and iron reservoirs, the tank-cars and cistern-steamers, of the black and busy-looking petroleum region. This striking analogy between the sabulous railway routes on both shores of the Caspian has, in fact, been practically illustrated by serious accidents due to the sand being blown over the rails, as in February last year, when a train of goods and petroleum ran off the track near the second station from Baku. Owing to constant complaints and mismanagement the Tiflis-Baku Railway has now been taken over by the Government.

The people of this district, as far as one could judge from the specimens lounging about at the railway stations, are chiefly Persians. Groups of swarthy, unkempt individuals stood about on every platform, with heavy black sheepskin caps, and beards painted dark saffron or deep red. In Baku I was surprised to see the legs of their droshky horses dyed with the same pigment, which made me think at first that the animals belonged to a circus. At many of the railway stations there were natives on duty in Cossack uniforms, shouldering muskets or repeating rifles, which showed that Russia had also organized these Persians into something of a militia or police force; while it was evident, by several officers met with in the train who were pure Persians, serving as chief police masters of districts, or in other positions of command, that they were not excluded from the local executive and administration. They all wore the same long Circassian dress,—that sartorial badge of the close and genial link between the Russian and the Asiatic, which is seen on the Cossacks who guard the Tsar at St. Petersburg, and on the Turkoman Khans who surround Colonel Alikhanoff at Merv.

In a country of so many intermingled types and languages, it was not easy to recognize in these men the Russified natives of Iran.

When I got out of the train at Baku I was at once taken in charge by the police. The assistant of the police master was waiting for me on the platform and calling out my name and nationality in order, as he politely stated, to acquaint me with the news, of which I was already aware, that there was no just cause or impediment to my further progress into the Transcaspian. He then recommended me to go to a certain hotel, and kindly had my luggage put into a droshky. I had some scruples, however, as to the convenience of following this police advice in the matter of hotels, and so had myself driven to quite a different hostelry. This independent line of action, it turned out, was calculated to lead to some annoyance, for I had not long been in the hotel of my own choosing when another police officer made his appearance, who seemed quite ignorant of the special orders received from St. Petersburg on my behalf, and requested me to hand over my passport. I lost no time in going to the Steamship Company's office, and, to my utter disappointment, found that the steamer which the agent in Tiflis had positively assured me was to start that very afternoon, had been countermanded, and there would not be another boat for two days. This was a good example of the dependence to be placed upon any kind of information in Russia, even in matters of business. The representative at Baku blamed the agent at Tiflis for not knowing better, but officially-subsidized steamship or other companies in Russia are not bound to be precise with the public. Among all the five or six steamboat and shipping companies of Baku, there was not a single craft, under sail or steam, going to Oozoon Ada for forty-eight hours. After all I had heard of the great traffic and daily transports across the Caspian since the construction of the Transcaspian Railway to the Amu Darya, I was very much struck with this fact, especially on an occasion when one would have expected even more than the usual number of vessels to be running on account of the inauguration of the last branch of the railway. There were several engineers and others connected with the Transcaspian line anxious to see something of the festivities who were forced to

Through the Caucasus to the Caspian. 105

wait like myself. Meanwhile I paid a visit to the Civil Governor of the town, and was received with the same obliging politeness which all the Russian officials showed me throughout the journey. It was only a pity that they could not curtail somewhat the delays to which I was all the time subjected from the Caspian onwards. His Excellency told me, somewhat to my dismay, that part of the Transcaspian Railway had been washed away by the floods, and that General Annenkoff's family party, which had just got over, had been obliged to halt in the desert until the damage could be repaired.

At the time I was in Baku the first annual trade fair was being held there. This new mart has been established for the purpose of co-operating with the Transcaspian Railway in inducing Asiatic merchants to send their goods here for sale in preference to the more distant fair at Nijni Novgorod. It was a very miserable beginning, and a large number of the wooden sheds of which it was composed outside the town were afterwards burnt down. It will be a long time probably before it attracts any considerable part of the Asiatic commerce of Nijni.

In due time I started for Oozoon Ada in the English-built steamer *Prince Bariatinsky*, engined by John Penn, and commanded by a Swedish captain. Several, if not all, of the other half-dozen passenger boats of the same company were constructed in England. It is remarkable, said a Russian to me, what a number of Swedes have taken situations on this sea since the two famous Scandinavians, the Brothers Nobel, created their great petroleum industry at Baku. With here and there an exception, you will always find foreigners in Russia the promoters and sustainers of non-official activity and enterprise. The *Prince Bariatinsky*, named after the General who took Schamyl and conquered the Caucasus, which shipped Skobeleff and his troops to Tchikishlar in 1879, and often conveyed the late Mr. O'Donovan, might have been anything but a Russian steamer on a Russian island sea. Besides the captain, the mate was a Swede, the chief engineer was a German, and the crew were chiefly Tartars and Persians.* There were Swedes, Germans, Poles, and Tartars among

---

* Ministerial orders have been issued that no more foreign subjects are to be accepted by the Baku authorities as ship-captains on the Caspian.

Through the Caucasus to the Caspian. 107

the first-class passengers. The decks were occupied with the usual motley crowd of turbaned Orientals with their prayer carpets and covered-up wives, Persians with their rosaries, Armenians, and smart dealers in cheap and generally spurious turquoises. There were a couple of young Poles on board who had not long ago finished the University course at Warsaw, and were going out to Bokhara on a speculation for some Polish firm of manufacturers. They gave me a deplorable account of the effects of the Russian Government's present policy of strictly excluding educated Poles from all employment under the Crown in their own country, and thus compelling them to seek their fortunes in other parts of the Empire. This to a certain extent is why there are so many Polish engineers engaged on Annenkoff's railway in the Transcaspian,— a fact which has already excited the surprise of the authorities in St. Petersburg. The architect of the Amu Darya bridges, M. Belinsky, of whose work I shall have something to say hereafter, is a Pole, and so is the engineer charged with the great task of restoring the Sultan Bent Dam on the Murghab, and of thus irrigating the Tsar's new Transcaspian estate. This gentleman, Mr. Kozell-Poklefsky, is at the same time a remarkable instance of a pardoned Polish rebel. He was police master of Warsaw during the revolution, and passed several years of exile in Siberia and abroad previous to receiving a pardon from Alexander II.

CHAPTER V.

OOZOON ADA AND KRASNOVODSK.

Arrival at Oozoon Ada — Wretched aspect — Delay — Floods — Interrupted communication — Description of town — Buildings and population — Shipping firms — Sand storms — Silting up of harbour — Inundations — No fresh water — Description of seaboard — Labyrinth of salt lagoons — Long Island — Dardja peninsula — Ancient channels and delta of the Amu Darya — Proposed restoration of old bed of the Oxus, now practically useless except for irrigation — General Glookhofsky's project and opinion — Dangerous proximity of railway to the Persian frontier — Necessity of supplementary communication by water — Oozoon Ada versus Krasnovodsk — Commission on — The question shelved — Reasons for — Transference of railway terminus unnecessary — Effect of proposed branch line to Krasnovodsk — Arrival of train from Askabad — No first-class carriages — Extent of rolling stock — Special accommodation for Mohammedans.

WE reached the Bay of Oozoon Ada, the Caspian terminus of the new Asiatic Railway, early in the morning, after a fair voyage of about 132 miles in nineteen hours. The aspect of the place was extremely wretched and melancholy,—hardly an encouraging introduction into a new country, although some amends were made for the barren and blighted character of the landscapes by the beautiful fine weather and a cloudless sky with 100 degrees of Fahrenheit in the shade.

The train was timed to start at six o'clock in the evening, which entailed another whole day's delay, and this time in such a miserable and uninteresting waste, that most of the passengers preferred to stay in the steamer until the hour of departure. Instead of six o'clock, it was nearly midnight before the train actually did leave, as the one due from the opposite direction had first to be waited for ; and there had been no communication either way for several days in consequence of the rails near Kizil Arvat and other places having been washed away by the floods. A whole day was certainly too long to inspect this bivouac on the edge of the desert ; and its description may be summed up in very few words. Eighteen low, and narrow wooden piers jutting out into the water round a semi-circular and sandy bay, with one or two

Oozoon Ada and Krasnovodsk. 111

larger and stronger landing stages belonging to the steamship companies; a few dozen sailing brigs, barges, and smaller craft; two or three steamers at anchor; with straggling rows and clusters of flimsy wooden houses, huts and warehouses, the whole enclosed by a background of bare hills and mounds of light yellow sand. Such is a picture of Oozoon Ada as I first saw it. The hurriedly built settlement had a very ephemeral and unsubstantial appearance, and in no way corresponded with the fanciful description of a Russian newspaper writer who had filled it with imaginary fine streets and squares. There was the green painted dome of the indispensable wooden church, dedicated to St. Michael the Archangel, or, as the Russians here, with very appropriate significance, prefer to call him, St. Michael, the Archistrategist; and large sheds for the weekly market or bazaar had also naturally been provided. The other wooden buildings now comprise sixty houses, one bad lodging-house, a few stores, including one for the sale of ready-made Vienna clothes, and one *dookhan* or Caucasian wine-shop. The small business of the place, such as it is, has, of course, been taken in hand entirely by Armenians from the Caucasus. The principal shipping and mercantile firms represented are "Lebedeff," "Droojina," "Nadiejda," and Koodrin and Company; and the inhabitants number from 800 to 900 souls.* The railway station, which has a buffet, is situated nearly a quarter of a mile from the landing-place, and passengers have to trudge ankle-deep through the hot sand to get to the platform; but the trains from the interior are run round the bay from the station to the head of the steamboat pier. During violent storms of wind the fine sand flies into one's face like spray, and nothing can prevent it from irritating the eyes and penetrating through the clothes to the skin. Sometimes ports of the bay, deep enough for all ordinary vessels, get sanded up to within five or six feet of the surface, and the floating dredger has to be set to work before the deeper draught steamers can reach their accustomed anchorage. This is precisely what happens in the Amu Darya and other Central Asian streams that are gradually disappearing under the sand. At the same time the sea occasionally floods the houses near the water's edge, and this necessitates the raising of some of them upon piles.

* The latest census of Oozoon Ada, made in October, 1889, gives 1,651 inhabitants, including 240 women and 130 children.

General Annenkoff is now about to construct a stone dam, or quay, on the north shore to prevent these inundations. At the time of my visit there was no fresh water supply at Oozoon Ada, as the condensing machine, which generally worked day and night, was out of order, and water had to be brought by every train in large vats, or cisterns, on wheeled platforms all the way from Kazandjik, 120 miles off.

The appearance of this dismal shore was not always perhaps so overpoweringly dreary as it is at the present day. If at this point the mighty stream of the Oxus, freighted with the wares of India and the East, once found an outlet into the Caspian Sea, the aspect of the desolate seaboard has probably undergone as striking a change as that in the course of the river itself. The part of the coast on which is situated the Caspian terminus of the Central Asian Railway now consists of a complicated and fantastic labyrinth of salt lagoons, the pale, green reflections from whose glassy surface contrast agreeably with the light yellow of the sand-hills on the numerous islands and peninsulas which they form. Oozoon Ada, or "Long Island," is an elongated strip of sand, connected with the peninsula of Dardja by a railway dam about a mile long. The watery labyrinth extends some fifteen miles beyond the railway terminus; and the lagoons only come to an end where the train enters the desert of the interior, after passing the second station at the now disused Michael's Bay. Near the coast are also numerous desiccated watercourses, which, together with the maze of sand and water, certainly give one the impression of being the remains of a vast river delta. Some explorers consider that these traces rather indicate the former existence of a broad gulf connected with the basin of the once existent Sary Kamish Lake, into which the Amu Darya emptied itself, instead of flowing directly into the Caspian Sea. But the question of the ancient channels of the Amu Darya has never yet been satisfactorily settled, and should any definite solution ever be arrived at, much of its practical value in furthering the creation of a direct waterway between Russia and Central Asia would now be lost, owing to the construction of the Central Asian Railway. On the other hand, it would be of great importance in facilitating the work of irrigation, and if the whole or the greater part of the Transcaspian deserts could be fertilized by

Oozoon Ada and Krasnovodsk. 115

diverting the river into any of its old channels, the railway would eventually reap the benefit by running through a flourishing country instead of a barren wilderness. Other authorities, who have not the same tender interest in the railway that General Annenkoff has, are of a very different opinion. The chief of these is now General Glookhofsky, who explored the old courses of the river at the head of a special commission between 1879 and 1883; and he believes that the reversion of the waters of the Amu Darya to the Caspian, so as to open up an alternative and supplementary route to that of the railway, is now more urgently needed than ever it was. In fact he considers that the safety and prosperity of the railway depends very much upon the accomplishment of this project, as the proximity of the line to the Persian fontier endangers the security of its communications, and the 300 versts of desert which it now runs through only increase the working expenses, whereas the proposed waterway, being farther from the frontier, would be less liable to attack, and besides fertilizing the country, would afford a much cheaper means of transport. Such are the arguments in favour of this gigantic engineering scheme, which would cost some

30,000,000 roubles, and take ten years to complete.

A far more pressing question, about which there has been a great deal of discussion, is the advisability of transferring the starting point of the Transcaspian Railway from Oozoon Ada to Krasnovodsk, on account of the deeper water and better accommodation for steamers at the latter place. General Annenkoff and his friends are naturally opposed to this projected change, especially after the expensive alterations already made in the Caspian terminal of the railway. With the exception of a few persons specially interested in Krasnovodsk, the principal or, at least the majority, of the shippers on the Caspian are reported to be of the same opinion. Krasnovodsk, which has sixteen or seventeen feet of water, was originally chosen for the starting-point of the railway; but St. Michael's Bay was subsequently preferred, because it offered a more direct and shorter cut to the first fresh-water oasis of Akhal Tekhe. The Gulf of St. Michael, however, was too shallow to receive the larger steamers, so that they still had to proceed to Krasnovodsk, and transship their goods for the railway into other boats of lesser draught.

Oozoon Ada and Krasnovodsk. 117

After the first section of the railway had been opened, this inconvenience induced General Annenkoff to look for a more suitable harbour. At first he was inclined to select the Bay of St. Xenia, named after the Emperor's eldest daughter, and even began some kind of preliminary work there; but this point was very soon abandoned in favour of Oozoon Ada. As soon as the Oozoon Ada branch of the line was accordingly made, the General's opponents began to agitate against it. Last autumn a commission was appointed to inquire into the matter; and it appears that no definite decision was arrived at, although the majority of the members were unable to find any very weighty reasons for the retention of Oozoon Ada. It was thereupon reported that the question had been indefinitely shelved on the following practical grounds:—

In the first place, the anchorage of the bay at Oozoon Ada (nine to ten feet) is as deep as the port of Astrakhan at the mouth of the Volga, which is supposed to regulate the draught of nearly all the vessels built for service on the Caspian. General Annenkoff says that boats drawing $9\frac{3}{4}$ feet can enter the bay of Oozoon Ada, while the deepest water of the port of Astrakhan cannot float vessels drawing over nine feet. Of all the 1,480 vessels on the Caspian, of which about 500 are steamers, only eight or nine of the latter, with a loading line of fourteen feet, and plying between Baku and the other seaports, are unable to enter Oozoon Ada without transshipping or lightening their cargoes outside the bay, off the island of Rau; therefore if Krasnovodsk is to be preferred to Oozoon Ada merely for the sake of these nine vessels, several more millions would have to be spent on a new railway branch 75 or 100 miles long between Krasnovodsk and Bala Ishem, or between Krasnovodsk and Molla Kari, which would increase the total length of the railway by twenty or thirty miles, and consequently augment the cost of freights. No adequate necessity can be shown to exist for such an outlay until the port of Astrakhan is deepened, or either of the projected railways between Vladikavkaz and Petrofsk, on the western shore of the Caspian, and between Vladikavkaz and Tiflis, through the mountain chain, has first been constructed. Either of these railway lines would carry goods direct from Russia into much deeper water, the one to the port of Petrofsk and the other to Baku, both of which have a depth of twenty to twenty-five feet. A great deal of money has already been spent on Oozoon Ada, and no great advantage could be gained in the present circumstances by its desertion in favour of Krasnovodsk. Oozoon Ada has now more inhabitants than Krasnovodsk, which, without its garrison, would be as completely deserted as Oozoon Ada without its railway; all necessaries have to be brought to both places from Astrakhan and Baku; both are obliged to distil their chief supply of water from the sea; and in no other respect can the one town claim any superiority over the other.

These are the arguments of General Annenkoff, who defends the existence of his pet offspring with all the courage of desperation. His opponents, however, flatly contradict many of his facts and figures. One side declares that the water-depth of Oozoon Ada is often less than seven feet; the other asserts that it generally reaches thirteen, and is never much under ten. A correspondent of the *Grajdanin* newspaper, writing from the spot, states that the depth in winter is ten feet; in summer eleven; and that in 1889 it reached as much as thirteen feet. The puzzled looker-on at this contest between the partisans of the rival ports can only come to the conclusion that there is a certain reckless disregard for accuracy in the statements of both parties. The drift of General Annenkoff's argument seems to be, that as long as the port of Astrakhan remains in its present shallow state, there is no necessity for any better seaport for the Transcaspian Railway; which is an indirect admission that Oozoon Ada is, in any case, only a temporary expedient until the improvement of accessory ways of communication on the western coast of the Caspian. His contention, it will be seen, is entirely based upon the connection between the Volga trade and the Central Asian Railway, to the exclusion of the shipping interests of the Caspian proper, which is said to be represented by only ten steamers incapable of entering Oozoon Ada. Another authority asserts that there are as many as seventy vessels of more than nine feet draught, which cannot always safely enter the port. As for the assertion that most of the Caspian steamers are built to suit the river depths of Astrakhan, it is well known that most of the steamers running between Oozoon Ada and the Volga have to receive or transfer their cargoes and passengers in the famous nine feet roadstead at the mouth of the river. There is also every reason to suppose that there will now be a tendency to build larger and deeper boats for the Caspian, in view of the imminent opening up of the deep ports of Petrofsk and Derbent by the projected railway from Vladikavkaz. Even at present the shipping trade of the Caspian is sufficiently independent of the Volga, and cannot be ignored in presence of the growing traffic on the Transcaucasian railways between Baku and Batoum, and the certainty of their junction, sooner or later, with the rest of the railways of European Russia. General Annenkoff himself tells me that he is now endeavouring to turn the cotton transport on to the Baku-Tiflis-Batoum lines, so as to avoid the accumulation of goods at Oozoon Ada during the long closed season of the Volga route. This, he thinks, will enable him to transport all the Central Asian cotton within the year of its growth, instead of during the following one.

There are other objections to Oozoon Ada besides its shallowness of water. It is objected that the entrance to the harbour is narrow and tortuous, and that the railway station and warehouses are built upon a low sand bank which is constantly overblown by the shifting sand from the hills and dunes. This movable ground is stated to be unfit for the erection of permanent stone buildings for workshops, railway depôts, etc.; and there is no accommodation for large numbers of troops in case of reinforcements arriving from the Caucasus. On the other hand, Krasnovodsk is recommended because it lies in a deep gulf; is sheltered from the winds by the Balkan hills, which would have to be cut through for a railway; and already possesses the necessary military requirements. The opponents of Krasnovodsk state that the coast-line of the latter is narrowed and cramped by the mountains; that there is not room enough for a first-class goods station; that sufficient fresh water will never be found; and that the weather in the harbour is often very boisterous and stormy; all of which allegations are positively denied by the opposite party. One point which has been alleged in favour of Krasnovodsk, namely, that the voyage thither from the Volga or the western Caspian would be shorter than the distance to Oozoon Ada, is not borne out by the facts recently given by the special correspondent of the

Oozoon Ada and Krasnovodsk. 123

Grajdanin, who states that the voyage from Baku to Krasnovodsk takes four or five hours longer than from Baku direct to Oozoon Ada; and that the proposed branch line from Krasnovodsk would entail another extra five hours on the railway journey; so that passengers and goods *viâ* Krasnovodsk would have to travel altogether about ten hours more than at present. The late General Paucker once suggested the choice of a spot near Cape Oofra, a few miles from Krasnovodsk, in lieu of the latter, as a more suitable place for the railway port; and others have proposed to run the railway on to the petroleum island of Tcheleken. Whatever may eventually be decided upon, the sooner some decision one way or the other is come to the better, as prolonged suspense will only stop further expenditure on improvements at Oozoon Ada, and hinder the development of trade.

The latest phase of the question is curious and characteristic. General Annenkoff had no sooner returned to the Transcaspian last autumn, after attending the Commission in St. Petersburg, by which the matter was supposed to have been virtually shelved, than another and different Commission followed closely on his heels in order to make further inquiries, and to survey the route for the line to Krasnovodsk, which, it was at the same time stated, had been positively resolved upon in the Ministry of War. This new Commission appears to have been despatched at the instance of the General Staff, and was headed by General Kopieff. One of its most prominent members, Colonel Shebanoff, who formerly managed the first section of the railway to Kizil Arvat, is regarded as the bitter enemy of General Annenkoff. Colonel Shebanoff was also for a short time assistant to Annenkoff in working the line, and a violent antagonism seems to have sprung up between them. Shebanoff made accusations against Annenkoff, who retorted in the same way; and at last Shebanoff left the Transcaspian, and rejoined the Staff in St. Petersburg. Shebanoff's successor, the late General Bazoff, who was in charge of the railway as far as the Oxus during the construction of the Bokharan half of the line, was also very hostile to the chief constructor. It was said that he not only would not himself attend the opening of the railway at Samarkand, but at first refused to facilitate the journey of Annenkoff's guests when they were detained by the inundation of the railway.

One can imagine the surprise of Annenkoff at the appearance of this Commission with Colonel Shebanoff as one of its principal members. It was at the same time reported that the construction of barracks and other official buildings at Oozoon Ada had been suspended by telegram, in consequence of the determination to extend the railway to Krasnovodsk. The Commission completed its work and returned to the capital, whither it was soon followed by General Annenkoff, who continues down to this day to express the most sanguine confidence in the perfect security of his precious creation. Nothing officially has transpired; but I am inclined to believe that the Krasnovodsk extension, although pretty certain to be made in the end, will not be undertaken for some time to come.

The train from Askabad which was to take me from Oozoon Ada to Samarkand, came in between ten and eleven at night, and started back again five or six hours behind time to begin with, as soon as the exchange of passengers had been effected. I was told there was not a single first-class carriage on the entire line, and such is the case up to the present day, with the exception of one or two special coaches reserved for General Annenkoff and the Governor-General. At the end of the train there was one very high double-storied waggon, second-class below and third on the top. There was no other second-class compartment, the rest of the train being made up of third and fourth-class cars. Several of the closed trucks, used indiscriminately on all Russian railways for cattle or troops, and marked "Eight horses or forty men," were filled by persons who found them much cooler. An official informed me that there were as yet only about 1,000 waggons and sixty locomotives for the entire distance of 900 miles, but these numbers have since been increased to 112 locomotives, 70 passenger carriages of second and third-class, 1,146 closed goods waggons, 570 open trucks, 62 water cisterns on trucks, and 82 tank-cars for petroleum. Many of the locomotives are always under repair in consequence of the sand getting into their wheels and machinery. As the Bokharan branch was not yet opened, there were no through tickets for Samarkand, and passengers could only book as far as the Amu Darya. I should not omit to mention that strict Mahommedan travellers have been specially thought of, and provided with separate waggons, lettered in two languages. A Persian time-table and guide has also been published by General Annenkoff, with a fine portrait of the Shah, for the purpose of inducing the Shiite Mahommedans to avail themselves of the Russian Railway in their pilgrimages to the holy city of Meshed.

CHAPTER VI.

OOZOON ADA TO GEOK TEPÉ.

Departure from Oozoon Ada — Howling wilderness — Desolation — Persian *hamals* — Railway dam — Blood-red water — Kizil-Soo — Michailofsk: the original terminus — Bala Ishem — The Balkans — The Kuren and Kopet Dag mountains: lifeless appearance and Turkoman avoidance of — Fertility of their Persian slopes — Insignificant valleys and streams on Russian side — Rise of Tedjent and Murghab — The mountains relieve the sight, and supply the water — Failure of wells — Memorial of Skobeleff's march — Gradients — The salt steppe — Mirages — Ninety per cent. of desert — Fast and movable sands — " White earth," or *loess* — Proposed colonization and irrigation — Expected results — Old channels of the Oxus crossed by the railway — Former bottom of the sea — Naphtha Dag and petroleum supply — Kazandjik: the first fresh-water source — Delays and damage caused by floods — Insufficiency of culverts — Easy construction of the line — Difficulties of the sand — Cuttings — Part of road re-made twenty times — Materials lost in the sand — Speed and cheapness of construction — Competition between General Annenkoff and the Minister of Communications — Effects of floods — Troubles and pastimes of Annenkoff's guests — Kizil Arvat: beginning of the Akhal Tekke oasis — Population —

Oozoon Ada to Geok Tépé. 129

Fountains—Bami—Junction with the Atrek—Character of the oases—Turkoman *obas*—Towers of refuge—Salt, sand, and grass steppes—Saxaoul—Discomforts of the railway—Military control—Turkoman platelayers—Turkoman dress—Cossack justice—Persian navvies and porters—Russian tenderness for the Tekkes and dislike of the Persians—Persia and the Yomud and Goklan Turkomans—Russia claims them—Treatment of Persians—Official monopoly of railway accommodation—Fellow-passengers.

WHEN I left Oozoon Ada it was a clear moonlight night, and the sandy desert could be comfortably surveyed from the rear of the train through the end door of the two-storied car which took the place of a brake-van. As we dragged along at the moderate rate of thirteen or fourteen miles an hour, the lone and desolate outlook recalled my school-day visions of the Great Sahara. I could compare this howling wilderness with nothing else that I had ever seen or read of; and all that was wanting to complete the picture were the bleached rib-bones of camel skeletons protruding through the yellow sand. After the noble and elevating scenery of the Caucasus, this violent contrast was all the more melancholy and depressing. The only signs of human kind on this part of the road were two or three *kibitka* tents, seen

K

between the hills, and half-buried in the sand. A French acquaintance boasted of having descried a jackal sneaking along in the distance, but I am pretty sure that it was only a stray dog, for no other animal would be likely to follow man into this wretched region. I do not believe there was a single other quadruped at Oozoon Ada, nor a single wheeled vehicle of any kind off the railway sidings; so that the traveller with luggage had reason to be thankful for the strong Persian *hamals*, who are able to wade through the hot sand with weights on their bent backs almost as heavy as the ordinary load of a camel.

The train first finds its way through a cutting between the sand dunes at a certain gradient, and then passes over the long dam or sand bank, which is very well laid across the estuary or lagoon that separates the island of Oozoon Ada from the peninsula of Dardja. This narrow trail of the water-flanked line is the only instance throughout the length of the railway, as far as my observation went, of the use of good stone rubble to strengthen the sides of the embankment. The thin telegraph posts seemed very infirmly stuck into the sandy bottom of the water along the side of this dam, and looked as though they would require frequent attention. Farther on we passed several pools of presumably briny, and decidedly blood-red water, which probably accounts for the origin of the name of Krasnavodsk, in native nomenclature Kizil-Soo, both meaning red water.

The first halt of the train is at the little station of Michael's Bay, which was the original terminus and landing-place from Baku and Astrakhan, but is no longer used as such on account of the shallowness of the harbour. Here the train has to retreat a few hundred yards in order to reach the platform bordering the first rails laid down in the Transcaspian. The first part of the twenty-five versts, or seventeen miles, to this station presents nothing but shifting sand driven up by the winds into hills of all shapes and sizes, destitute of vegetation, and interspersed with salt lakes and pools. At Michailofsk the sand hillocks are varied by the kitchen middens of the former settlement, which has now entirely disappeared, and a rough wooden cross or two mark the sites of human graves. Nothing else has been left, except the small station building, and two or three scattered wooden houses belonging to the half-dozen employés.

Morning dawned upon us near Bala Ishem,

and we soon saw the last of the Great and Little Balkan mountains, between which the train had passed during the night ; while in return for this loss to the view we came in sight of the steep, rugged range of the Kuren Dag, continued opposite Kizil Arvat by that of the higher Kopet Dag, rising 6,000 feet above the sea. These mountains, which form the natural frontier of Persia, run parallel with the railway on the south for 350 miles, until the line bends off near Dooshak on its way to Merv. When one sees the sterile and lifeless character of their Northern or Russian slopes, it is no longer surprising that the Turkoman enemies of Russia preferred to remain and accept defeat upon the open plains, rather than retreat into their mountain recesses and imitate the opposition of the Caucasus. This side of the Kopet Dag is bleak and bare. All the fertility, and all the best water-sources, are on the opposite side in Persia, where the rainfall is just about double what it is on the Russian side. There are no Alpine pastures, says M. Semenoff, and no very deep and sheltering valleys for the refuge of independent mountaineers, as in the Caucasus ; and none of the streamlets that fertilize in a very half-hearted sort of fashion the oases of Akhal

Oozoon Ada to Geok Tepé. 133

Tekke, take their origin on the snowless crests of these scabrous heights : they nearly all rise from underground sources at the foot of the mountains, and the valleys which lead to them are of small and insignificant extent. An exception to this rule occurs on the eastern part of the range, where the rivers Tedjent and Murghab, rising on the Persian and Afghan slopes, break through to the Russian side.

These mountains are said to almost overshadow the railway the whole of the long distance of some 400 miles as far as Dooshak ; and, indeed, it would be a great blessing if they actually did so in such a way as to moderate the excessive heat. They have their uses, however, of another kind. Happily for the weary vision of the traveller, compelled for several days together to gaze across this sorrowful expanse of unvaried flatness, they constitute the one relieving feature of the endless plain extending in every other direction ; and without them, in fact, the railway would have been quite impossible, for they furnish the greater part of its fresh-water supply, though often, it must be confessed, in far too great abundance to benefit the line. The system of wells, which was to provide all the necessary water, has turned out a failure.

An artesian well bored at Molla-Kari, a small station beyond Michailofsk, has never yet produced anything but salt water, and has now been abandoned. A natural source, it is said, formerly existed here in the so-called "Sacred Mountain," but this has also become brackish, owing to the infiltration of tainted water from the salty surface of the soil.

On this first waterless section of 115 miles, on one of the hills of the Little Balkans, near the station of Pereval, there is a small stone shrine commemorative of the passage of the Russian troops in the Expedition of 1881, when Skobeleff and his men took two months to cover the distance along this road to Askabad, which can now be traversed in twenty-four or thirty hours. Although the railway seems to be everywhere built on low level ground, it is said that at Molla-Kari, passing the Little Balkans, there is a gradient of 0.018 fathoms, and between the small stations of Aydin and Pereval, the latter meaning "pass," a lesser one occurs of 0.015. There is no other rise worth mentioning as far as the Amu Darya.

The flat plain on all sides for many miles along this part of the line, after quitting the mobile sands near Molla-Kari, is caked over with a thick crust of whitish clay or marl, impregnated and faced with salt, which crystallizes perfectly white on the surface like snow, especially in the sunken spots and salt pans left by the rain pools. Salt here, for the most part, takes the place of sand, and glitters brightly in the glare of the sun. It is probably this top dressing that helps to form the distant mirages of the Tekke desert, which I more than once saw from the windows of the train, presenting the appearance of sheets of cool inviting water with islets of rich vegetation floating on their surface, and tremulously glistening in the lambent atmosphere.

In order to appreciate the little there is of variety in this ill-favoured country of Transcaspia,—which is larger than France, and contains 10,000 geographical square miles, with no less than ninety per cent. of desert,—it is necessary to distinguish between two kinds of sandy surface, in addition to the more argillaceous and saliferous districts just mentioned. The sand wastes are divided into shifting sands, billowed up by the force of the winds, and fast sands covering a very hard clayish level, sometimes with the smallest possible sprinkling of vegetation, but oftener with none at all. These fast sands are especially noticeable between Aydin and Aktcha Kuima, near Kazandjik, between Askabad and Giaours, and after passing Merv towards the Amu Darya, before reaching the shifting sands of the Kara Kum. The Russians call this particular kind of sand steppe by the name of *takir*, which is apparently a Turkoman form of the Turkish word *taq* or *tak*, to fasten or attach. There is even a station named Takir next to Dooshak, where the railway turns off towards Merv.

Another uncommon term—*loess*—is used to denote the rich, compact, loamy soil found over a great part of the Transcaspian steppes, which is said to resemble the fertile mud of the Nile and the alluvium of the Blue and Yellow Rivers of China. Russian authorities state that the whole of the distance between Kizil Arvat and Askabad, after discounting the intervals of sand, is covered with this kind of soil, and the possibilities of its productiveness, when properly watered, are said to be boundless. It is from this wonderful *loess*, or "white earth," as the Russians also call it, in contradistinction to the "black earth," or "chorny zem" of their southern provinces, that the Turkomans, according to General Annenkoff, have lately obtained

Oozoon Ada to Geok Tepé. 137

as much as one hundred and seventy fold from their crops in the oases of the Tedjent and the Murghab. They told M. Semenoff, the vice-president of the Imperial Geographical Society, during his visit there last year, that eighty fold, and over, was the average yield in the most favourable years. The General believes, that with the aid of this soil, and the indispensable auxiliaries of a vast system of irrigation, such as the Government has already begun on the Murghab, and of Russian colonization aided by the State, the Transcaspian deserts may in time be made as flourishing and populous as the best parts of China. Let us hope that this marvellous transformation may one day be effected, in spite of ninety per cent. of desert at present absolutely incapable of producing anything. Many Russians think it could be accomplished in time by the diversion of the waters of the Amu Darya into its old channels, which are also bordered by abundant deposits of this rich soil of *loess*. Six of these channels have been traced between Askabad and the present stream of the river, and the railway crosses three of them between Merv and Chardjui. The line also cuts the Uzboi, or principal ancient arm, east of Molla-

Kari. But these old delta ramifications do not force themselves upon the attention of the ordinary traveller. They have to be carefully looked for, or to be pointed out by some one who knows the country well. Their very existence is apt to be forgotten under the strong impression that within a very appreciable distance of time the whole of this expanse must have been at the bottom of a sea which washed and abraded the slopes of the Balkans and the Kopet Dag; and if the waters of the Caspian could be let in to cover it over again, that would perhaps be the best solution of the problem.

Some twenty miles west of Bala Ishem, and connected with the railway by a Decauville line, is the Naphtha Dag, or black petroleum hills, which formerly supplied the locomotives and stations with fuel and light. At first, when the wells yielded an average of five tons of oil per day, the supposed total quantity of the source was estimated by the engineer, Kanshin, at 9,677,420 tons; but the supply gradually diminished until the last three borings produced none at all. The railway has now, therefore, to procure its petroleum from Baku at the rate of about 25,000 tons a year. There is a reasonable prospect, however, that the coal recently discovered at Penjakent, thirty to fifty miles from Samarkand, or the seams long worked at Hodjent, may be made available by the extension of the railway to Tashkent; so that the line may not be always dependent for its fuel upon petroleum.

At the station of Kazandjik, the first freshwater source from the Caspian, and eleven miles from another station misnamed Oozoon-Soo, "Long water," where there was not a drop of water to be had from any local supply, we heard of passengers ahead of us having had to wait as long as three days until the repairs on the inundated section had been completed. We afterwards passed the places where the damage had been done, between the small station of Ushak, or Ooshak, and Kizil Arvat, which is the first of the larger stations on the line; and there we saw the old rails bent and curled into all manner of shapes, lying hundreds of yards off from the line, where they had been thrown by the force of the water. I could never have believed in such hydraulic power on a perfectly level plain, had I not seen something more of the water's violence on my return journey, when I narrowly escaped the consequences of another destruction of rail and roadway. General Annenkoff had not then paid enough attention to this important matter. The line was not destitute of culverts through which the water would find its way in ordinary cases, but there were evidently far too few of these structures. Perhaps the Transcaspian Railway is not much worse off in this respect than many other Russian lines on which the traffic is often stopped for days together in spring-time by the floods from melting snows and swollen rivers; but this does not justify the appearance of floods on the rails in Central Asia, where they might be avoided. Without being a professional engineer, it was not difficult to see that there were many old waterways and depressions crossed by the railroad, which had not been provided with the requisite water passages ; and although this defect had in some degree been remedied by trenches cut parallel with the road, about eight or ten feet broad and half as much in depth, there was still a great deal to attend to in this respect before the line could be pronounced perfect. After heavy storms, such as at that time burst over the mountains, the rain-water rushes and bounds across the plain in turbulent torrents and overflows these trenches in a very few minutes. Neither was there any ballast worth speaking of, which could offer the slightest resistance to attacks of this nature. With few exceptions, the rails have been laid down along the perfectly flat plain of alternating desert and oasis almost without any embankment whatever; and it struck me as well as several other persons, who like myself were travelling over it for the first time, that this must have been one of the most easily constructed railways in the world. There is not one tunnel along the entire distance of nine hundred miles; and the only engineering difficulties, properly so called, have been the bridging of the Amu Darya,—no slight undertaking, however,—and the two or three cuttings through the moving sands. These sand cuttings, it must be admitted, have been exceedingly difficult work, and quite out of the range of ordinary railway engineering. It would not be easy to say which has given the most trouble,— the making of them, or the keeping them open now they are made. A gentleman who helped to supply materials told me that one bit of the line at Michailofsk had to be re-made twenty times before the attacking sand could be finally held at bay; and in the meantime several barrels of fastenings completely disappeared beneath the sandy deluge. It certainly needed the discipline of the railway battalions to build these sections of the line ; and the indomitable perseverance of a man like General Annenkoff was none the less necessary in directing the work. As to the other parts where no difculties or impediments existed, they might perhaps have been made more substantial and secure, had more money and time been devoted to them at the very outset ; but the main considerations which guided the construction, irrespective of the pressure of military necessities, and the danger of Afghan frontier troubles, were cheapness and speed in getting the work done.

It was all the time a contest between General Annenkoff as the representative of the Minister of War, and the Minister of Ways of Communication, in order to prove which of the two could build strategical railways cheapest and quickest. This competition between the military and civil engineering departments had been going on ever since General Annenkoff built the Jabinsk-Pinsk line in Poland, which was severely criticized by the opposing authorities at the Ministry of Communications ; but up to the present the energetic constructor of the Transcaspian Railway has managed to hold his own, and even to get the better of his rival.

It seems strange to be writing about so much water in this desert country, which has been generally regarded as quite destitute of it; but my experience impressed me almost as much with the water nuisance, as it did with the dangers and troubles of the sand. I was told that these destructive floods had never been known before, and were quite exceptional. It was not the first time nor the last that the line has been inundated, but never to the same disastrous extent. Between Ushak and Kizil Arvat the damage extended over some six versts and a half. At one place every sign of the iron road was obliterated for 1,000 yards, as though there had never been any railway at all, while the rails and sleepers were carried half a verst away. It was a poor treat for General Annenkoff's daughters and their party to be on their way to Samarkand at this unfortunate juncture, though at the same time it was fortunate that the "representatives of all nationalities," so pompously proclaimed as having been present at the inauguration, only existed in the Russian imagination. Their accounts of the journey, had they been there, would hardly have been enthusiastic descriptions of triumphant railway progress. The General's relatives and French friends and admirers had to be carted through the water to Kizil Arvat, or wheeled there on trollies in the middle of the night, in order not to delay the opening of the Samarkand branch beyond the anniversary of the Tsar's coronation. They were first delayed at Kazandjik, where there is a tiny oasis supplied with water brought in canals cut by the Russians from a mountain stream into a reservoir, and then conducted two versts to the station through 4-in. pipes into six tanks, each holding 700 pailfuls. The Oozoon Ada-Kizil Arvat section is supplied with water from this station. There is also a very flourishing garden and a quantity of acacia, pistachio, and other trees planted as experiments. The belated guests had plenty of time during three days here to visit a cotton plantation and small house, with bathing accommodation, belonging to Prince Khilkoff, and occupied by the engineer of the section. This district I heard is also prolific of scorpions and tarantulas, some of which, I was told, the detained passengers had procured from the Tekkes, and beguiled

Oozoon Ada to Geok Tepe. 145

the time in verifying the suicidal instincts of the scorpion by worrying it with the more active tarantula. The worst awaited the festal party two stations beyond Ushak, where they had to abandon the train, and camp out after dark in the wild open, with soldiers' rations of black bread, mutton, and onions, until they could be sent for, as already stated, from Kizil Arvat through the intervening waters. These rain floods, however, quickly disappear without any apparent benefit to the land. When I passed over this part to Kizil Arvat, the water had already subsided, having been rapidly absorbed by the earth, or evaporated by the great heat, and the ground had even begun to split into cracks and fissures.

Kizil Arvat, generally recognized as the beginning of the Akhal Tekke oasis, is a fertile spot with a number of houses and barrack buildings of white stone from the Kuren Dag, and an important point as the head-quarters of the railway battalion and the principal depôt of the line as far as the Amu Darya. The town contains 210 houses and 3,296 inhabitants, including 1,700 Russians, 660 Armenians, 60 Georgians, and 816 Persians. There is a splendid fountain at the station, and the

L

waiting-rooms are even furnished with the electric light. Two stations farther on, at Bami, there is another fountain, and still two more beyond at smaller stations towards Askabad. General Annenkoff has certainly made a conspicuous show of water wherever he has been able to obtain it, and these jets and basins of the indispensable element are very refreshing after the sight of so much salt and sand.

Bami, which is celebrated as one of the principal *étapes* of the Skobeleff expedition, and the point of junction with the line of the Atrek on the opposite side of the mountains running from Chikishliar, presents a green and flourishing appearance, with a few clumps of small trees near the foot of the mountains, and a sparkling rivulet or two winding towards the station. A few versts more of comparative desert separate it from more streamlets and verdure, and even some thinly-sown wheat fields.

Most of these small oases very poorly justify their name, and are chiefly conspicuous by the utter barrenness which prevails between and around them. They are nearly all confined to the mountain base on the south of the railway, while beyond a short distance on the northern side of the line the great desert of the Kara Kum rarely gives any signs of life. The vegetation, excepting the saxaul, comes to an end where the puny streams from the foot of the mountains exhaust themselves in the sand, or are tapped for the purposes of the railway. It was not till we reached this point in the journey that the *kibitkas* of the Turkomans, with their numerous flocks and herds of camels, were at all noticeable by their numbers. The first Turkoman village, after leaving the Caspian, is situated two versts east of Molla Kari, but we had only seen an occasional Turkoman horseman sometimes careering across the plain, or a few camels browsing off the short camel-thorn, called *yangut*, while the Turkoman *aouls*, or *obas*, clusters of dingy dome-shaped tents pitched near the mountains, had hitherto been few and far between. Dotted all over the plain in their neighbourhood, were generally to be seen the mud-built towers of refuge, which now serve no other purpose than to mark the rude and lawless life of these sturdy brigands before the Russian conquest.

The best characterization of the whole surface of the country is to divide it into sand steppes, salt steppes, and grass steppes, the last named being the so-called oasis interspersed between the other two. It is only between Oozoon Ada and Molla Kari on the Caspian, and between Merv and Chardjui on the Amu Darya, that the sand steppes exhibit any dunes or hills, and are regarded as being dangerous; the other parts are deadly flat and uninteresting. With few exceptions, all the sand steppes manage to nourish the short and knotty shrub called the saxaul, which strikes its hardy roots down to a wonderful depth, sometimes ten or twelve feet, into such soil as it can find, and appears on the surface like a thin and scanty gooseberry bush, varying from a foot to five feet in height, at intervals of five, ten, twenty, or, perhaps, forty feet, all over the plains as far as the eye can see. Between Oozoon Ada and Michailofsk, the first two stations from the Caspian, there is not even this saving sign of vegetation, for not a speck of verdure of any kind is visible, while the dunes here are larger and higher than those of the Kara Kum on the other side of Merv. Strangely enough, the saxaul grows most luxuriantly, if such a word may be applied to anything in a desert, on the first part of the sand steppe bordering the Amu Darya, which is the most abominable section of the whole road. As soon as the great heats come on, the saxaul gets scorched up, and assumes a similar colour to that of the dusty drab steppes.

But it is one thing to describe the Central Asian Railway, and quite another to travel over it and experience its many discomforts. It was naturally not to be expected that a purely military railway not yet quite finished would afford all the comfort of first-class lines to every ordinary passenger, and it is from the ordinary passenger's point of view that I feel bound to regard it, at least as far as the Amu Darya, where I received my first recognition as a special visitor for the opening at Samarkand. A big cattle van or goods truck without seats, for instance, when placed at the disposal of one or more persons in 100 deg. of heat, is a very agreeable change from hot, dusty cushions and close, stuffy compartments; but this is what may be called the *maximum* of room with the *minimum* of comfort. There was such a lack of respectable passenger waggons for the inauguration that the first train from the Oxus carrying the constructor's family and Parisian friends was composed of simple goods platforms, upon which a number of deal boards had been roughly knocked together into the form of a Russian peasant's *eezba*, or hut, with a lining of common cotton print loosely tacked up inside to cover the chinks between the planks, and furnished with rough wooden benches and tables. A few of these platforms were only shaded with an awning for those who preferred to sit out in the open. One of these gipsy-like house-trucks was kindly reserved for me on my return from Samarkand to Chardjui, and I succeeded in making it tolerably comfortable with the aid of a Turkoman carpet and a travelling pillow. My only trouble was after dark to prevent the candle, fixed in an empty wine-bottle, from being shaken against the loosely hanging cotton lining and setting it on fire. There was no lavatory of any kind, and other conveniences were of the most primitive description. The thing was certainly original, but uncommonly rough.

The entire line, as may be supposed, was under strictly military control; and I was sadly disappointed to find that what many enthusiastic Russians had told me of the Turkomans having been already so far Russified as to be employed on the trains, was nothing but a miserable hoax. There were sometimes a few of them mixed to-

Oozoon Ada to Geok Tepé. 151

gether with the Persian navvies and assisting the Russian platelayers in repairing the line, and this was evidently the only kind of work they as yet aspired to. I saw a good many of them staring and gaping about at some of the stations, and wearing such gigantic black sheepskin hats, that how they managed to support such heavy head dresses in a climate like theirs was to me a mystery. Imagine a round hat of black sheep's wool half as large again as a Grenadier's busby, often with its long curly wool hanging down all round over the face and neck of the wearer, like a most abnormal crop of hair, and you will have some idea of the savage-looking Tekke's headgear. A long, reddish-coloured cotton gown, generally with a sash round the waist, and thick slippers or Russian top-boots, complete the costume. None but soldiers, I found, were employed as conductors and railway servants generally. All the telegraphists, ticket-sellers, and collectors were also soldiers. The stationmasters were generally officers, except at the very small stations, which were left in charge of subalterns. There are no blue-coated gendarmes at the stations, as in Russia, but a Cossack parades the platform, when there is one, and administers summary justice with his short whip.

His principal duty seems to be to dictate and shout to the lazy, slipshod Mahommedans, who jump out to fill their pitchers from the water-tubs sunk deep into the ground, or to perform their religious ablutions at a fountain basin and make the train wait. Any unruly person of the lower civil orders, or in fact any misdemeanant out of uniform, is not taken before a gendarme and the station chief to have a protocol drawn up as in Russia, but is simply thrashed over the head without more ado. All the dirty work of the line is done by the Persians, who are very numerous as porters at all the principal stations. They seem to prefer to come over the border and work for the Russians in the desert, in spite of the Cossack whip, at a miserable pittance that defies all competition, rather than stay to be harassed by tax-gatherers in their own beautiful and flourishing Khorasan. Six or seven years ago they would never have ventured here among the man-stealing Turkomans, who used to sell them in thousands to the slave-markets of Khiva and Bokhara. It was highly interesting to see the Tekke marauder and his would-have-been slave peacefully labouring together on the Russian railway as though they had always been the best of friends. The Russians now seem to be affected with a certain tenderness towards the Turkoman Tekkes, perhaps in a kind of inverse ratio to the mercilessness of Skobeleff's treatment of them at Geok Tepé; but the Persians, on the contrary, come in for a good deal of rough handling. Their Russian employers deny them all the manlier virtues; and are filled with endless amusement at the stories spread about of the way in which the Shah's troops, on the other side of the frontier, have to be concentrated in thousands from all points during several months in order to punish a few hundred Turkomans of the Goklan or Yomud tribes. Of course, say the Russians, these Turkomans left over in Persia, as well as those still wandering and oppressed within the Afghan boundaries, will all have to come over to Russia before they can be properly dealt with and licked into respectable order. This is regarded as inevitable, and only a question of time. I several times saw a whole crowd of dusky, ragged Persian *hamals*, strong as horses, being driven away from the train by a single Cossack, until they fell over each other in their flight, and fairly screamed for mercy. Every officer, as may be inferred, is master on this military railway, and I presume that a full general could stop a train without having to answer to anybody who might object. Any military officer, or, for the matter of that, any of the numerous engineers of sections, as they are called, who should consider himself of sufficient importance, can easily occupy a whole carriage or truck, and nobody complains except the ordinary passenger, who finds no available carriage to correspond with the class of his ticket. An enormous number of officials and officers seemed to be travelling about in this way on service, some with their wives and children. At different times nearly half the carriages of our train were separately engaged. One was occupied by a scientist who was studying the flora and fauna for the Emperor's cabinet, another by the Postmaster who was organizing the post, and so forth. In my compartment was a young officer, who was the first to be sent by this route to reach Eastern Siberia, where his regiment had long been stationed. He was bound for the far-distant Amoor, and the War Office had made out his march route over the Samarkand Railway as an experiment. He was very doubtful about reaching his destination within the allotted time, considering the great delays; but as it was only a trial case, there was no anticipation of blame being attached to him for arriving late. The other non-military passengers were Poles, Germans, and natives of the Caucasus and Armenia, going, as they said, to see if any business could be done; and a Persian Prince, in the uniform of a Russian colonel, was taking his wife and daughter on a pilgrimage to Meshed. Although the daughter had been brought up in a Russian educational institute at Tiflis, and had always been accustomed to European dress, both she and her mother were attired for this occasion in Mahommedan costume, and strictly veiled. Many other Mussulmans sat among the Russians, and did not seem to be particularly anxious to avail themselves of the waggons reserved for their separate use.

CHAPTER VII.

GEOK TEPÉ TO MERV.

Arrival at Geok Tepé—The fortress—Disease—Removal of the Russian settlement—Siege and slaughter—Burning the dead—Skobeleff the "Split Beard"—Unjust criticism of Skobeleff— Dr. Heyfelder's opinion of—Author's acquaintance with Skobeleff—His typical Russian character—A great leader of men—His cruelty at Geok Tepé explained—Difference between his mode of warfare and the English method—Killing of women inexcusable—Mr. Marvin on the subject—Remains of the siege—Alleged neglect of the Turkomans to use their water supply against the Russians—Their chivalrous bravery—Osman Pasha's mistake repeated at the Turkoman Plevna—Arrival at Askabad—Akhal Tekke oasis—Giaours—Ak-soo —Artik— Luftobad — Its retention by Persia disapproved of by Skobeleff—Dooshak—Nearest point to the Afghan frontier—Future junction of Russian and Indian railways—Refusal to permit Englishmen to go to Kelat—Tedjent river and oasis—Sarakhs and Zulficar—Population and administration—Fever—Tigers, boars, lizards, and tortoises—Losing sight of the mountains—Camels—Their proposed introduction into Russia—Depilation of—Present style of caravan progression—Arrival at Merv—Delay—

Geok Tepé to Merv. 157

Merv station—Garden irrigation—No native town—
Russian town—Floods and draining—Koushut Khan
Kala—Forced growth of business—Turkomans in
the hands of Jews and Armenians—Attempt to bathe
in the Murghab—The " Penjdeh sore "—Filters—A
wash in a bath-house.

ON arriving at Geok Tepé, after passing six stations from Askabad, and altogether eighteen from Oozoon Ada, it was our second evening in Transcaspia, and fortunately not too dark to get a view of the famous fortress where 35,000 Tekkes made their last desperate stand for independence. As we slowly approached it from the west, the great ramparts of earth and clay composing this formidable-looking stronghold loomed up immensely high in contrast with the flatness of the surrounding plain. I just had time to pay a flying visit to the crumbling ruins of its southern wall, close to the railway station, where the final assault was delivered, and to observe that its spacious interior, which once contained the entire population of the Akhal Tekke oasis, was now quite empty and deserted. This great earthwork has not yet been utilized by the Russians, like the other Turkoman fortress at Merv, owing, probably, to the terrible epidemic which broke out immediately after the slaughter of its defenders, and caused the removal of the small Russian settlement to a much healthier spot, two or three miles nearer to the mountains. Its huge, thick walls are as much as four miles in circuit; and near the north-eastern corner is the large aperture or break in the unfinished wall, through which the panic-stricken crowd of defeated Turkomans, with their women and children, fled out before the murderous onslaught of Skobeleff's troops, and were ruthlessly mown down by their pursuers without distinction of age or sex. Eight thousand of the besieged perished in this disastrous rout, besides 10,000 or 15,000 more slain during the siege and capture. So great was the carnage that thousands of bodies had subsequently to be burnt to prevent the spread of disease. After this terrible decimation, the Turkomans called Skobeleff "Quenz kanli," or "Bloody Eyes," which corresponds with the late Mr. MacGahan's description of the General's bloodshot eyes after an attack on one of the redoubts at Plevna. They have since enshrined the memory of the cruel exterminator of their freedom in native verse, under the more agreeable name of the "Sakal airi ooroosi," or the "Russian Split Beard," in allusion to the Dundreary form of his whiskers.

GENERAL VIEW OF THE STATION OF GEOK TÉPÉ.

Geok Tepé to Merv. 159

Skobeleff has been severely criticized in England for his massacre of the Turkomans at Geok Tepé; and his character has lately been subjected to the most reckless kind of dissection on the strength of conversations with Dr. Heyfelder, the obliging host of all foreign visitors to Bokhara. This amiable gentleman has consequently been attacked in the Russian Press for communicating disparaging anecdotes about Skobeleff to foreign tourists. The fact is that Dr. Heyfelder has published the most exhaustive accounts of Skobeleff and his personality, the sum total of which is quite the reverse of defamation of the late General's character; and it would be very strange if he now entertained any other feeling than that of admiration for the Russian popular hero. In recent English criticism Skobeleff has been called "eccentric ; a jumble of nobility and meanness, with a childish temper, and a petulant, ill-assorted, and unprincipled nature, querulous and morose, sanguine and despondent; without stability and without faith." A more terrible array of disreputable qualities could hardly be attributed to the most degraded character. The mildest view that can be taken of them, is that they represent a very hasty and superficial estimate of a Russian of Skobeleff's stamp. No other Englishman has ever made such an attack on the modern Suvoroff, as the Russian Staff Academy christened him over his grave; and Mr. G. K. Gradofsky, the only one of Skobeleff's own countrymen who ever ventured to publicly question his right to fame, has never pushed his adverse criticism as far as that. The author of this sweeping condemnation, who admits that in Russia every man who raises himself above the crowd has a host of enemies always trying to pull him down by the most despicable means, seems to have forgotten that, although in Skobeleff's case it was the crowd which raised him aloft on the pinnacle of fame, he still had enemies, mostly among the foreign elements, who always placed the lowest construction on everything he did. If General Annenkoff were also judged by the gossip of his much wider circle of enemies, he would not be a second Lesseps, but the greatest charlatan in Russia. The vast majority of a people do not elevate a man into a hero for nothing; and now that Skobeleff is dead, foreigners might be generous enough to admit that he was a great man, at least in his own country. I was closely acquainted with the General for some years, both in war and peace, and may be allowed to add my small quota to what has already been said on the subject. I saw him lead his men up to the Turkish redoubt at Plevna, and was subsequently in his company at Constantinople when he wept bitterly over the death of our mutual friend MacGahan. He was not only in some respects, as described by the writer referred to, but wholly and entirely the typical representative of his nation ; the personification of all its merits and defects ; and doubly endowed with the virtues and vices of his fellow-countrymen. And yet no one would seriously think of condemning the entire Russian people in the terms used by our critic against Skobeleff. If his passing humours, as gathered from trumpery anecdotes, were to be taken as the touchstone of his genius, he would no more stand the test than a good many other great men. A great many other equally, or even better, authenticated stories show him in the light of one of the best-natured and most magnanimous of men and soldiers. He certainly never pretended to be a moral or a religious genius, nor could he have ever been mistaken for one. It would be odious, for instance, to compare him with General Gordon, who was just as much the outcome of British

M

civilization, as Skobeleff was the product of his Russian surroundings. In her present state Russia could no more produce a Gordon than England could tolerate a Skobeleff. If a Russian soldier is religious at all, it is rather in the spirit of the Old Testament than in that of the New. Skobeleff was, perhaps, overrated as the idol of the Russian people ; but he was undoubtedly a great soldier and leader of men. As to his cruelty at Geok Tepé, he always indignantly repelled the charge of wanton bloodthirstiness or unnecessary destruction of human life. The Russian traditions of Central Asian warfare, and the fact that he was not fighting a settled and peaceful population, compelled him to do what he did, and not any personal lust for blood. He was cruel, if at all, only to be kind. The crushing blow dealt the Tekkes in their flight after the capture of the fortress was considered necessary to break their determined spirit and force of resistance, which had been immensely elevated and increased by the disastrous failure of his two predecessors. Had he not completely routed and cowed the Tekkes in this way, it was foreseen that they would probably continue their resistance from the position on the Murghab, and by thus drawing on

Geok Tepé to Merv.

another Russian attack, Merv, instead of being peacefully annexed, as it eventually was, by the diplomacy of Konshin and Alikhanoff, would have had to submit at the expense of a much greater sacrifice of life than even that incurred at Geok Tepé. Skobeleff's cruelty consisted in his adoption of a policy the very reverse of the English plan of sparing the enemy to fight him again another day, instead of finishing the war at one fell stroke. The killing of women, however, is the one black feature in the battle of Geok Tepé, which no explanation will ever excuse in the minds of English readers; so that it would be useless to discuss the point here, especially after Mr. Marvin's exhaustive treatment of it in his account of conversations with Skobeleff and his officers.*

To return to Geok Tepé, there was still the breach made by the Russian sap and mine, visible from the station, and the ground for hundreds of yards outside the wall presented a puzzling confusion of irrigation canals, now mostly dry, rifle trenches, and minor earthworks. This Turkoman Plevna, as most readers are aware, was built over a rivulet brought from the mountains, only a mile or two off, which

* See accounts of Tekke women in Chapter XIII.

creates the oasis here at the foot of the range. Possessed of this stream, and well aware, as they must have been, by the experience of their own history, of the importance of water as a weapon of war, it seemed strange to Dr. Heyfelder that they did not use it against the Russian troops. Had they dammed up their canals, and thus flooded that part of the stream which led into the Russian camp, the latter, with all its trenches, would have been completely swamped, and while the Russians were in this predicament, had the Tekkes accompanied the manœuvre with an energetic sortie, the Russians would in all probability never have been able to extricate their horses and guns from the mire. This was the opinion of Dr. Heyfelder, who took part in the expedition, and was afterwards medical adviser to General Annenkoff during the railway construction. But against this theory it has been advanced by Grodekoff, Lessar, and others, that the Tekkes could not have cut off the water supply of the Russian camp, which was situated upstream, without exposing themselves to the deadly fire of the besiegers, or without swamping their own retreat, and undermining the walls of the fortress. Another notion is that the Tekkes fought with the most unselfish and high-minded bravery, and scorned to use the tricks of war which even Europeans do not despise. It appears, however, that they used all the tricks which they knew, and that was not many. They did not cut the Russian field telegraph when they could have done so, because they were ignorant of its use and importance; and they were not magnanimous enough to let a Russian prisoner remain among them without flaying him alive, because he refused to fire upon his comrades. As far as my own observation went, it occurred to me that the Turkomans had neglected another advantage in selecting the site of their fortress. They seemed to have imitated the blunder of Osman Pasha at the real Plevna in Bulgaria, when he pitched upon the more or less isolated town on the Vid for his fortifications, instead of choosing Loftcha, with the Balkans at his back. Had the Tekkes built their great mud work closer up against the mountains, the Russians would not have been able to get round it, and they would apparently have been able to retreat through the passes, with much less risk of pursuit.

Forty-two versts, or twenty-eight miles, from Geok Tepé we arrived at Askabad, the capital of the Transcaspia, in the middle of the night, and were only able to observe that this station was decidedly the best in every respect that we had yet seen. There was an excellent buffet and well-furnished waiting-rooms, which were very comforting during half an hour's stay, after the wretched places hitherto passed. I was only sorry that I was unable to see the town until on my return journey from Bokhara.

From Geok Tepé onward to Askabad there were more signs of fertility and nomadic population than had hitherto been seen on the green patches which determine the beginning of the Akhal oasis from Kizil Arvat. The belt of country so called is reckoned about 145 miles long, of oval shape, with an average breadth of four to ten miles, and is supposed to come to an end at Giaours, the second station after Askabad; but as there is more sand, and even salt steppe, between these two places, this theory seems to be rather incorrect. About thirty miles more of desert country intervenes between Giaours and the northern end of the Tedjent oasis; and in the name of another waterless station, called Ak-soo, or "white water," we come across the second misnomer of this kind since leaving the Caspian. Artik, the

RUINED MOSQUE NEAR ASKABAD.

fifth station beyond Askabad, is only a few miles from the Persian town of Luftobad, which forms the one single piece of Persian territory penetrating through to the Russian side of the mountains, and was left to Persia by the boundary arrangement of 1881, much to the disgust of Skobeleff, who strongly opposed its concession.

Passing two more stations, we reach the southernmost bend of the railway at Dooshak, which is also the point of the line nearest to the Afghan frontier. If the Russian and Indian railways are fated ever to meet, the Russian branch will probably start from this station, or somewhere near it, to join the lines of Chaman, Candahar and the Bolan Pass. This station was selected by three other English tourists, several months after my journey, as the starting point for an intended visit through the mountains to the Persian Khanate of Kelat, which a short time ago was erroneously reported to have been ceded to Russia; but on telegraphing to the Russian authorities for permission to make the excursion, it was peremptorily refused. Here the railway makes an angle to the north-east, and we rapidly lost sight of the Kopet Dag mountains, whose company we had enjoyed for more than three hundred miles, as they turned off in the opposite south-easterly direction towards Sarakhs. The railway soon afterwards enters the Tedjent oasis and crosses the river of that name,—called also in its upper course the Heri Rud,—not far from where its fan-shaped extremities, like those of the Murghab, farther on, are swallowed up by the sandy ocean of the Kara Kum. The station of Tedjent appears to be the nearest to Sarakhs, which is only about eighty-five miles off, and about 160 miles from Zulficar. The Tedjent oasis is peopled by about 30,000 Turkomans under the administration of Makhmud Kuli Khan, son of the famous leader against the Russians, Noor Verdi Khan, with a Russian Lieutenant-Colonel, or *pristav*, as his assistant. According to Doctor Heyfelder, the locality is a fever nest for Europeans, and swarms with gnats and mosquitos. M. Semenoff says that tigers are sometimes found lurking here along the banks of the river in search of the wild boar, and the same authority reports having seen between the Tedjent and the Murghab lizards (*Varanus stincus*) nearly five feet long, resembling young crocodiles. I did not come across any of these reptiles myself, but I saw a great many tortoises crawl-

Geok Tepé to Merv. 169

ing among the scanty shrubs of the semi-sand steppe which separates the Tedjent oasis from that of the Murghab.

Our parting with the mountains was the subject of lively regret, as now on either side there was nothing to relieve the eye from these staring wastes, except the isolated station huts and perhaps a few solitary *kibitkas*, or now and then a camel or two leisurely browsing on the scattered tufts of herbage, and exhibiting the most supreme indifference to the passing of their new steam rival.

It is not to be supposed that the ship of the desert has been altogether superseded here by the railway, which ought, on the contrary, to bring this ungainly beast into even more than usual requisition at places like Merv and Chardjui, where large quantities of goods have to be transported to and from the railway station, especially as the Russians have not yet introduced anything but droshkies, and the nomad Tekkes have never possessed wheeled conveyances of any description. But if the camel in the new towns of Transcaspia is likely to be supplanted by Russian, or even Bokharan, carts, there seems to be just as much chance of the animal in revenge entering into competition with the horses and oxen of Southern Russia. An enterprising proprietor of coal mines in the neighbourhood of the Don told me that he had seriously thought of purchasing camels to carry or draw his coal to the nearest railway station, as they would be much cheaper, and could be easily procured from the Calmucks living close by. Camels already carry coal from the Hodjent mines to Tashkent. While I stayed on the Murghab and the Amu Darya, there was constant loading and unloading of these animals, and long caravans of them laden with bales of cotton were all the time coming in or going out of the town. I was rather puzzled at first to account for the hairless state of their tawny bodies, with tufts of dirty wool hanging from the neck and feet; but upon inquiry I found that this unsightly depilation was caused by felt wrappings during the winter. Their present style of progression when in caravans, thanks to the Russian occupation, is apparently no longer that of a military transport attended by an armed convoy. I am not sure that they go through the more remote parts of the deserts in this lightly equipped fashion; but I often saw long trains of them walking into Merv with only a single nomad, sometimes two together, striding a donkey in front and guiding the leading camel by the nose chain.

In twelve hours from Askabad, at about noon the next day, we glided into the historical capital of Turkomania, or rather the "tented field," which has generally passed under the name of Merv in Western Europe. As soon as we reached the station, we were informed that the train would go no farther until the evening, the reason being that the next desert, or sand steppe—the bugbear of the entire route—was dangerous, and in order to avoid accidents or delays in the dark in the midst of this veritable wilderness, all trains from Askabad were detained at Merv until nightfall, so that the worst part of the way to Chardjui might be got over the next morning in daylight.* The station of Merv, though not so large and handsome as that of Askabad, was still very comfortable and cool after the trying heat and closeness of the railway waggons. There was a large fountain-basin between the platform and the station building, forming the centre of a newly-laid-out garden, as yet without cultivation, but being prepared for it by a deluge of water run

* I am told that the trains now often run through this desert during the night.

through a number of small conduits and ditches —a miniature copy of the irrigation in general. The parched-up soil refuses to yield to the labours of the tiller without being constantly flooded by artificial means.

Until the Russians began to build here no city of Merv had existed for more than a century, and there is still no native town beyond the tents of the Turkoman camps, pitched some distance off from the railway. The Russian town behind the station is composed of about a score of unpaved, dusty streets, also irrigated by deep ditches filled from the Murghab on both sides of the way, and uniform rows of low brick houses, mostly with Persian fronts, and open shops in Eastern bazaar fashion, all bearing the impress of hasty and unfinished construction. It seemed to me that the deep gullies of the streets, while helping to water the young acacias planted along some of them, could hardly be intended to drain off anything but the subsiding floods, which, in the first place, they probably assist in spreading. These inundations, one of which occurred only a few months before my visit, have already once or twice half drowned the town, and many persons were seriously contemplating the removal of their residences to higher ground on the other side of the river within the walls of Koushut Khan Kala, which is now cut by the railway, and already contains the white stone, or stuccoed houses and flourishing gardens of all the principal officers and officials. The shops of Merv are all tenanted by Armenians, Greeks, Georgians and Jews, who complain that their former brisk trade has dwindled down to nothing since the railway advanced to the Amu Darya, and took with it all the officers, contractors, and workmen. It was these departed customers who gave the impulse to the rapid expansion of the town ; and those attracted by the temporary activity of the railway construction now find that Merv has grown too fast. The Turkomans who do any business at all remain content with their bi-weekly market held within the walls of the late Koushut Khan's fortress, over on the other side of the Murghab, which is here crossed by a wooden bridge, belonging to the railway. Should any of the Turkoman natives attempt to open transactions in the Russian town, they are pretty sure to fall into the clutches of the more wily Armenians and Jews, who have quickly succeeded in finding "fields and pastures new" where the Russians have only found deserts. While negotiating for the purchase of a small Turkoman carpet with a group of Tekkes standing outside one of the shops, I soon discovered their connection with the Armenian or Jew inside, who was paying them a small commission to sell their native work at double the usual price.

The heat was so oppressive that many of the passengers, profiting by the delay, started off to take a cooling dip in the celebrated Murghab, and with the same intention I wandered for some time along the fusty, crumbling banks of the river outside of the town, vainly searching for a suitable bathing-place, until at last I came to the conclusion that the water was everywhere too dirty and muddy; besides which I had heard so much about the " Penjdeh sore " originated by the impurities of this turbid stream, that I was far from anxious to put myself into closer contact with it than was absolutely necessary in a filtered condition. Nowhere in the world is the water-filter a greater blessing to the community than at Merv and Bokhara, and, thanks to the forethought of General Annenkoff, it has now been supplied at most of the larger stations.

Dr. Heyfelder, on taking final leave of the Ameer a few weeks ago, very appropriately presented him with a filter of the Pasteur system. Instead, therefore, of bathing in the Murghab I took a Russian bath in a small wooden house, also kept by Armenians or Jews, where the water was cleaner, and the broiling heat of the weather outside was increased in the furnace-like bath-rooms by another twenty or thirty degrees. As there was not yet any fixed time-table, and the starting of the train seemed to depend very much upon the will of the station-master, I was rather afraid of being left behind, and so hurried back to the station after a rapid wash, resolving to see more of Merv if possible on my return from Samarkand.

CHAPTER VIII.

MERV TO SAMARKAND.

Departure from Merv—Bairam Ali—Ruins of four cities—Woman's influence in the destruction of ancient, and capture of modern, Merv—Transcaspian Sahara—Abomination of desolation—General Tchernaieff's attacks and General Annenkoff's success—Moving sands—Intense heat — Refreshments — Improvised restaurant of trucks—The stations—Protection of rails from the sand—Saxaul and its uses—Wooden palisades—Wells—Abrupt termination and vagaries of the sand—Oasis of Chardjui—Russian Chardjui—Cutting in two of the railway bridge—Further detention — Night drill of Russian troops — Colonel Alikhanoff—A nice opening of the railway!—Reasons for cutting the bridge—It breaks down—Description and cost of the bridges—Uncertain navigability of the Amu Darya—Its rapid current—M. Charikoff's voyage to Kerki—Dinner to Alikhanoff and the author—Farabia—Train of house-trucks—Repair of the bridge—My hut on wheels—The start over the river — Reception by the Bek of Chardjui — The festival-train—More sand—Kara Kul—A Bokharan bombardier—Arrival at Bokhara—Our reception by Generals Rosenbach and Annenkoff—Lunch—Bokharan guests refrain — Re-departure — Station of Bokhara—Valleys of Miankul and the Zerafshan—

Merv to Samarkand. 177

The "devil's wain"—Astonishment of Bokharans—Katta-Kurgan—Turkistan frontier—Arrival at Samarkand—Construction and condition of the railway—Annenkoff's reward—Cost and rapid building of the line—Defects: culverts and weakness of the bridges—Important significance of the railway—General Prjevalsky's opinion.

WE started from Merv as soon as it began to get dark, and seventeen miles farther on stopped for a few minutes at the station of Bairam Ali, close to the extensive ruins of the finest cities that ever flourished here in the palmiest days of Turkomania. The railway runs through a striking confusion of dilapidated houses and temples, tumble-down mud forts and crumbling caravanserais, and buildings of every kind, which thickly encumber the plain with heaps of mouldering bricks and clay over an extent of many square miles. Although sometimes called old Merv, these immense ruins include the remains of no less than four different cities, whose inhabitants, in the heyday of Mervian prosperity, are said to have numbered more than a million souls. The latest Mervian city of Bairam Ali was laid waste at the end of the last century by the Bokhariots, who at the same time destroyed the great river dam of Sultan Bent, thirty miles off, by which the water was once diverted into canals to supply the town, and which is now being restored by order of the Tsar. According to a native legend, this final devastation of the urban magnificence of Merv is accounted for by the maxim *cherchez la femme*. The ruler of Bairam Ali set his affections upon a beautiful member of the harem of his commandant of the *kala*, or fortress, guarding the Sultan Bent, and when at length he succeeded in gaining possession of her, the commandant revenged himself by surrendering the position to the Bokhariots. It will be remembered that a woman—the celebrated Goolijama Bai, widow of Noor Verdi Khan—was also very deeply concerned in the easy acquisition by the Russians of the mud huts and tents of modern Merv.

Two miles from Bairam Ali lie the remains of the two more ancient towns of the Iranian period, Giaour Kala, the oldest of all, and Iskander Kala, founded by Alexander the Great, or by one of his generals; and not far off the ruins of the tomb and city of the great Sultan Sandjar, destroyed by the ferocious hordes of Chingiz Khan.

The night was passed in crossing another extent of barren steppe, and the next morning we entered the dreaded Sahara of the Transcaspian. This savage desert is the very abomination of desolation, and no words can adequately describe it. I am now better able to appreciate General Tchernaieff's attack on the project of a railway through this terrible wilderness—an attack, by the way, that put the final nail in the coffin of the ex-Governor-General of Turkistan's official career, and all the more credit therefore is due to General Annenkoff, for having performed the feat for which utter failure was anticipated by many acquainted with the difficulties to be encountered.

The sand here is not blown up into hills quite so high, perhaps, as those near Oozoon Ada, but is more undulating, and, worst of all, more movable. As far as the eye can reach, in all directions stretches a restless sea of sand, driven up into successive billows and ridges, most of which are curved into crescent-shape on the side sheltered from the direct impact of the prevailing north-east winds. The lightest breeze raises the fine sand along their summits like spray, and very distinct lines of wavy indentation are imprinted upon the face of their slopes, like the ripple on the surface of water. As the train moved slowly through the midst of this dismal waste, imparting no doubt a certain amount of vibration to the dunes, the sand trickled down their sides close to the fascines of saxaul planted here to protect the rails, while the tops of the more distant hillocks appeared wreathed in light clouds of smoke as the sand was agitated by the breeze. I cannot say that these gentle zephyrs were very effectual in mitigating the intense heat in the railway carriages, where it was almost unbearably hot, the thermometer registering thirty-eight degrees Reaumur in the shade, or nearly 120 degrees Fahrenheit. By this time I had exchanged my second-class seat on the double-storied car at the end of the train for one in a third-class carriage, where there was more breathing space. There was only one second-class compartment, and not a single one of first class in all the train. Other passengers took to the horse-boxes with the doors open on both sides. In our third-class waggon a contractor, on finding one of the windows nailed up, smashed out the pane of glass with his stick, and paid the soldier-conductor the fixed fine of two roubles for the damage. There were only two or three ladies, in special carriages or compartments, and most of the men were in shirt-sleeves, and all the time engaged in the

Merv to Samarkand. 181

consumption of prodigious quantities of lukewarm seltzer-water and lemonade. This kind of refreshment, as well as Russian beer and Caucasian wine, was generally obtainable at the stations supporting buffets, which are all kept by Armenians; and for eatables there were rye bread, hard boiled eggs, and cucumbers. It was only at the half-dozen larger stations that a well-served substantial meal could be obtained. The only respectable place of the kind on this horrible part of the line was at a station appropriately named Peski, "the sands," where there were a couple of railway trucks propped up in the sand, with ladders up to the doors, serving respectively as restaurant and kitchen. The stations here were wretched little wooden dens, not so large as signal boxes, and often mere huts, with the bedstead and bedding of the inmates deposited outside or on the flat roof, either for want of room in the interior, or because it was too hot to sleep indoors.

This section of the line exhibited the best examples of General Annenkoff's arrangements for screening and protecting the rails from the insidious approach or sudden overspreading of the shifting sand. The saxaul, which has chiefly been employed for this purpose, appears to grow even here at great intervals. How it finds sufficient nourishment in so many feet of sand is very mysterious, and can only be compared with the way in which pine-trees often grow on the surface of stone and rock in Finland without an inch of soil to cover their roots. The smaller-sized shrubs of saxaul were thickly planted along several portions of the line, just beyond the rails, while the larger bushes were stuck along in lines over the sand hillocks. The necessity of thus employing these shrubs, and the fear lest the steppe should be gradually denuded of them for fuel, as at one time seemed imminent, thus increasing the danger and mobility of the sands, were the principal reasons that induced the constructor to turn his attention seriously to the supply of petroleum for the locomotives and stations. I saw long stacks of the gnarled and knotty saxaul wood at several places, but it appeared to be very sparingly used, and is no longer allowed to be pulled up. Another method of warding off the sand is by palisades or battens of lathe wood, such as are used in Southern Russia as a protection against the snow. These are placed so as to face the prevailing winds, and, together with the small barricades of saxaul, appear to be the only

Merv to Samarkand. 183

means possible at present of meeting the difficulty. The first sandy portion of the railroad between Michailofsk and Molla Kari has thus lasted, it is said, for six years without being buried, although nothing is said of the clearing of the rails, which in all probability is constantly necessary. There are said to be two wells on this part of the road at Repetek and Karaul, but fresh water is preferred from Chardjui, brought in vats on trucks attached to nearly every train.

This sand steppe continues as far as the Chardjui oasis, where it comes to an abrupt termination, and is at once succeeded by fields and gardens. It is plain that the sand has been gradually and recently advancing here towards the river, or else has been blown back from its western bank, for many gardens are half buried, as though either freshly covered over by the one process, or slowly emerging by the help of the other. Exactly the same thing is repeated on the opposite side of the Amu beyond the fertile banks of the river, where there are another fourteen miles of sand steppe without a single blade of grass. In fact, the Chardjui Bekdom is about thirty miles in circumference on both banks of the river, and outside this circle there is nothing but bare sand, while within it there flourishes the richest vegetation. The new Russian town of Chardjui, if it can yet be called one, is situated some distance from the Bokharan fortress of that name, and at the time of my visit was a confused agglomeration of new and of still more unfinished buildings, including the railway station, heaps of railway material, numerous sidings, and two or three roughly improvised eating-houses built of logs, all stretched out along the river's bank. The railway embankment here rises twenty feet or thirty feet to meet the level of the bridge.

On arriving here two important pieces of information immediately reached us. One was that the Governor of Merv, the well-known Colonel Alikhanoff, had come with us from the Murghab, and was also bound for Samarkand, and the other that the bridge had been taken to pieces, and there would probably not be a train going any farther for several days. It was of no good to go over the river in a boat, as there were no carriages or locomotives on the other side to take us forward, all of them having gone on to Samarkand. This news was a heavy blow after having been sixty hours on the road from the Caspian instead of thirty-six, which General Annenkoff had proclaimed as the longest time taken to cover the distance. There was nothing, however, to be done but to make ourselves as comfortable as we could without hotels or other necessaries of civilized life. I was fortunate in finding sleeping accommodation in a tent pitched close to the principal restaurant frequented by the officers of the garrison, but a lady and gentleman from Vienna walked about all the first night, and the next day started back to the Caspian in disgust. After nightfall the Russian battalion turned out for their drill on the dusty plain between the Russian settlement and native town, and a Pole informed me in a mysterious manner that, as Chardjui was still Bokharan territory, the Russian troops were always exercised after dark in order not to offend the natives ; but this was absurd, as it was evident that they could not exercise in the overpowering heat of the day. A little later, while I was in the restaurant, a tall officer with a red beard, and walking with the aid of a stick, came in and addressed himself in an authoritative manner to the station-master, who was sitting at one of the tables, and asked him when the train for Samarkand would start. The station master replied that he "thought" it would be the next day, or the day after. " I don't wish to know what you think," retorted the officer, " but I desire to be informed when the train will really go." " I really cannot tell," responded the station-master, " as it depends entirely upon when the repairs of the bridge are finished ; it may be to-morrow, the day after, or next week ! " " A nice opening of the railway," observed the tall officer as he sauntered away. This officer, whose acquaintance I afterwards made, was Colonel Alikhanoff, the Governor of Merv. Indeed it was a nice opening, not of the railway, but of the bridge, for two sets of pile supports or wooden piers had been taken away from the latter in order to let through one of the two flat-bottom boats lately built in St. Petersburg, and which in a few days was to take the Governor-General of Turkestan, General Rosenbach, up the Amu Darya to Kerki. It never seems to have occurred to anybody to keep one boat on one side of the bridge and one on the other ; but as a part of the centre of the bridge was specially made to open for the passage of these boats, there ought to have been no need of any further aperture. Upon inquiry I was told that the proper opening could not

Merv to Samarkand. 187

be used on account of the silting up of the sand, and consequently of insufficient depth of water to carry the steamer through. A gap had therefore to be cut through the bridge near the western bank. Another version of the affair was given to me by a well-known and competent authority, and this was that the section of the bridge or span constructed to swing off in the middle of the river turned out to be too small by several inches to admit of the passage of the steamer. The steamboat, which was brought in sections from St. Petersburg, had been made too broad to pass through the bridge. Such an absurd miscalculation is almost incredible; and there is no doubt that the bridge, which is by no means one of the strongest, has been seriously injured by cutting it in two. This has since been proved by the fact of it having already had to undergo repair three different times. When I returned two weeks later from Bokhara, we had to leave the train three parts across the river and descend into boats in order to reach the opposite bank; and since then the same part of the bridge has again suddenly given way. The passenger who informs me of this accident says that while the train was passing the bridge shook in such a way as to be positively dangerous, and afterwards during the night a crash was heard, and some of the woodwork had fallen into the river.* The structure is of a light description, on low wooden piers or clusters of piles stretching over the main stream of the river for more than a mile, after which come three other short bridges connected by three dams. The first and principal bridge is 820 Russian sajenes or 5,740 English feet in length, and the three others are respectively 560, 392 and 196 feet, with the intervening dams of 2,429, 750 and 2,527 feet making a total length of bridges and dams from one bank to the other of two miles and 678 yards. This great work of bridging across the mighty and capricious waters of the Oxus cost altogether 301,674 roubles, of which 141,674 roubles were for labour, tools, &c., and 160,000 roubles for material, all of which had to be brought from Russia. At first the intention was to make shift with some kind of a ferry to connect the two ends of the railway, and a considerable amount of money appears to have been wasted over premature contracts made in England. A bridge

* The bridge has again been temporarily put out of use by the destruction of one of the dams between the shorter bridges near the right bank (August, 1889).

RAILWAY BRIDGE ACROSS THE AMU DARIA (LENGTH 1 MILE 992 FEET).

of iron would have cost some six or seven millions, which was more than the estimates would bear, and so finally M. Bielinsky, a Polish engineer, was engaged to build the present one of wood. It is expected to last at least ten years. The trains at present only crawl over it; and I am inclined to think that heavy war material would soon put it out of order. "But it does not matter," said many Russians, "what now becomes of the bridge; the railway is ready on the other side, and having got over all our material, we can dispense with the bridge if necessary."

Another difficulty which the Russians have to cope with here is the uncertain navigability of the upper course of the river. The current of the water, which is of a deep chocolate colour, and seems to be loaded with sand, is said to be one of the fastest in the world. I think it was Lieutenant Burns who calculated its flow at the rate of 6,000 yards an hour, but the Russians assert that it runs as fast as twelve feet per second. The bed is constantly changing, and one Russian at Chardjui told me that where he bathed in six feet of water one day there were only two feet the next. After cutting open the bridge, the Governor-General of Turkestan did not venture to go to Kerki while I was in the country, but M. Charikoff, the political agent in Bokhara, essayed the voyage instead, and was grounded for three days on the sand-banks. Kerki, it will be remembered, is the last place on the Afghan frontier occupied by the Russians since the boundary settlement, and is now an important military post with several battalions of troops under the command of General Krestianen.

On the day following our arrival at Chardjui, Colonel Alikhanoff and I received an invitation to cross the bridge and dine with the engineer of the first section of the Bokharan part of the line, M. Konsky, also a Pole. We walked over the gap in the bridge on planks, and were then wheeled on trolleys by the workmen. The station on the other side is called Farabia, and a very picturesque spot it is, in the midst of a wooded country with broad-spreading mulberry-trees shedding their white berries on the ground like snow, young cotton plantations, and fruit gardens. Two or three engineers have built quite handsome villas here, and there are also machine shops, engine-house, and other appurtenances of a railway depôt. During the day the news came that the train of house-trucks

Merv to Samarkand. 191

which had conveyed General Annenkoff's family to Samarkand had been sent back for other visitors, and might be expected that night ; so we waited for it, and were duly conveyed back over the bridge as far as the gap. After some delay the repairs were hastily completed, and the train was able to clear the bridge. The station-master of Chardjui then informed me that he had just received a telegraphic order from General Annenkoff to send me on to Samarkand as quickly as possible, which was some little consolation for a detention of two days and nights at Chardjui crowning the delays of the earlier part of the journey. The train was to return to Samarkand at five o'clock the next morning, and separate house-platforms were allotted to the Governor of Merv and myself in which to pass the night, in order that we might be all ready to start on the morrow's dawn. My hut on wheels, surmounted by a flag, was furnished with a rough corded Bokharan bedstead, without anything whatever on it, a deal table, and two seat forms. The train, as usual, did not leave the next morning at five, but at nine. When we again reached Farabia, across the river, we found the Bokharan Bek of Chardjui waiting to welcome us under a splendid spread of native tenting of variegated colours, close to the platform, and surrounded by his officials in their best dressing-gown attire and turbans. The grass under the tent was carpeted, and the table was covered with the customary *dostarkhan* of sweetmeats, which answers to the Russian bread and salt, always offered to guests whom the host delights to honour. Colonel Alikhanoff and I took seats on the Vienna chairs at the table opposite the Bek, and after a pause, during which glasses of hot Russian tea were brought in, his Bokharan Excellency began in the usual Asiatic manner to inquire after the respective healths of ourselves and relatives. This is the Asiatic substitute for European commonplaces on the weather. After about a quarter of an hour passed in desultory conversation between the Colonel and the Bek—I must here remark parenthetically that Colonel Alikhanoff is a practised Oriental linguist as well as a soldier—we re-entered the train and continued our journey.

It will give a better idea, perhaps, of the festival-train that carried the visitors to Samarkand if I mention that our house-trucks were without any steps, and it was not very easy or agreeable to get in and out of these new-fangled

Merv to Samarkand. 193

cars, five feet above the ground, without assistance, especially too as most of the stations in Bokhara which had yet got beyond the paper-and-project stage, were also without platforms. Therefore we were thoughtfully furnished with ladders, which we had to let down and haul up after us like Robinson Crusoe. We had another twenty-one versts of sand to go through after leaving Chardjui, and when we came to Kara Kul, thirty-eight miles distant, and famous for its black lambskins, we began to enter the fertile valley of the Zarafshan. At one of the stations the commander of the Bokharan Artillery got in with Colonel Alikhanoff to go to the capital, and I joined them out of curiosity to see a specimen of the Ameer's officers. This Bokharan bombardier wore a black sheepskin cap instead of a turban, and had a scimitar girded round the waist over his long gown. In the course of a very serious conversation, which, I presume, was on military matters, the native adjutant of the general, unused, no doubt, to any kind of elevated seat, tilted up the form by sitting right on its edge, and fell down. The Oriental gravity of his superior was in no way disturbed by this ridiculous incident, and Alikhanoff and I kept our countenances as well as we could.

On arriving at the station of Bokhara, about sixty-two miles from the Amu Darya, another surprise awaited us. General Rosenbach, the Governor-General, and General Annenkoff had just arrived from Samarkand, and were being entertained by M. Charikoff, the diplomatic agent, in the shade of a magnificent embroidered tent or marquee, surrounded by a large particoloured crowd of turbaned natives. The band of the Russian Railway Battalion was playing at the entrance, the men in white caps, white tunics, and top-boots, over red-stained leather breeches—the latter being a distinctive feature of uniform among all the Turkistan troops; and at a further and more respectful distance stood a Bokharan guard of honour, in dark dress and black sheepskin hats. Our train had no sooner come to a standstill than we were sent for and invited to lunch with the Governor-General and other guests. After a very hasty toilette in the trucks, without water—for there were no lavatory arrangements of any kind—Colonel Alikhanoff and I were soon sitting at the table listening to well-deserved compliments and speeches in honour of the constructor, and for the success and prosperity, of the railway. Both Generals Rosenbach and Annenkoff expressed their re-

Merv to Samarkand. 195

grets at my having been so much delayed, and were exceedingly amiable. The lunch was served in European fashion to about fifty persons, comprising officers of the diplomatic staff, members of the Russian commercial colony, and two or three ladies. All round the sides of the tent a number of gorgeously-dressed Bokharans, including one or two ministers, stood in solemn attitudes over tables loaded with the inevitable *dostarkhan*, and seemed to me, unless they only wore their habitual expression, to look most intensely bored. They took no part whatever in the repast, as it was then the Mahommedan fast, and they were forbidden to touch food until after sunset. In less than an hour the Governor-General and General Annenkoff were again in their special train—the only respectable set of carriages I had yet seen—and on their way to inaugurate the navigation of the Oxus as described above. We also resumed our course in the opposite direction towards Samarkand.

The site for the station of Bokhara has been selected in the midst of a cultivated plain, ten miles distant from the populous capital city which gives its name to the Khanate. This is much complained of by visitors to Bokhara, but it evidently has its very good reasons. It is the intention of the Government to build a large Russian town here like the one at Samarkand, as well as a large mansion for the Political Resident. So far, there was nothing but a chaos of wooden shanties, Armenian eating booths, and bare brick walls, the latter being rapidly shaped into houses by Persian bricklayers under Russian masters. There was no station building yet ready, and the stationmaster lived in a shed with a frontage of two big doors exactly like a coachhouse. With the exception of some little steppe land the remainder of the line from Bokhara to Samarkand runs through the beautiful valley of Miankal, the "Garden of Central Asia," fertilized by the "gold-strewing" stream of the Zarafshan. The view in all directions is one of richly cultivated scenery, with cornfields, meadows, orchards, here and there rude and primitive water-mills, presumably for irrigation, with curious earthenware jars fixed round the wheels, and tall clay walls surrounding gardens in which the Bokhariots live during the summer. At the stations village boys come across the fields with baskets full of apricots to sell for a few *puls*, or farthings; and troops of turbaned horsemen came galloping out to see

Merv to Samarkand. 197

the "fire-arba," or the "Shaitan arba" (Devil's wain), as they call the locomotive. The Turkomans had long since got accustomed to the smoke and whistle of the iron invader, but the Bokhariots were then at the very height of their astonishment and wonder. We passed Kerminé, once the capital of the Khanate, where the Ameer was then residing; and near Katta Kurgan we saw the ruined fort and works where Kaufmann finally defeated the army of the late Ameer and secured the capture of Samarkand. The frontier between Bokhara and Russian Turkistan was crossed at a place called Sara Boulat, and on the morning after our start from the Amu Darya we reached the Samarkand terminus just as the festivities of the opening were drawing to a close.

I have thus endeavoured to give an impartial account of all I saw and experienced on the new Central Asian Railway, which, if prognostics do not deceive, will prove to have been one of the most important undertakings of the present century. Some further historical and technical particulars will find their place in another chapter; but a few words here on the construction and condition of the line will fitly close the account of my journey to Samarkand.

The only great difficulties which had to be surmounted,—the shifting sands, and dearth of water,—have been met in a way that is so far practically successful. To a certain extent the work must necessarily have been scamped, through the extraordinary haste displayed in its construction. General Annenkoff was in such a violent hurry to get the first train over the final section that on the last day before the appointed time of opening he had no less than six versts of rails laid down, of which the last verst was placed in thirty minutes. Among the workmen he was sometimes called the *nagaika*, or whip, because he urged everybody on with an energy and untiring perseverance that in apathetic Russia is a very rare and valuable quality. Although the Imperial reward was rather long in appearing, owing probably to the General's enemies, whose name is legion, it came at last in the shape of the St. Alexander Nevsky order in brilliants, accompanied by an Imperial rescript, in which the Tsar said, " For three years you have laboured with characteristic energy at the accomplishment of this task, sparing neither strength nor health in a constant struggle against natural obstacles which seemed almost unsurmountable." The General has now

Merv to Samarkand. 199

been appointed chief director of the line for two years, under the joint supervision of Generals Rosenbach and Komaroff, with a credit of four and a half millions of roubles for putting on the finishing touches. The Commission of Investigation, under General Paucker, said that it would take fifteen millions to put everything in proper order; but this estimate was subsequently cut down by the Imperial comptroller to ten millions. General Annenkoff then offered to do all that was necessary for two millions, so great was his desire to show that he could build the railway cheaply as well as rapidly. The General received the two millions, and afterwards obtained four millions more. The total cost of the line has been estimated at forty-three millions. The whole length of the railway from the Caspian to Samarkand, 1,345 versts, or 900 miles, including the section to Kizil Arvat, built for the Skobeleff expedition, was about seven years and a half in process of construction; but the major part from Kizil Arvat was built in three years; and the terminal section from the right bank of the Oxus to Samarkand, a distance of 346 versts, or 230 miles, was begun in January 1887, and opened in May 1889. The officially stated total cost of this last section is 7,198,000 roubles, or 20,823 roubles per verst; but well-informed persons consider that it cost 500 roubles per verst more.

What struck me most in the circumstances was the insufficiency of culverts and water ducts, preventing the line from resisting the effects of floods like those which interfered with the progress of the visitors to the inauguration. It was also evident that the bridges, especially the first frail structure across the main stream of the Amu Darya, were the weakest parts of the railway. But after taking into account all its faults and defects, many of which, I am informed, have been remedied during the present year, it is impossible to deny the enormous importance of this new railway, or to refuse to admit that General Annenkoff's work is already producing a revolution of a stupendous character in the drowsy world of Central Asia, which must certainly tend to still more surprising changes in the future. Its condition and significance is best summed up by a short and pithy description in one of the last letters written by the late General Prjevalsky while on the expedition to Tibet in which he lost his life. The intrepid

Merv to Samarkand. 201

explorer wrote, under date of 10th September, 1888, as follows :—

" In two weeks we have traversed 5,000 versts from Moscow to Samarkand. We first went by the Nijni Novgorod Railway, then down the Volga and across the Caspian to the Transcaspian Railway, which is simply a marvel in these deserts. You are carried along in a waggon through shifting sands or over barren waterless plains as in some fairy tale. One night's journey from the Caspian brings you to Kizil Arvat, towards evening the same day you are in Askabad, next morning at Merv, and so on to Samarkand. A bridge has been thrown across the Amu Darya which certainly oscillates and creaks under the weight of the cars, but the trains run over all right from Turkomania into Bokhara. Altogether the railway is a bold undertaking, of great significance in the future, especially from a military point of view. It is true one meets with many inconveniencies and deficiencies, but these shortcomings do not in the least lessen the great services of General Annenkoff. The greatest trouble is to master the moving sands. An active struggle with this enemy by means of hedges or fences is impossible, but a passive contest with it, as at present carried on, may be successfully maintained by continually sweeping the wind-driven sand off the track, and by plastering the latter over with clay. Briefly, in my opinion, the Transcaspian Railway merits very much more praise and wonder than condemnation and attack."

CHAPTER IX.

SAMARKAND.

Arrival at Samarkand, "the Face of the Earth"—Inauguration festivities—The station and the town—Situation of the city—Zarafshan River and Siob Canal—Gold-strewing—Russian town—Fortress and citadel—Coronation stone—Execution block—Contrast of Russian and native quarters—Russian and native art—Deterioration of native talent—Clumsy attempts at restoration—Military club and amusements—Orthodox temple—Site of Russian town—Native town and its ruins—Principal mosques and colleges—The shepherd saint—Mausoleum of Shah Zindeh—Legend concerning Kazim-ben-Abbas—His tomb—Mohammedan votaries—Bibi Khanum College—Slanting minarets—Tamerlane's tomb—Kala Afrosiab—Oldest irrigation canal in the world—Valley of the Siob aryk—Primitive mills—Tomb of a giant prophet—Alikhanoff in the mosques—Jews and Hindoos—Population.

COLONEL ALIKHANOFF and I reached Samarkand, "the Face of the Earth," just in time to hear the last echoes of the revels which celebrated the arrival of the first locomotive in the city of Tamerlane. The Governor-General of Turkistan and General Annenkoff, attended by Mr. Charikoff, the Political Resident, had gone to open the navigation of the Amu Darya, which was accomplished, as already related, with very indifferent success, and many of the other guests at Samarkand were on the point of leaving in various directions. These departures were lucky for us, as they made room for our reception in one of the houses hired for the occasion by General Annenkoff, in default of which we should have found but very poor accommodation. There were no hotels, properly so called, and it was due to the kindness of Mr. Milutin, a former aide-de-camp of General Annenkoff, who kindly installed us in spacious apartments just vacated by the French visitors, and richly furnished with native carpets and broad divans, that we were not obliged to put up at one of the dirty little lodging-houses where travellers are generally compelled to stay. The 38,000 inhabitants had been sorely tried in providing sufficient house-room for the large number of natives and Russians, the latter being mostly officers and officials, who had flocked into the town from all the surrounding districts. The small number of visitors from

Samarkand.

Russia proper and abroad had been somewhat disappointing, but this deficiency had been made up by the influx of a great many persons from all parts of Turkistan and Transcaspia.

The Bokharan Ambassador and the Begs of Shahrisabs, Chardjui, and other places had witnessed a sight which must have moved even Asiatic apathy and unconcern. They had stood and watched, no doubt with new and strange thoughts and feelings, the first train being dragged up to the terminus by the magical "fire-arba," decorated with flags and inscribed with the names of Rosenbach and Annenkoff, followed by the railway battalion standing and shouting in the open trucks. Then had followed in rapid succession illuminations, balls, and banquets, at the Governor's house and in the station building, lighted by electricity, and ram fights and *batcha* boy dancing in the native town. Some very fair horse-racing was also got up by a local society of patrons of the turf, in which both Russian and native horses and riders took part, and the principal prize was appropriately carried off by one of the *employés* of the railway.

There was every sign of the hasty inauguration that had taken place, and the work of building was still going on. The station was a very respectable one-storied edifice of stone, with ticket office, buffet, and waiting-room, and a garden and large fountain-basin in the rear.

It is only a figure of speech to say that the Russian locomotive runs to the tomb of Tamerlane, as the town surrounding the site of the great conqueror's resting-place is situated two or three miles off, along a dusty, though picturesque road, which may, however, be very comfortably traversed in good Russian droshkies and carriages driven by native Sart and Tartar coachmen. The Russians have followed out their usual strange plan of establishing stations as far off as possible from the towns through which the railway passes according to time-tables and guides. This inconvenient characteristic of many railways in European Russia is often accounted for by the pencil-and-ruler principle of construction first adopted by the autocrat Nicholas. In Bokhara there is some justification for this arrangement, in the commendable desire of the Russians not to thrust their conquering railway too close under the noses of the natives; but in Samarkand, where they have been perfectly at home for many years, the terminus of the railway might

Samarkand. 207

have been taken closer into their own quarter with considerable advantage in many respects.

This marvellous city, whose past glory has so long fired the imagination of the world, is now one of the most charming spots in all the broad dominions of the Tsar. Its situation is almost perfection, inasmuch as it lies higher than the rest of Transoxiana traversed by the new railway, and the heat is nearly always tempered by gentle breezes and naturally moderated by the rich and umbrageous flora. In full view to the south rises the snow-clad range giving birth to the Zarafshan river, which flows through the city in several streams and ancient *ariks*, or irrigation channels, and literally gives life and being to the entire district. It has been thought that this "gold-strewing" river was so called figuratively because it spreads rich vegetation and golden crops throughout the Bokharan Khanate; but I was shown a place on the Siob, one of its tributaries or artificial channels running through the oldest ruins on the outskirts of the Mohammedan town, where particles of gold are frequently found in the sand along the banks. The present Samarkand is divided into two distinct parts, the new Russian quarter and the old native portion, or Sart town, as it is commonly called, which lies rather higher than the other, and contains very much, and indeed all, that is of the greatest interest to the visitor. Between these two towns stands the fortress and citadel, with the famous reception court of Timur, which holds the coronation-stone, the *Kok-tash*, or Central Asian stone of destiny, enclosed within a modern iron railing on the end part of the covered verandah that runs round three sides of the court. The open end forms the entrance, barred at present by large iron gates, through which we were obliged to be content to look at the interesting interior, as the sentinel on guard could not open them without the orders of his officer, and the latter was just then not to be found. We also caught a glimpse of the other historical stone, standing like a baptismal font in the centre of the court-yard, which is believed to have served as the block whereon high criminals were executed when condemned to the *kokserai*. The Russian town is all buried in thick foliage, and looks like an immense park full of villas. Nearly all the wide streets form shady groves and avenues of trees, and all the white brick or stone houses have large gardens, watered from the clear brooks which flow along the edge of the

Samarkand.

pathways on both sides of the road, and pass through conduits under the garden walls. Kaufmann Street and Abramoff Boulevard, named after the two celebrated Governors-General, are immensely wide, and the latter has no less than twelve lines of trees along its central and lateral footways. All modern Russian towns, whether in Europe or Asia, are begun on these thoroughly broad and straight principles, so that there never need be any fear of overcrowding or subsequent necessity for widening thoroughfares or removing obstructive blocks, however enormous the populatron may eventually grow. In this respect the Russian forms a marked contrast with the native town, although the latter has always been considered the largest and grandest in all Central Asia, renowned also for its great science and learning. But vast and imposing as may be the Russian cities in their own particular way, they can never vie with such places as old Samarkand in the beautiful and durable architecture and ornamentation given to it by its great "barbarian" rulers, and the influence of which is still traceable in the rude imitations of style and design on many a tumble-down mosque or tomb on both sides of the Oxus.

When I remembered the massive cathedral of St. Isaac at St. Petersburg, half hidden in unsightly scaffolding during the last fifteen years, with its marble façade and granite monoliths continually cracking and crumbling away, I could not help asking myself what Russia was bringing here to compare with the noble ecclesiastical architecture which, though now dilapidated, has withstood so well the ravages of time and siege for more than 500 years that it still excites the wonder and admiration of all beholders. Take a common native *dootara*, or two-stringed guitar of Persian shape and finely-rounded artistic lines, such as I was fortunate in securing, and compare it with the rude *balalika*, or triangular banjo, of unstained wood, played by the Russian *moujick*, and you have exact types of the art and taste that are rapidly disappearing from this historical ground, and of those now being introduced by its latest conquerors.

But one civilization after another, planted thickly on each other, like geological strata, has been the fate of the medley of races who have jostled each other in ancient Sogdiana, and nobody will for a moment deny the great benefits of quite another kind which Russia is now imposing. It is also perfectly true that the natives themselves have now quite lost the cunning of their great teachers whom Timur sought out and brought to Samarkand from every part of his great empire, stretching from the Irtysh to the Ganges, and from the Desert of Gobi to the Sea of Marmora. Clever stonemasons from Hindustan, architects and workers in mosaic from Shiraz, potters from Kashan, modellers, moulders, and artists from Ispahan and Damascus — all these craftsmen were liberally encouraged by the great Mongol in perpetuating each victory or domestic event of his life and reign. The present descendants and successors of these artificers have produced almost as much disfigurement by their clumsy attempts to restore some of the mural ornamentation of their mosques and colleges, as the Russians have bungled in repairing and trying to remodel the delicate contour of the cupola of Timur's tomb. The rest of the magnificent ruins seem to have been left by Russians and natives alike to the gradual process of decay, and the vandal hands of hunters after souvenirs.

But, returning to the Russian town, we find there nothing artistic or old, and little movement of any kind. The few shops are scattered about among the trees like the private houses, and are difficult to find. Of course, there are all the usual adjuncts of a Russian garrison settlement. Society and its amusements have their centre in the officers' club, which is a whitewashed and pretentious edifice, with a thickly-wooded park attached, and a bold frontage composed principally of a covered colonnade. Here there is a great deal of billiard-playing and gambling at cards, and a weekly dance on Saturday evenings, when members invite the ladies. The private soldiers take turns in doing service as waiters, and they serve up very fair cookery and excellent wines of the country at moderate prices, as I had the opportunity of proving during five days' experience as a visiting member. Opposite the club house is a Russian church, looking, like most of the Russian orthodox temples, as if built of whitewashed and painted wood, with dark blue domes bespangled with gilt stars. There is nothing to be seen of historical or other importance. Whatever treasures may have lain hidden in this quarter were probably doubly buried in the laying out of the present town. Recent investigators state that some Græco-Bactrian remains have been discovered near the Russian camp, which lead to the belief that

Samarkand. 213

the Russians have built on ground once occupied by an extension of the Maracanda of Alexander the Great.

Despite its stiffness and monotony, the Russian town is yet a pleasant and sequestered spot, and so quiet withal that it has not yet been thought worth while to provide lamps for people out of doors after dark.* Not so, however, with the native town, where all is bustle and colour, mingled, it is true, with a good deal of the customary dirt of the East. Leaving the trashy architecture, the stucco, and the white caps and tunics of the Russian Christians for the artistic ruins and kaleidoscopic panorama of the native Mahommedans, we ascend the rising road on the other side of the citadel, and come upon a totally different and, indeed, a unique sight. Out of a forest of old garden trees—luxuriant willows, tall poplars, and spreading elms and planes—with the flat-roofed, mud-built houses clustering between, rises the faded splendour of Tamerlane in the form of ribbed, melon-shaped cupolas of mosques and colleges, with gigantic cufic inscriptions in colours; lofty mosaic, arrow-headed portals, and beautifully tiled and slanting

* The municipality of Samarkand are now discussing the question of introducing electrical lighting.

minarets. It is only when arriving on the Rigistan, or public place, which on bazaar days is all astir with the bustle and chatter of a dense, turbaned, and many-coloured crowd, that an idea of the magnificence of the place in the days of the Timurides and Sheibanides can be gained. On three sides of the square are the celebrated Medressés or theological seminaries of Tilla Kari, Shir Dar, and Ulug Beg, or respectively the gold-covered, the lion-bearing, and the name of Timur's grandson, who was the great patron of astronomy, and who built an observatory on the Tchupan Ata hill on the north-eastern suburb, where now remains nothing but the small tomb of the shepherd saint of Samarkand. These three original and grand-looking piles of well-made brick and stone work, as well as others yet to be noticed, are all faced with glazed tiles and bricks of palish blue, white, green, and yellowish-brown, forming beautiful artistic designs, arabesques and illuminated texts from the Koran. So gigantic are the letters of some of these exterior inscriptions that, according to Mahommedan writers, they may be read by the naked eye more than a mile away.

Some distance farther on the other side of the busy bazaar, and approached by a narrow road cut deeply through a very ancient cemetery, where the bones of generations of the faithful lie exposed in layers, one above the other, on either side of the way, and which is much patronized by beggars and lepers, is another of Timur's handsome relics—the Shah-Zindeh, or living king. This is more properly the mausoleum of Kazim-ben-Abbas, a relative of the Prophet, who is said to have come here in early Moslem times to preach the Koran with the sword, and to have been defeated and captured. According to one absurd legend he was then beheaded, whereupon he caught his falling head and popped into a well, where he still exists; and, according to another fable, he retired for prayer and fasting into the caverns of the earth, where he is still waiting for the purification of Islamism to come forth and expel the Russians. In any case the saint is supposed to be still in the flesh, as the name of Shah-Zindeh indicates; and yet the Mollahs, who gravely relate this arrant nonsense in apparent good faith, are in no way struck by the contradiction when they show at the same time the tomb where they say the self-same Kazim lies dead and buried. The worshippers of Allah and the Prophet will have to get their heads a little clearer before they can hope to revive the power and glory of Mahommedanism in Central Asia. Even a curious lock in the shape of a fish on one of the doors of the tomb is supposed to symbolize the silence imposed upon the still living Kazim. As a symbol of living silence, it might have been more appropriately hung up before the curtains and rugs which I saw here in the dark corners of the mosque, and which concealed, not fictitious or mythological beings like Kazim-ben-Abbas, but real men, who were remaining voluntarily mute for forty days at a stretch. On having one of these sheets pulled aside, we beheld a sitting and perfectly motionless figure with his hands on his knees and his gaze steadfastly fixed in melancholy contemplation. Our intrusion seemed to be absolutely unobserved and unheeded, and his whole body had such an utterly inanimate appearance that he might have been taken for a squatting mummy. When we expressed fear that we were disturbing this votary in his prayers, our guide said that it did not matter in the least, and that a Russian cannon fired off in his close proximity would have left him equally unmoved and impassive. This tomb of the Shah-Zindeh is really a cluster of small mausoleums and mosques erected on the side of a hill

Samarkand.

on which is an extensive cemetery, used, I believe, down to the present day. The cluster must have been gradually formed about the beginning of the fourteenth century. The entrance from the road up a small flight of steps originally paved with marble, and under a graceful pointed arch decorated with glazed earthenware, leads into a long, narrow, ascending, and uncovered passage, with walls on either side, once faced with coloured tiles, but now for the most part quite bare. Along this gallery are several *mazari* or mausoleums, all beautifully enamelled and surmounted by cupolas, containing the tombs of some of Timur's relatives. On one side is the miraculous well connected with the strange history of Kazim-ben-Abbas, while at the end is the mosque, with seven domes, though not all visible from this point of view, where the remains of this saint are dimly seen through a grating, and covered by a heap of cloths and prayer carpets placed there by pious worshippers. The mosque is composed of several chambers, in which may also be seen a finely carved door inlaid with ivory, an immense Koran about six feet square, written by some one still living, or, as Krestofsky informs us, by the grandfather of the present Ameer of Bokhara, the horse-tail banner of the saint, before which women occasionally pray as a cure for sterility, plenty of alabaster, stalactite decoration, and many other curious and very beautiful objects. On regaining the Tashkend road, and proceeding still farther from the centre of the town, the sightseer arrives at what is, I think, the grandest and most imposing building of all—the medressé of Bibi Khanam, the Chinese consort of Tamerlane. The spectator feels dwarfed in presence of the colossal proportions of this magnificent structure, although it may perhaps appear higher than it really is by comparison with the small houses and stalls of the Mussulman vendors around. Its main gateway is very broad, with a most gracefully-pointed arch, and beyond, in the middle of the spacious courtyard, and facing the principal door, is a huge marble lectern on nine low feet, with steps on all sides, and cleft in the shape of a half-opened book, in which was formerly placed for public perusal the blood-stained and much venerated copy of the Koran, now in the Imperial Library at St. Petersburg. The façades and cupolas, as well as the lofty minarets, are all faced with the remains of beautiful tiling. There is a great deal of *débris*, and large portions of the walls seem ready to

Samarkand. 219

fall. The towering minarets of these palatial monuments are nearly all on the slant like the tower of Pisa, especially the two on either side of the Ulug Beg College. Some of them look as though they must certainly fall sooner or later, and at first sight appear really dangerous. There has been much controversy about the cause of this leaning. Schuyler attributes it to an optical illusion caused by one-half of the column being vertical and the other inclined, while Krestofsky thinks they were originally built thus to exhibit the skill of the builders, and perhaps to convey some religious signification. But these seem strange explanations in view of the pure symmetrical lines and regular taste displayed in all the other parts of these magnificent structures. Most of the Russians on the spot attribute the peculiarity to the shocks of earthquakes, which all admit have cracked and damaged many of the buildings, including the dome of Tamerlane's tomb. But whatever may be the true cause of these minarets, 150 feet or 200 feet in height, being apparently out of the perpendicular, nobody has ever yet failed to remark the striking fact, except one of the latest English writers on the subject, Dr. Lansdell. This gentleman says in his book on Central Asia that he saw no inclination at all, although he mounted one of the minarets and surveyed them from below with the greatest attention. This is a curious case of obliquity of vision, in the paradoxical sense of seeing things straight that everybody else sees to be crooked.

I have not yet said anything of the tomb of Tamerlane, which is naturally the first thing that the visitor inquires for, although certainly, to my mind, its appearance does not equal in interest that of the antiquities already referred to. It is called the Gur-Emir, and must be pretty familiar to the public through Verestchagin's pictures. It is not so large as the other medressés and mosques, and is splendidly decorated with the usual enamel and alabaster work without and within. The roof is topped by a melon-shaped dome, like the ancient Russian helmet, or *shelm*, which was a copy of the *shishak*, or Asiatic casque, and it also has two ruined minarets. An elaborately-decorated, though broken gateway, leading to a paved court, with various fruit trees, form the approaches to the steps and entry of the building containing the tombs of Tamerlane, his preceptor, his grandson, and other members of the family. These are marked by squarish coffin-shaped blocks of grey marble,

THE TOMB OF TAMERLANE.

except that of Timur, which is of greenish-black stone, supposed to be nephrite or jade, and a low, flat slab, all placed together in the centre of an octagonal chamber, and surrounded by a square railing of fretted alabaster. At the head, pointing towards Mecca, is a tall arched recess with a window and a short pillar, in the niche of which rests a votive lamp, and a couple of tattered standards on high, bent poles. A narrow winding staircase in one corner descends into a well-kept vault of brick, which contains the actual graves, covered with similar blocks of some kind of limestone, and set to correspond exactly in position with the cenotaphs above.

It would take up an entire volume to give even a cursory notice of all the other interesting objects of this old town, so I shall content myself by concluding with a reference to the oldest and most legendary part of the ancient city called Kalai-Afrosiab, hill or fortification of Afrosiab, a semi-fabulous hero and giant who, local tradition says, was able to sit upon the wall of his capital and bathe his feet in the cooling water of the Siob Canal. This hill or fortress of Afrosiab is on the north-eastern outskirts, and is nothing but a raised accumulation of graveyards, tumuli, and rubbish, extending, perhaps, for a mile. It was in much the same state in the time of Tamerlane as at the present day; and report invests it with the most wonderful store of hidden treasure and prehistoric remains. The Russians have hitherto made but few excavations, and have not even explored the subterranean passages and caves which are said to undermine the whole of this district. A steep hill of some 100 feet in height is still shown as the site of Afrosiab's castle ; and on the north of this, spanned by a Russian stone bridge over the Siob stream, reputed the oldest irrigation *arik* in the world, and approached by the Tashkend road, cut through part of the hill, lies a beautiful flourishing valley, with a number of the most primitive water and other mills in the midst of flourishing gardens and purling streams. I visited several of these native mills, and found the machinery of the very rudest description. One, for cleaning rice, had a long beam slowly knocked up and down by a water-wheel in the stream outside the mud house, and the other end, inside, had a vertical piece, which was thus each time thrust down the side of a hole full of rice. There was also a curious oil mill, which consisted of a thick beam suspended by one end to the roof of the house, with the lower end rest-

Samarkand. 223

ing, like a pestle, in the hollow of a big wooden mortar, made of the trunk of a tree and filled with cotton seed. An old horse dragged the lower end of this pole round the sides of the wooden mortar, and thus crushed the seed until oil made its appearance. This part, also, has its relics of saints and prophets. Clambering up the side of the hill, I found the giant tomb of the Mahommedan prophet Daniel. If his remains really occupy the whole length of his tomb, which is twenty feet long at least, he must have been as tall, or even taller, than the Persian Afrosiab. Of a truth giants walked the earth in those days. At the head is a horse-tail banner and a fine pair of ram's horns, as well as a quantity of stones, laid on the top of the tomb by pious pilgrims. The hillside is burrowed with catacombs, caverns, and cells. According to local and Iranian tradition, Afrosiab ruled here no less than 3,000 years ago and 1,700 years before Mahomed.

I may mention that during part of my sojourn in Samarkand I had the benefit of the agreeable company of Colonel Alikhanoff, the Governor of Merv, who came here, like myself, for the first time, quite as a private visitor, and was just as eager as I was to see all the wonders of the city; besides which it must be added that, although, perhaps, somewhat lax in practice, he came also as a pilgrim and true follower of Mahomed. Among the crowds of mullahs and students who followed us about were many who wondered who the Colonel could be, for he talked Arabic as glibly as I afterwards heard him talk in the language of his Turkoman subordinates at Merv. When he recited from memory whole verses of the Koran in the mosques, with his forage cap removed in Christian fashion, and deciphered the cufic inscriptions on the walls, I wondered almost as much as the turbaned crowd around us.

We afterwards visited the bazaar, and were much amused with the Jews who hang about there watching the chances for doing a little business. The few Hindus here, with red smudges in the centre of their foreheads, are nearly all usurers, like the Jews. Those we met seemed very much interested in me as an Englishman. The Jews ran after us at every turn with offers of their services in negotiating for our purchase of curiosities, and, although cursed and reviled by the stall-keepers and repulsed by ourselves, they nearly always managed to get some little trifle out of our bargains.

Samarkand.

The rest of the population includes Tadjiks, Uzbeks, Kirghiz, Persians, Khivans, Arabs, gipsies, and Afghans, with an occasional Turkoman. Of the total of 36,000 or 38,000 inhabitants—although there are probably now many more—the proportion of Russians amounts to 5,500, and of Jews to 1,500. There are 113 different factories and 246 cotton and silk manufactories.

CHAPTER X.

SAMARKAND TO BOKHARA.

Departure from Samarkand—Our Anglo-French Embassy—Impressions on a Russian railway through foreign territory — Russia's careful absorption of Bokhara—Numbers and particulars of Russian and native troops—Russia holds the key of Bokhara's existence—Quarrels over water, and their consequences—Water police — Water as a measure of wealth and position—Schemes and difficulties of irrigation — Valley of the Zarafshan — The " fire devil "—Origin of the name of Samarkand—Russo-Bokharan frontier — Resemblance and difference between the two conquests under Alexander of Macedon and Alexander of Russia — Kerminé — The " Father of Bokhara "—Arrival at the station of Bokhara — Bad accommodation — We retain our house-car—Journey to the capital—Native carts—Electricity in Ameer's palace—" Shaitan Feringhee " —Contempt for Europeans—Gates and walls of the city—Difficulties of progression—Conolly's fate—An Englishman photographs the Ameer's lunatics—Russian Embassy — Influence and abilities of M. Charikoff and his secretary — Native women — Various races and their dress—Jews—Persian Shiites, Bokharan Sunnites, Orthodox Russians and Russian Tartars—Arrival at Embassy — The *dostarkhan* — Ablutions—Doctor Heyfelder—A Russian ambulance

Samarkand to Bokhara. 227

—Disease and rate of mortality—Hospitality of the Ameer and Russian Embassy—Ameer's presents—Ambassador's establishment.

I LEFT Samarkand, as I had reached it, in one of a train of General Annenkoff's house-cars, which I this time shared with the last of the French guests, Vicomte C——, a delegate from the French Minister of Commerce. We had both received invitations to visit the capital of Bokhara under the powerful wing of the Russian Diplomatic Resident, and we agreed to throw in our lot together, and form a kind of Anglo-French embassy of our own to the Bokharan Government. It was rather difficult at first, when we recrossed the Bokharan frontier about fifty-five miles from Samarkand, to realize the fact that we were no longer on actual Russian territory, and that the Government of the Tsar was only served here by a resident agent or ambassador. The railway and the continual contact with Russian officers and soldiers all the way was a sufficiently representative display of Russia's presence to give us the impression that we were only passing through one of the numerous Asiatic provinces of the Russian Crown,—one that was certainly very distinctive in local colour and peculiarities, but still a part of Russian Central Asia. In reality, such was the case; but for the present Russia prefers to temporize with Bokhara, and studies her own convenience in maintaining a show of diplomatic intercourse—or rather of diplomatic dictation. At Samarkand the *Ooroosi*, as the Bokhariots call their virtual masters, have planted their standard as firmly as at Kazan or any other semi-Asiatic centre of Russia proper; but in Bokhara, " the strength of Islam," and especially in the city and heart of the Khanate, they have not yet altogether settled down to the conviction that their prey has been sufficiently tamed and overawed to undergo incorporation without kicking against the pricks. The Bokhariots are a very peaceful, cultivated, and commercial nation, and do not require crushing at one fell blow on the Skobeleff principle, like the kidnapping and slave-trading Turkomans. A great deal of caution and no little careful dealing are therefore necessary in order to avoid unpleasant friction, especially with the religious and fanatical element, and to prevent any undesirable precipitation of matters towards a crisis. With troops on three sides of the Khanate, north, east, and west, Russia can have no other

Samarkand to Bokhara. 229

reasons or fears for not rounding off her actual frontiers and making them identical with the Bokharan - Afghan boundary on the south. Besides the railway troops distributed along the Russian line, there are other battalions at Kizil Arvat, Askabad, Merv, Chardjui, several at Kerki, farther up the Amu Darya, and two or three more at Samarkand on the other side, as well as detachments at several other places.*

* As the number of Russian troops permanently quartered in the Transcaspian has often been either much underrated on the one side, or greatly overrated on the other, it may be useful to give a correct account of the forces stationed at all points along the railway, including the Afghan frontier, Samarkand, and Tashkent. The Rifle battalions in Central Asia are always kept at an increased peace strength, and generally number about 800 men each. Altogether the total of Russian troops in the Transcaspian, Bokhara, and Samarkand, is about 16,000 men. The native Bokharan troops, all told, are reckoned at 15,000. At Tashkent there are about 7,000 more Russian troops, who could be marched on to the railway in two or three days. The following are the Russian troops and their headquarters. They are only temporarily moved from one place to another, according to the state of affairs on the Afghan frontier. Since the pacification of Ishaak Khan's rebellion, at least one battalion, the 17th, has left Kerki and returned to Samarkand :—

Germab (between Askabad and Geok Tepé), 1st, 2nd, 3rd, and 4th Transcaspian Rifle Battalions, 1st regi-

Should the Bokhariots, to put a case of remote possibility, ever attempt to cut the railway communication, the Russians could easily inflict a deadly retaliation, without railway or even troops. This could be effectually accomplished by cutting off the Bokharan water supply at the head course of the Zarafshan river, and the Ameer's smiling country would become a famished steppe in the course of a few weeks. Just as the Bokhariots themselves in the last century destroyed the great Sultan Bent dam on the Murghab,

    ment of Taman Cossacks, 4th Battery of Horse Artillery, and the Transcaspian Sapper Company.

Merv, 6th and 7th Transcaspian Rifle Battalions, 1st regiment of Caucasian Cossacks, and 296 Turkoman militiamen.

Old Sarakhs, 5th Transcaspian Rifle Battalion.

Sary Yazi, 8th   ,,   ,,

Chardjui, 3rd Turkistan Line Battalion, and 2nd Transcaspian Railway Battalion.

Samarkand, 6th and 11th Turkistan Line Battalions, and 2nd regiment of Ural Cossacks.

Katti Kurgan, 8th Turkistan Line Battalion.

Kerki, 9th, 14th, 17th, and 19th Turkistan Line Battalions.

Kizil Arvat, 1st Transcaspian Railway Battalion.

Tashkent, 1st, 2nd, 3rd, and 4th Turkistan Rifle Battalions, 6th, 10th, and 12th Turkistan Line Battalions, Turkistan Brigade of Field Artillery (56 guns), 5th regiment of Arenburg Cossacks, and half a battalion of Sappers.

which M. Poklefsky is now restoring, and reduced a great part of the Turkoman oasis to a desert, the Russians in their turn could stem the flow of the lower Zarafshan with much more disastrous effect upon Bokhara, for the whole country depends entirely on the irrigation from this stream for its very existence, and the Russians have the key of it within their own boundaries, on the other side of Samarkand.* Cutting off the water supply in these countries is a much more serious calamity than the same operation in London for nonpayment of water rates. From time immemorial nations and races as well as individuals have fought and harassed one another in this part of the world by destroying irrigation works and damming up rivers and canals. Strange pranks have they played with the land as well as with themselves by this process. Large tracts of country have alternately

* The drought and disease this last summer in Bokhara was attributed by some to the checking or diminution of the usual flow of water into Bokharan territory, and by others to the increase of rice plantations, and consequent increase of irrigation in the district of Samarkand. Other rumours insinuated that the proper amount of presents had not been forthcoming from Bokhara.

become waste and fertile, rich and poor, populous and deserted many times over, until the very sources of fertilization have become perverted or exhausted. Rivers and streams have become lessened in volume and shortened in length, and, instead of reaching their original outlets, now lose themselves in the sands, while others have found new and strange beds and courses. Whatever other agencies may have been at work in the freaks played by these eccentric rivers of Central Asia, one cannot help thinking that the circumstances of the irrigation system, and in fact that system itself, badly carried out, must have been the main cause of these vagaries.

At present, as for many years past, there exists both in Bokhara and Turkistan a very important body of water police, named after a compound of the words *mir*, ruler, and *ab*, water, with others of subordinate rank, whose duty is to see that every person gets his fair share of the precious fluid, and does not suffer from the greediness or enmity of his neighbours. The wealth and social position of a native in these parts are estimated to a great extent by the quantity of water to which he is entitled. At the same time the higher authorities of Bokhara are so anxious about their proper water supply that they have the permission of the Governor-General of Turkistan to send their own officials every spring to look after the dams and dykes of the river near Samarkand. The great difficulty would seem to be to turn the water as much as possible back again by other channels, so as not to overdrain and exhaust the river. This is what the Russians are devoting their skill to at the present moment on the Imperial estate of the Murghab, where an elaborate scheme of canalization is expected to fertilize no less than 300,000 desiatines, or more than double as many acres of land, and produce cotton enough to supply two-thirds, if not the whole, of the quantity required by Russian manufacturers.

We steamed along the beautiful valley of the Zarafshan in our novel train of house-cars behind a petroleum-fed locomotive during the best part of the day, having started from Samarkand at six o'clock in the morning. On all sides were thriving villages of flat-roofed mud houses half hidden in verdure, very different from the bare, wretched-looking hovels and treeless hamlets of the North Russian peasantry; and luxuriant fruit gardens and square-walled mud enclosures, shaped liked the usual Asiatic forts, with corner towers and bastions. The golden harvest was already ripe, and the busy Sarts in the fields rushed to hold the heads of their frightened horses, or stood in wondering groups at the stations and crossings. Occasionally the women would come out and sit at a considerable distance to take a peep at the Russian self-moving fire devil—a fit compliment to the Russian "self-boiling" tea urn, or samovar, which they have long since thoroughly adopted—but they quickly replaced their veils as soon as they discerned any one staring at them from the train. As we passed through this pleasant scene, and tasted the delicious apricots and peaches brought to the stations, it made us dread all the more the repetition of our thirsty experiences over the sand steppes and arid plains, which we had to go through again after our visit to Bokhara. No wonder the ancient denizens of other parts of Central Asia called Samarkand and its district an "earthly paradise," especially if they had to reach it through the wild wastes and desert places of half the surrounding country. The very name of Tamerlane's famous capital is supposed to mean a land, or rather a city, flowing with milk and honey. Among the many interpretations put upon the meaning of Samarkand, such as its derivation from the name of a certain chieftain or King Samar, who settled here in times whereof the memory of man runneth not to the contrary, the most probable and now generally received translation is that the word *siamiar*, or *samar*, in both Arabian and the Turanian dialects, is employed in the sense of fruitful, fruit-bearing, and useful, to which has been added the suffix *kand*, *kent*, or town. Even the ancient Maranda or Maracanda of Alexander of Macedon is now thought to have been nothing but a Greek corruption of Samarkand, just as the Russian names of many places and things in Central Asia of to-day are the product of a bad pronunciation of native sounds.

It was still morning when we arrived at the Bokharan frontier near Sara-Bulat, ten miles past Katta Kurgan and fifty-five miles from Samarkand. There were no signs of any frontier division, but there were still the mud fort and mounds where the late Ameer's army suffered such a dire defeat at the hands of General Kaufmann. True to their principle in Asiatic warfare of *j'y suis, j'y reste*, the Russians, it seems, made their frontier exactly on the limit of their advance. It is curious to note, in connection with the overthrow of Bokharan independence near this spot on the occasion in question, that what happened to the Russian army, also befell the troops of Alexander the Great. When the latter marched to the Jaxartes, now the Syr Darya, the people of Samarkand, or Maracanda, raised a rebellion behind his back. Similar treachery was practised on General Kaufmann by the inhabitants of modern Samarkand, after its submission, when the Russian commander had followed the retreating Ameer up to this place between Katta Kurgan and Sara-Bulat. The people of Samarkand had actually shut their gates against the flying Bokhariot soldiers, and had welcomed the Russian wounded and a small Russian garrison; but when Kaufmann turned off into Bokhara to give the *coup de grâce* to the routed Bokhariots, near the present frontier, they shut up the garrison and attacked the Russians in the rear. Kaufmann speedily returned and administered punishment. Here, however, ends the resemblance and begins the difference between the two conquests; for what Alexander of Macedon could not accomplish in firmly establishing his power and connecting this new

Samarkand to Bokhara. 237

possession by secure communication with the rest of his empire, Alexander of Russia has certainly thus far done with a success that promises to be as lasting as anything in this world can ever be.

Three stations farther, at Kerminé, as we learnt afterwards, the Ameer was then staying in a country seat some distance away from the railway. It was at this station that His Highness not long before had received General Rosenbach, the Governor-General of Turkistan, presented him with many costly gifts, and called him the Father of Bokhara.

When we arrived at the station of Bokhara it was already dark, and as the capital to be visited was ten miles distant, and there was very poor accommodation to be had in the shanties and restaurant booths grouped round the station, my French companion and I importuned the station-master to let us have our house-car uncoupled and left at the station to sleep in until we started again for Chardjui. With great good will the station-master acceded to our request, and we were very soon engaged upon some roast mutton in the Armenian restaurant close by. This establishment, I may state for the benefit of intending travellers before the erection of better buildings, has a row of ten very small bedrooms like police cells in a yard at the back. We had not yet got through our meal when the station-master came in out of the darkness and said that he should advise us not to leave our truck with baggage unguarded, as a Russian soldier had just brought him a small revolver and note-book, which he supposed to be our property and had sent back into the waggon. Acting upon this advice, we very soon turned into our trucks for the night.

Early the next morning, before the sun got too hot, we begged a little soap and water of the Armenians again, hired a native *arba*, and started off bag and baggage for the city of the Ameer. There were several very decent open Russian carriages for hire, but we preferred a native cart as an experiment. These single-horsed *arbas*, which appear to be the only conveyances of the country, are simply composed of a couple of long shafts mounted very high at one end between a couple of immense wheels, two or three planks placed across with some matting to sit or lie upon, and a matting cover for shade bent over above the shafts and between the wheels, with both ends open. The boy driver usually sits upon the shafts, and

sometimes on the horse's back. This curious vehicle seems to have been specially invented to imitate the height of the camel; but the camel kneels down to receive its rider or burden, whereas the cart cannot, unfortunately, be let down for the same purpose. The wheels are quite ten feet high, and can go through most of the rivers without wetting driver or passengers. The whole Bokharan army, it is said, once crossed the Amu Darya over a bridge made of these *arbas* on its march against Khiva. It was in one of these springless and uncomfortable equipages, therefore, that we jogged along slowly into Bokhara. The dusty road gradually got narrower, and the fields and gardens by degrees became interspersed with habitations and enlivened by population, until we knew that we were in the extramural suburbs of the city.*
We met a continual stream of natives riding away from the town on horses and donkeys, very often two or three on one animal, dressed in all the colours of the rainbow, and apparently

---

* A large walled garden, or park, on this road encloses the favourite summer palace of the Ameer, which is now being prepared for the electric light. Civilization is thus advancing with rapid strides.

returning from some great fair or holiday *fête*. Many had their wives, completely concealed in black, baggy clothes, perched up behind them on horse or donkey like sacks of potatoes or bundles of goods being carried home from market. I overheard one young man as he passed call us " Shaitan Feringhee," or diabolical foreigners, accompanied with other ejaculations, which were probably not more complimentary. Others regarded us with that "silent, deep disdain" characteristic of Asiatic contempt for Europeans. This was enough, perhaps, without the otherwise distinctive Asiatic aspect of all the surroundings, and the absence of any other Europeans or their traces, to convince us that we were here away from the Russians in a part where Russian contact with the natives was yet scarcely appreciable. At some narrow places on the road our clumsy cart and driver were so near the edge of the stagnant canals and crazy bridges that we considered it prudent to get out and walk.

We entered the city through one of the eleven gates that pierce the crenellated and buttressed mud walls, which are eight miles in circumference. The first wall is said to have been built in 830, and the present one, twenty-five

Samarkand to Bokhara. 241

feet high, after the destruction wrought by Genghis Khan in 1234. The watchmen at these gates live in holes in the walls of the arches, and allow none to enter or leave the town after seven o'clock at night, except, of course Russians and their guests. The general practice is to mount horses at the gates and ride through the narrow streets, as there is really not room for the passage of vehicles; but as we had our luggage in the cart we insisted upon taking it with us. The so-called streets might compare with the narrowest and dirtiest alleys of old London, filled with a motley crowd of busy Asiatics and long rows of open shops. Many of these alleys were covered over with various kinds of awning, especially those through the bazaars, which made them dim and cool. It was a very difficult and awkward piece of business to get our cart through these narrow labyrinths, for if a donkey happened to stand across the way there was not sufficient room for a foot-passenger. One of us had to walk far ahead and shout at approaching horses, camels, and *arbas*, which we unceremoniously jammed into by-paths and recesses, or made go back to wider thoroughfares in order to let us pass. We did not feel called upon to be over squeamish about native etiquette, as we considered that the Bokhariots ought to have got accustomed by this time to being shocked by European visitors. One of the first to disturb their solemn gravity was Captain Conolly, who was murdered here in June, 1848, for insulting the Ameer's Kush-begi, and another English visitor, but a few months before our arrival, had set at nought the precepts of Mahommedan law and Bokharan custom by photographing the inmates of the Ameer's lunatic asylum, in opposition to the request of the dragoman of the Russian Embassy. This was told me with much bitterness in the Embassy itself, and the dragoman said that he had been obliged to leave the enthusiastic traveller to his fate, whereupon he was hustled out of the establishment with his apparatus. We did not, however, go to this extent; and were not at all surprised that the Bokharan officials were often afraid of letting foreigners see their various institutions. I fear that we did not cut a very dignified figure in the eyes of the natives as an Anglo-French embassy, as we pushed our way forward and made our own paths straight without the aid of the usual Eastern pomp and heralding in advance of

Samarkand to Bokhara.   243

djigits and officials; but we made up for it afterwards in our visits about the city. Whenever any difficulty arose we referred to the Russian Embassy as our destination; and when that was not understood, we had only to pronounce the name of the Russian Ambassador, M. Charikoff, and the way was cleared for us at once. The name of Charikoff is the talisman to be used here in all difficulties. I was surprised at the popularity of the Russian representative, and am sure that an appeal to him in most matters would be more likely to be effective than an address to the Ameer. In point of fact the present Ameer is hardly more than a Russian chinnovnik, and cannot help himself. Most of our inquiries were answered by a reference to Charikoff, and when we applied to the Bokharan Government about trade, we were also told to ask Charikoff. Unfortunately, M. Charikoff, who speaks English perfectly, and was once a member of an English Debating Society in St. Petersburg, was away on the Amu Darya during our visit, and the secretary left in charge, M. Klemm, who is also a great linguist, speaking no less than ten languages, had only just buried one of his children, which accounted for our not being welcomed in the usual manner at the gates of the city. Before the completion of the railway to Samarkand, the few Russian residents in the town felt so isolated, that they often went to the railway station to look out for strangers, and offer them hospitality. As we pushed on through the variegated throng we occasionally met the sombre figures of women, much more strictly veiled than their Mahommedan sisters in Samarkand, and they nearly always turned off and set their faces against the wall, or retreated into some corner or doorway until we infidels had gone by. The only women permitted to go unveiled in Bokhara are professional female beggars, mostly widows, in the hope that compassionate husbands may be attracted by their looks and induced to take them into their harems. Little girls under ten run about with the boys quite uncovered, and are distinguished from the latter chiefly by their two long, thin plaits of black hair falling from under the small skullcap worn by both sexes. The greatest variety, after the gaudy robes common to all the men, is seen in the different turbans and other head-gear. The Jews are the only persons forbidden to wear turbans, and until lately, when they gained the right, by purchase, of wearing a thong round the waist, they were compelled to girdle their long gabardines with rope. Their head-dress at present is mostly a dark, flattish kalpak, four-cornered above the rim, something like the cap often worn by the Poles. The Hindus and Parsees wear no chalmas or turbans by choice. The Russian Mahommedans, Kirghiz, Turkomans, and Tartars generally keep to their national black sheepskins. I may mention here that the Shiite Persians are as much looked down upon by the Bokharan Sunnites as they are despised for their want of character by the orthodox Russians, while the Russian Tartars in Bokhara, who have long been settled there as merchant clerks and agents, are very highly considered and esteemed by the natives of all ranks and classes.

We reached the Russian Embassy at the farther end of the town in the afternoon, and were received at the gate by half a dozen Bokharan guards, with queer old halberds, and much salaaming on the part of the native servants. We had long been expected, and a little whitewashed room with carpets and beds, and the indispensable *dostarkhan*, spread out on a table in front of the window, was quite ready for our reception. The welcoming spread, which was soon supplemented by Russian tea, consisted of about a dozen plates of sugared pistachios, almonds, balls of honey and sugar, white sugar plums, raisins, and other dainties, more likely to be appreciated by children than by tired and thirsty travellers like ourselves. We were not allowed to have these sweets taken away the whole time of our stay, and so at last got rid of them by distributing them into the corners of the room. One of the first things we did was to have our feet washed in true Eastern and Biblical fashion, sitting on the threshold of our apartment, after which lunch was brought in, with more tea. Owing to M. Charikoff's absence and the recent bereavement in the family of M. Klemm, we were entertained by Dr. Heyfelder, the medical chief of Skobeleff's Tekke expedition, the doctor of General Annenkoff's railway staff, and the well-known author of " Transkaspien und seine Eisenbahn," lately published in Hanover. The abounding local knowledge and talents of this gentleman were placed at our disposal throughout our visit with a willingness and courtesy that won our sincerest gratitude. Dr. Heyfelder is reputed the most popular man in Bokhara, which is greatly owing to his ever ready attention to the Bokharan sick, who come every morning to see him in the Embassy, or send for him to their houses at all hours of the day and night, and also to his scrupulous consideration for the native customs and prejudices.*

The Russian Embassy in Bokhara has undertaken a difficult task now that the railway is bringing more and more visitors to see the country. It has taken upon itself, no doubt for political as well as other reasons, to dispense the Ameer's hospitality and look after the foreigners who would otherwise have to put themselves under the guidance of the Bokharan officials. This is advantageous in many respects to all parties concerned, as it relieves the Ameer from much costly ceremony and the custom of giving

---

* Dr. Heyfelder has helped to establish an ambulance hospital and dispensary for the natives in the Ameer's capital under the direction of a Russian apothecary, and there is now a doctress for attendance on the Mahommedan women. Owing to the total absence of all sanitary conditions, as well as of rational medical treatment, disease and death are rampant to a frightful extent. In July and August, 1889, the death-rate in the city was said to have reached 700 per day, and gave rise at first to fears that cholera had appeared; but the increased mortality was ascertained to be due to certain kinds of malaria fever. The Russian Embassy distributed a large quantity of quinine on the occasion.

presents;* it suits the Russian representatives politically, and to some extent financially, for the Embassy receives large subsidies from the Bokharan Sovereign in provisions and service, and it enables visitors to get on better with the Russians than they could with only the native authorities to depend upon. The Ameer supplies the Embassy with meat, pilaff, tea, sugar, *dostarkhans*, horses, servants, and in fact nearly everything. I was informed that it only cost the Russian Foreign Office about £2,000 a year to keep up the whole concern. There is a native Mirakhur, who is appointed by Said-Agat-Khan-Bogadoor to live in the Embassy and rule over all the arrangements of ceremony and service, and the Bokharan attendants, who must number a score, are made to serve as a sort of *corvée*, or it may be even as a punishment for certain periods, when they are relieved by others. In any case they do not seem to get any salaries worth speaking of, but they pick up a good deal in the way of backsheesh from visitors. There are twenty Cossacks of the Ural

* The Ameer's presents to visitors whom he receives are generally three or four khalats, or robes, several pieces of silk, nearly always a horse, and if the guest be a married man, which is ascertained by the officials after the audience, also a shawl.

as an escort, who are relieved every six months, and several Tartar and other interpreters. One of the most interesting of the servants was an old Persian water-carrier, who had been sold into slavery by his Turkoman captors, and subsequently liberated by the Russians.

The various buildings and courts of the Embassy occupy a considerable space of land, and are enclosed by high mud walls, above which can just be seen the citadel, called the *ark*. The first court is the residence of the Mirakhur, who was generally squatting outside on his carpet watching the tea-bearers, water-carriers, cooks, and other servants at their various duties ; and in a further court are the stables and barracks of the Cossacks. An inner courtyard contains the guest rooms on one side of the square, and the different rooms of the native servants and their supplies of provisions on the other. In one corner is also the Chancellerie and general dining-rooms for visitors. In a smaller court entered from this one is the house of the Ambassador, before which a Cossack sentinel with drawn sabre paces day and night ; and at the back of all these courts is a very large garden of apricot, plum, and cherry trees.

We were well regaled with pilaff and sweetmeats from the Ameer, as well as with European dishes from the table of the Secretary's family, and always had horses and guides ready to take us about the town. What we did and saw during these excursions I will recount in the following chapter.

CHAPTER XI.

THE CITY OF BOKHARA.

Stay in the capital—Civilities of the Russian Embassy—
Inadvisability of going about unattended—Necessity
of a guide—Ameer's chamber of horrors—Visit to the
prison—Its inmates and filthy interior—The sheep-
tick dungeon and black hole—Conolly's subterranean
cell now closed—Manner of feeding prisoners—
Kalian minaret : a place of execution ; ascent of by
an Englishman—Ameer's palace and clocks—Official
visit to the Ameer's Minister of Commerce—Our
procession through the streets—Bokharan guard of
honour—Reception by the Minister—More sweetmeats—Pilaff and tea—Conversation on trade—
Diplomatic answers—Inspection of the guard of
honour—Objections to making presents—The reshta
worm—Dr. Heyfelder's experiments—Spurious Bokharan postage stamps—Russian and native transmission of correspondence—Ameer's absence from
the Railway inauguration—Opening of the line to
Bokhara, and invasion of the capital by Russians
and Turkomans—Assassination of the Divan Begi—
Lex talionis, and torture of the assassin—Ameer's
executioners—Originality and population of the city.

DURING my stay in the Bokharan capital with
Vicomte C——, we were escorted about the

town by the native djigits of the Embassy and Atobai, the Tartar kavass. The latter was a magnificent specimen of the Russian remnant of the Golden Horde, tall and handsome, with a small-brimmed, soft, white felt hat pulled straight in front to shade the eyes, and disclosing the embroidered skullcap behind in the nape of the neck, and with a gorgeous silver belt round the waist of his long black coat. He informed us confidentially that he had just married a second and younger wife, the first being still alive, but old and peevish. I do not know what the increasing number of foreign visitors will have to do in the future; but it was still considered advisable not to go about the crowded streets and bazaars altogether unattended, and the Embassy, only a short time before, had even showed some objection to Dr. Heyfelder going out alone, especially at night. No doubt, however, the Bokhariots will soon get accustomed to the sight and inquisitive manners of Europeans prying about in their mosques and holy places, so that precautionary measures for their safety will be gradually relaxed. In fact, the Russian Embassy will never be able to keep up an hotel for the ever-increasing number of distinguished Russians and strangers, unless the right of

The City of Bokhara. 253

travelling over the Central Asian Railway continues to be as severely restricted by the Government as it has been up to the present moment.

Apart, however, from the above considerations, it is almost impossible for a foreigner to thread his way through the maze of crowded streets and alleys of Bokhara without the assistance of a guide and interpreter. To take a native one is not the best way of obtaining admission to the buildings which the Bokhariots still try to keep shut against Europeans, and only the Russians know how to pronounce the "open sesame" which discloses the Ameer's treasures and chambers of horror. By this last epithet I refer to the famous prison or zindan and dungeon of torture, to which we were very fortunate in gaining admittance, though not without trouble. After a good deal of urging, we were at last conducted to the spot by the djigits and kavass of the Embassy. The guides rode on in front, clearing the way where necessary by a flourish of their whips, and we followed on horseback behind, in the usual Eastern manner of progress. The poor Bokhariots who can afford it generally ride on *ishaks* or asses, the better off on horses. We arrived by tortuous alleys and dirty thoroughfares at one side of the artificial hill which supports the citadel and the Ameer's palace. The stout, swarthy governor and gaolers, with rattling keys, were ready to receive us, and as soon as we had dismounted they led the way up the mound to the door of the prison. All the building and walls, like the houses everywhere around, seemed made of dried mud and clay, supported by wooden beams and frames. We were first taken into a small uncovered yard with two or three patches of garden and a large tomb half sheltered by a shed with open front. At the head of the stone were laid a pair of fine ram's horns, and three tall bent poles were fixed in the ground, with rags and horsehair dangling from their tops, reminding one of the distant gibbets in some of Gustave Doré's illustrations of Balzac. We were told that this was the tomb of Kusk-Kara-ta, the protector of shepherds, though why he was buried in this prison yard we could not understand. A small iron-barred door of a low building, surmounted by a dome at one end, like the top of a Turkish bath at Constantinople, was then unlocked, and we all peered in, but the darkness was so great in contrast with the glare of the sun outside that at first we could see nothing. We then bent down, and went just

A STREET IN BOKHARA.

The City of Bokhara.

inside; and as soon as our eyes had accustomed to the gloom, we discerned a number of men standing round close together against all the four walls, except just near the doorway through which we had entered. The room was not more than fifteen feet long by ten feet broad, with a low ceiling that we nearly touched with our heads. In this den were crammed no fewer than twenty-five half-naked, dirty prisoners, with filthy rags littering the earthen floor, and a few shelves on the walls with gourd water-bottles, pieces of bread, and other odds and ends. There was no ventilation or light. A few chains were hanging round the walls, but none of the men appeared to be in irons, and all were free to sit down when we had gone. I subsequently ascertained that their gyves and manacles had been removed in anticipation of our visit. Another small door was then unlocked in the right-hand wall of this chamber, and we looked into a kind of well, entered by a descent of several broken steps, and lighted from the open top of the dome which we had noticed outside. Here we saw twenty more men huddled together, with hardly space to move. Some had chains on their limbs, and, altogether, it would be difficult to imagine a more wretched collection of human beings. Notwithstanding the aperture above, there was such a foul stench in this den, worse even than the sickening odours of the adjoining room, that I had to make a rush into the yard before our inspection had ended in order to breathe fresh air. We did not descend into this reeking hole, but only stood on the steps. These two cells, according to the Governor, constituted the whole of the prison; but we insisted that there must be an underground chamber somewhere, and called his particular attention to the reports of the horrible sheep-tick cell into which Captain Conolly and Stoddart were let down to be eaten up alive by vermin. After some conversation with the interpreter, he ordered several prisoners sitting in the middle of the well to get up, and then pointed to a stone slab exactly in the centre of the floor. This, he said, was the entrance to the dungeon below, but he assured us that it had been filled up and closed for ever in honour of the arrival of the Russians. The stone certainly did look as if it had been plastered down, and was not intended to be further removed. This black hole contained no less than 110 prisoners at the time of the death of the late Ameer, father of the present ruler, and one of them told the Russian Resident that no

The City of Bokhara. 257

inmate had ever been known to sustain life longer than three years. Before leaving we requested permission to give the prisoners some money, but Atobai suggested the better plan of giving them something to eat, as the money would only be taken away as soon as we had turned our backs. Accordingly we sent one of the gaolers for bread, and he quickly returned with a pile of flat brown cakes in the lap of his robe. These were at once distributed among the men, who invoked upon our heads the blessings of Allah as the heavy clanking door was shut behind us. Outside we noticed, hanging upon the wall, a thick stick with a large knob like a big drum-stick, and were informed that this was used for belabouring the prisoners when they became obstreperous. On descending into the street we saw a couple of the prisoners chained together, begging, as we were told, for the rest. Bokharan prisoners are each allowed only one thin cake of bread per diem, besides what is procured by those let out, two at a time, to beg.

We next made an attempt to ascend the great minaret Kalian, but in vain. No European has ever yet been allowed to mount this great tower, and we were no better favoured than our prede-

S

cessors.* It stands over 200 feet high, by the side of the Medressé of the same name, and is used as a place of execution, the condemned criminal being hurled from its summit down on to the flagstones below. A request which we made to be taken into the great mosque of Mir Arab, with its fine columns, which is close by, was equally unsuccessful. We were put off with the usual story that the Mollah Moutevalli was not at home, and the key could not be found without him. So also was refused our application to see the interior of the Ameer's palace, which faces the Rigistan, or large public square and market-place. We rode up close to the steps leading upward to the great portal of the palace, flanked on either side by round towers, and surmounted above the arch by the only public clock in all Bokhara, but here we were made to dismount. Most authors on Bokhara say that this clock over the palace gate was made by Giovanni Arlandi, an Italian slave, but the Russians assert that it was the handiwork of a Russian Tartar prisoner. Report has it that the Ameer now

* This tower has since been ascended by an Englishman in the employment of General Annenkoff, which shows how great and rapid is the change being effected by the Russian contact.

The City of Bokhara.

employs a German to wind up his clocks and pocket watch; but Dr. Heyfelder says he has never met any of his countrymen engaged in that capacity.

The most interesting incident of our stay was a ceremonious and official visit which we paid to the Ameer's Minister of Commerce, the Inak, or chief treasurer and collector of taxes. A long cavalcade of *djigits* or mounted guides heralded our approach through the streets. To any European we must have cut a most ridiculous figure; but the natives, who stared and ran after us, appeared to think it all very grand. My French companion and I were attired in evening dress, and mounted upon two of the finest chargers kept in the Russian Embassy. I had tacked on to the left lappet of my coat all the decorations that I could muster, including the medals for the Russian war in Turkey, and for the coronation at Moscow, as well as the Roumanian Cross. My billycock unfortunately had been much damaged by travel, and my friend's crush-hat, which had also suffered the effects of too much packing, looked very much like a stretched-out concertina. But the medals had a surprising effect. In front of us rode a big-bearded Russian in frock-coat, who was also to take part in the interview for the purpose of arranging for the erection of buildings round the railway station. Further ahead rode two turbaned *djigits*, and right in front slowly paced the chief guide of the procession. The rear was brought up by another Bokharan and by Atobai, the Tartar, in his finest parade uniform. We were not allowed to hurry, as that would have been undignified and improper. About every five minutes our caravan was joined by other horsemen from the Minister to see that we were coming, and these galloped back at intervals to report our stately progress like aides-de-camp on a field-day. In this grand style we arrived, covered with dust, at the Minister's residence.

A file of fifteen native soldiers was drawn up as a guard of honour outside the gateway where we dismounted. They were dressed in an imitation of the Russian uniform, dark tunics, top-boots, and black lamb's-wool caps, with Russian letters on their red shoulder straps. Their officer was dressed very much like his men, only with a longer coat, and, besides a curved sword hanging from the belt, he carried a battleaxe in his right hand. The men were armed with some antiquated system of rifle which I did not examine very closely. I had never seen such an ungainly-looking set of soldiers since the formation of the raw levies of Bulgarians at the beginning of the Russo-Turkish campaign in 1878. Indeed, there seemed to me to be a great resemblance between these Bokharan infantrymen and the raw recruits whom I saw in the Balkans, both as regards uniform and general appearance.

We were received at the gate by a crowd of gorgeously-robed officials, and I suppose attendants on the Minister, who marshalled us up the courtyard to a slightly raised verandah, where his Excellency was already waiting. With a flabby shake of the hand and a profuse deal of bowing we were invited to seat ourselves at a table spread out with the never-failing *dostarkhan* of cloying sweets. No word was uttered on either side for several minutes, and we had plenty of time to survey each other and get ready our questions and answers. The Minister was dressed in a brilliant gown of Moscow silk and gold brocade, and wore a very large fine turban. At his side stood his own interpreter, as a check upon Atobai, who stood at one end of the table to interpret on our behalf. Presently the conversation was opened with the customary inquiries after the state of our health, and how we liked Bokhara. Then the Russian architect entered into professional details about house construction in the projected Russian town, and laid stress upon the fact that the Ameer's Government must first of all provide him with a house for himself and family.

Meanwhile the *dostarkhan* was cleared away, and a very excellent set of dishes of pilaff, roast chickens, and fruit were set before us with Russian lemon-flavoured tea, in glasses in Russian fashion. My French friend soon opened fire on the subject of Bokharan commerce, about which he desired to collect statistics for his Ministry at Paris. The chocolate-coloured features of the Minister looked puzzled and perplexed, and he took plenty of time to consult with his attendants before giving any reply. The Vicomte inquired if the Ameer would like to send his representatives with samples of Bokharan products to the Paris Exhibition. His Excellency asked what was an exhibition, and after some difficulty it was explained to him as a large bazaar of international trade exhibits. He said he would submit the matter to his Sovereign, and let us know through the Russian Embassy. We then both asked whether his

The City of Bokhara. 263

Majesty the Ameer would like to see British and French merchants in Bokhara, and what we should inform our respective Governments on the subject. The Minister said that that was a matter on which we must really talk with Charikoff, the Russian Ambassador. English and French goods were already to be found in Bokhara, and he believed Bokharan wares had also found their way to London and Paris. All our other questions were parried in the same diplomatic way with appeals to the Russian Ambassador; so that we soon withdrew from the Ministerial presence with a great many parting compliments and salaams. The Minister insisted, however, on accompanying us down to the gate with all his retinue. When we had mounted and distributed the usual backsheesh, I noticed the Bokharan guard of honour presenting arms again; so I rode up to the line and greeted the men with the Russian salutation of "Zdorovo molodtsi!" "Health to you, my braves!" at which there was not a word of response, such as Russian soldiers would have given, but the officer with the axe walked up and shook me cordially by the hand. We then rode back to the Embassy in the same order, but with the addition of several more *djigits* from the Minister. Vicomte C—— was desirous of sending a few unconsidered trifles to the Minister, in the hope of getting something handsome in return; but the Embassy rather objected to this, as they have recently advised the Ameer and his Ministers to discontinue the ruinous practice of giving presents.

One of our excursions into the bazaar was made with Dr. Heyfelder for the purpose of seeing the operation of extracting the reshta worm from the afflicted natives. This worm, *filaria medinensis*, or *Bukharinensis*, is the veritable scourge of Bokhara, and is introduced into the system by the consumption of stagnant and filthy water. It was described by the traveller Jenkinson some 300 years ago; and as it seems to be as prevalent now as it was then, we may measure by this fact alone the rate at which civilization has hitherto advanced in Bokhara. There is another disease called the Afghan plague, or Sart disease, which exhibits itself in sores on the face, and I believe is one of the forms of leprosy, but the reshta is much more disagreeable and common. No one can drink raw water in Bokhara with impunity, and among the Russian residents the samovar tea-urn is boiling all day long. As Dr. Heyfelder says, it is a parasite imbibed with impure water, which, after nine to eleven months' development in the organism, finds its way into the subcutaneous and muscular parts of the body in the form of a long, milky-white, and rather elastic worm. In autumn and winter the water is seldom dangerous; but in summer the city of Bokhara is reeking with stagnant pools and basins where the water containing the germ of this reshta is used indiscriminately for bathing, washing, and drinking, with the lamentable result that it is a rare thing to meet a Bokharan who has not been attacked.* They seem to think that water cannot be impure if prayed over and used for religious ablutions. Europeans, who do sometimes drink the water, are believed to escape the disease through their use of alcohol and other strong liquors, which probably

* Dr. Heyfelder informs me that this summer (1889) quite half of the inhabitants were afflicted with the reshta, many having several worms at a time. He thinks that the careless manner in which the extracted worms are often thrown on to the ground, and probably allowed to crawl away into the water, may help to distribute the germs. It appears that the present Ameer has only once been attacked by the reshta, and then strangely enough on his visit to Moscow during the coronation in 1883.

destroy the germ. At Samarkand it is hardly known at all, and at Kerminé it is rare. It only becomes more prevalent as the Zerafshan river nears the capital, thus proving that its origin must be in this city. The worm generally appears under the skin like a strong vein in the legs, arms, or back, and is accompanied with itching. Its head, which is hard and pointed, pierces a small hole, and then gradually comes out of itself when fully developed. It is not unusual for a man to go to the barbers, who act as the extractors, with the worm half hanging out of his calf. Sometimes it dies under the skin and causes gangrene. Dr. Heyfelder once supplied certain antiseptics to the wound made by the head, and after the patient had rested twenty-four hours the worm came out without further assistance. Many persons have two or three reshtas regularly every year, and they may have ten to twenty in different parts of the body at one time. They often put the feet and legs in cold water in order to send the worm up higher. Not a single case, however, I am told, occurred among the Russian soldiers and workmen employed in building the railway, owing to General Annenkoff's strict orders that they were not to drink the Zarafshan water, and to the supply of

The City of Bokhara. 267

a number of Pasteur filters. Many of these filters are now in the different railway stations. Annenkoff also prohibited the eating of fruit, and especially of melons, as equally liable to contain the germ. We saw a number of men operated upon in the barbers' shops in the bazaar. They sat or lay down on the floor while the barbers cut the skin with a sharp razor, and after probing about with a small piece of wire, and finding the head, they carefully drew the worm out by constant massage of the flesh round the wound. Such crowds surrounded us, thinking, no doubt, that we were all foreign doctors, that our *djigit* felt called upon to use his whip rather roughly. This offended our amiable doctor, Heyfelder, and he took the whip away and administered a severe reprimand ; but the man at once pulled out another one from under his gown, which very much amused the bystanders, in spite of the thrashing they had just received. I bought one of the worms that I saw extracted and brought it with me in spirits as a specimen and curiosity to St. Petersburg. If the worm coils itself under the skin it may be tied into a knot in the course of extraction, and then the operation becomes very painful. I watched some experiments made on this vermicular parasite by Doctor Heyfelder in the Embassy with the aid of the microscope, which were very interesting. Being oviparous, every drop of fluid pricked from the body of the adult worm contains myriads of minute living copies of the parent. The effect of several chemical solutions were tried upon these minute organisms, and they generally revived after some time. Some lived for twenty-four and others as long as forty-eight hours after being put under the lens.

While I was in Bokhara, some ingenious persons in Europe were endeavouring to take advantage of the credulous by representing the Ameer's country to be so far advanced in modern civilization that it had long been included in the International Postal Union, and possessed an organized penny post. A number of spurious Bokharan postage stamps appear to have been circulated among collectors; and Doctor Heyfelder had the satisfaction of exposing the fraud, by informing the numerous correspondents who wrote to him on the subject, that no native postal service or postage stamp had ever existed. Since the completion of the railway to Samarkand a regular Russian

The City of Bokhara. 269

post has naturally been organized all along the line, and Bokhara has thus been brought within the reach of the letter post of Europe. Previously to this, one of the Russian commercial houses represented in Bokhara had a private post office attached to its place of business, and undertook to transmit correspondence between Russia and the Bokharan capital; but the Ameer and the natives among themselves still send their epistles rolled up and tied round with silk by means of mounted *djigits*.

I further learnt in Bokhara that the presence of all the petty potentates of Russian Central Asia at the inauguration of the railway in Samarkand, as depicted in glowing colours in the French Press, had also been an invention. Not even the Ameer of Bokhara, near as he was all the time to the scene of jubilation, thought fit to put in a personal appearance. His reserve in the circumstances is easily understood. It was certainly not for the ruler of a country which has been cut in two by a Russian military railway, and reduced to a position which gives Russia all the advantages of actual possession without any of its burdens, to personally rejoice in the depreciation of his own dignity and importance. He therefore very naturally confined his participation in the rejoicing to the despatch of Ambassadors and the usual presents. His Highness must have had enough of Russian festivity in connection with the progress of this railway when the line reached the neighbourhood of his own capital. The Russian railway advance has, in fact, been celebrated by General Annenkoff and his officers at every important point from Askabad onwards, and the *fêtes* at Samarkand were only a repetition on a larger scale of those previously held at Chardjui and Bokhara. When the line was completed to the latter station, a large party of Russian officers—some say nearly a hundred—entered the native town, ten miles off, to attend a banquet in honour of the occasion at the Russian Agency. This triumphant entry of the Ooroosi into the town must have appeared to the Bokhariots something like an invasion, and was certainly calculated to wound their national pride. What made the matter worse was, that Colonel Alikhanoff rode over from Merv with an escort of sixty Turkoman horse. As may well be imagined, the invasion of the narrow and crowded streets by this numerous convoy of former bad neighbours, as well as bad Mussulmans, was highly displeasing to the Bo-

The City of Bokhara.

kharan Government, whether prompted merely by a love of military display, or adopted as a measure of personal security. If for the latter reason, it must have been equally offensive, as showing a most uncomplimentary want of confidence in the Bokharan authorities, who are still treating the Russian Embassy as guests of the Ameer. Even the Russians themselves soon saw that they were giving a dangerous provocation to the more fanatical portion of the populace; and the Governor of Merv had the prudence—or perhaps he received orders—to send his Turkoman retinue back to Merv. When staying in Constantinople in 1878, while the Russians stood round the defensive lines of that coveted city, after their hard-fought victories in Bulgaria, I well remember that only a very limited number of their officers were permitted to enter the town at one time, and those were compelled to appear in mufti. Even Skobeleff was not exempted from this regulation. The Russians evidently see no necessity for repeating such a precaution in their peaceful and easily won conquest of Bokhara. There is no need to mince matters with the Bokhariots, as they can be swallowed up at any moment. Yet, however strong may be the Russian grip on the country, a fanatical outbreak, a last expiring effort, is not at all impossible. It would certainly be the final doom of Bokharan semi-independence, but might entail an unnecessary and frightful amount of slaughter. But the Russians know what they are about with Asiatics, and, fortunately, on the occasion in question the Bokhariots took the matter coolly. Some, however, say that it was not altogether without its consequences, and a competent person expressed the belief that this incident may have had something to do with the assassination of the Ameer's Russophile and unpopular Divan Begi several months before my visit. This murder was generally attributed to private revenge, but there was also suspicion that motives of political and religious fanaticism were at the bottom of it. The Russian officials seemed to be very little enlightened on the subject. In any case the murderer was punished with one of the cruellest and most barbarous deaths that Asiatic justice has ever invented. There appear to be three kinds of capital punishment—throwing the criminal from the highest minaret; cutting his throat in the Rigistan, or market-place; and handing him

The City of Bokhara. 273

over to the relatives and servants of his victim to be tortured to death. The latter system of *lex talionis* was adopted for the assassin of the Ameer's chief Minister. The wretch had his eyelids cut off, his limbs broken and hacked away, and when the relatives and menials of the murdered Minister had done their horrid work the mutilated body was tied to the tail of a donkey and dragged through the town, to be thrown to the dogs outside. The proceedings are described as having been revolting in the extreme; and I heard blame cast upon the Russian Diplomatic Resident for seeming to countenance such an atrocious system of execution. Russia's humanizing mission might well have come in here. If Russia's representative had no immediate power to prevent such a savage kind of punishment, he should have quitted the town with all his staff during its infliction, by way of showing his decided disapproval.*

The thorough accounts of Bokhara given by Eugene Schuyler and other English travellers

---

* The Ameer employs several executioners. The chief one attached to his palace is called upon to deal with only high criminals, and he receives £2 per month. The others receive from £1 to £1 10s. per month.

T

are all so well known that I shall not enter into any fuller description of this curious old stronghold of Asiatic manners, exclusiveness, and Mahommedan fanaticism. But I would advise those who wish to see it in all its originality, dirt, and splendour to make haste and do so before the Russian contact becomes too close for things to remain as they are. Its 140 mosques and eighty Medressés are not to be compared with the ruins of Tamerlane's beautiful structures at Samarkand, and altogether the city, which contains 170,000 inhabitants, has a cramped and over-populated appearance, which Samarkand has not.

CHAPTER XII.

BOKHARA TO MERV.

Departure from Bokhara—Breakdown of the Amu Darya bridge—Descent into a barge—Boundary between Iran and Turan—Hardships of Russian Expeditions—Difficulties and dangers abolished by the Railway—Peter the Great's instructions—Expeditions under Tcherkasky and Bucholtz—Peter's efforts to open up roads to India—His apocryphal testament—Perofsky's failure — Successes of Kaufmann and Tchernaieff— Peter the Great's dream realized—Speed and method of constructing the Railway—Comparisons with American construction — The Railway's receipts and traffic—Arrival at Merv—Welcomed by Colonel Alikhanoff—The Governor's house—Turkoman carpets — Alikhanoff's escort—Bathing—Snakes in the Murghab—Origin of the river's name—Alikhanoff's trophies—Relics of the disastrous English retreat on the Koushk—a Turkoman Khan's opinion of the English, Russians, and Afghans—Introduced to the Khans of Merv—Alikhanoff and his Turkoman subordinates.

WE left the capital of Bokhara in much finer style than we had entered it. The Russian Embassy sent us off in a four-seated landau

T 2

drawn by four horses, with Bokharan outriders, and we were escorted by a convoy of Ural Cossacks, native *djigits*, and clouds of dust. We had with us in another carriage, which went ahead, the Secretary and Chargé d'Affaires of the Agency, M. Klemm, who was also going by the train as far as Chardjui. It was a marvel how we got through the narrow thoroughfares with our big carriages; but as it was rather late in the evening the streets were not so crowded as in the daytime, and we dashed along at a pretty good pace, until we reached the station, ten miles off. We resumed our places in the house-truck in which we arrived, and were soon on the road back to the Amu Darya. We started from Bokhara at nine o'clock at night, and arrived on the bridge over the Oxus at six the next morning. To our disappointment the train, which crept and creaked along over the rapid, coffee-coloured river, at last came to a dead stop near the opposite bank. The bridge had again broken down just in front of us, and the train could proceed no farther. After a long delay we had to get out and descend into a big barge with our luggage. The Persian porters somehow reached our part of the bridge, and performed wonderful athletic feats in carrying enormous boxes and bundles single-handed along the narrow plank, guarded by a slight hand rail, at the side of the train as far as the barge. When we got into the flat-bottomed barge we found everybody's luggage mixed up in confusion, and the crowd of Mahommedans, Armenians, Jews, and Russians were wrangling and pushing one another about to find their respective effects. Without waiting for all the long-skirted Mahommedans to get down the ladder, we pushed off to the shore; and on landing, I had only just time to buy my ticket at the unfinished station, still surrounded with scaffolding, and mount into a fresh train that was just on the point of starting.

We soon lost sight of the verdant scenery of Chardjui, and again entered the terrible sands of the Kara Kum, the boundary between Iran and Turan. We had quitted a country of fertility and wealth, and were now re-entering one of deserts and comparative poverty, or, to make another comparison, the Russian locomotive had brought us out of a land possessing wheeled conveyances, such as they are, and was re-introducing us to one which had none. I was reminded, as we again passed into this billowy sand steppe that here, in sight of Chardjui, was supposed to be the scene of that magnanimous act of Alexander the Great, when he took the water brought to him in one of his soldier's helmets and poured it out on the sand, saying that he had no right to drink while his army was dying of thirst. Many other expeditions had failed to reach the Amu Darya since that far-off time. Markozoff's detachment in the Khiva campaign could not get there, and was obliged to return, while Kaufmann's column had to contend with enormous difficulties and perils in view of the river. Not only armies, but travellers, had met with unheard-of privations and hardships. Twenty-five years ago Professor Vambéry said that the wayfarer or explorer in this region must expect to encounter insurmountable obstacles. What, therefore, can be more important than a railway enterprise that has abolished all these difficulties and dangers? In 1714, a certain ukase of Peter the Great to the Senate ran thus :—

"Send to congratulate the Khan Shirazy on his accession, and go to the Bokharan Khan under the pretext of commercial business, but in reality to find out where Yarkand is situated,

Bokhara to Merv. 279

how far it is from the Caspian, and whether any rivers debouch into the latter sea."

In 1716 this expedition started under Lieutenant Bekovich Tcherkasky to Khiva. At the same time another expedition was organized at Tobolsk under Bucholtz, and charged to construct a fort near Lake Tamysheff. After wintering at this place, Bucholtz was ordered to advance and capture Yarkand, and investigate the exploitation of gold on the Amu Darya. By means of these enterprises the great Russian reformer hoped to establish commercial relations in Central Asia, and eventually to find a way of communication with India. He knew that India had enriched every country which its commerce had gone through, as witness the once rapid development of Babylon, Egypt, and the Genoese colonies; and he was eager to draw some of its fabulous wealth into his own promising Empire.

These attempts at opening up ways of communication through Central Asia were gradually abandoned, it is true, but only for a time. The so-called testament of Peter the Great is not the document of disputed authenticity which generally passes under that name, but the sum total of all the great Emperor's acts and far-seeing views, which have become the precedents and traditional inspiration of Russian policy. In pursuit of this policy of Peter I., expeditions into Central Asia were afterwards renewed by one sent to Khiva in 1839, to force the Khan to release his Russian prisoners and cease to interfere with Russian caravans. This mission, under Perofsky, like others before it, turned out a failure. In 1865–1868 and succeeding years, however, the Russian arms, under Tchernaieff and Kaufmann, took Tashkent, Samarkand, and Ferganah, and subsequently established the power of the White Czar on the littoral of Transcaspia and over the Turkoman steppes. Finally comes the Russian Central Asian Railway ; and the dream of Peter the Great has been almost realized.

While travelling back over this railway I cannot refrain from making a few more observations on the speed and method of its construction, especially after all that has been written on the subject in the Russian press ; and a comparison with American railway enterprise in these respects may perhaps be interesting. It may seem unfair to compare Russia with a fast-going country like the United States ; but

Bokhara to Merv. 281

in many respects the Russian Central Asian line, barring, perhaps, the difficulties of the sand and lack of water, seems to be much like the lines laid down with more astonishing rapidity across the American prairies. And General Annenkoff has certainly imitated the American system in more ways than one. In all probability he received his inspiration from one of the members of his staff, Prince Khilkoff, an Americanized Russian, who is still the acting manager of the traffic. When I met this gentleman at Samarkand, with a Yankee tuft on his chin and the real American accent in his speech, I took him to be one of the most typical citizens of the States I had ever seen.

Now, the greater part of this railway in Central Asia, from Kizil Arvat to Samarkand, 740 miles, was built in about three years. The last part, of 230 miles, from the Oxus to Samarkand, was made in four months. According to recent accounts of American engineers, the extension of the Manitoba system last year through Dakota and Montana, a distance of 545 miles, was done in six months and a half. This makes about eighty-three miles of road per month constructed in America and only fifty-eight per month in

Russian Central Asia, both over a flat country. When, however, the wide difference between the two countries and circumstances generally are taken into consideration, the quicker rate of building in the United States is not, perhaps, so much to the disadvantage of General Annenkoff's degree of speed as the figures seem to imply. The description of the making of the Manitoba extension may be fitly applied to that of the Russian Central Asian line, which again shows to what a great extent General Annenkoff has adopted the principles of American railway construction. The American line referred to was laid down over the prairies by 10,000 workmen, with all materials and provisions hauled up from the base of supplies. This working army, like that commanded by Annenkoff in the Transcaspian, slept in its own tents, shanties, and cars. When the rails were laid down, and able to bear the trains, the railway was not more than half finished. The track had to be better ballasted, and the wooden structures replaced by buildings of brick and stone ; but it began to earn money from the very day the last rail was laid down, and out of its earnings and the credit thereby acquired it subsequently completed itself. It

Bokhara to Merv. 283

seems to be a general practice in America to get a road open for traffic in the cheapest manner and in the least possible time, and then to complete and improve it out of its surplus earnings. This is precisely what General Annenkoff claims for his railway in Central Asia; but whether it yet produces any surplus to pay for its completion I do not know.* The stationmaster at Samarkand told me that he

---

* The following are the official figures of receipts, expenses, and traffic of the Central Asian Railway for the last two years :—(For later figures see the last chapter.)

		Roubles.	Kopeks.
Receipts in	1887	1,535,802	88.
,, ,,	1888	1,965,218	20.
Paid by the Government for working expenses in	1887	1,921,355	
,, ,,	1888	2,264,563	

1887.
Passengers of all classes   41,793
Officers and soldiers   .   10,803
Private goods   .   .   3,609,158 poods, about 60,000 tons.
Military goods   .   92,495 poods, about 1,500 tons.

1888.
Passengers of all classes   110,497
Officers and soldiers   .   19,485
Private goods   .   .   8,600,835 poods, about 138,724 tons.
Military goods   .   158,501 poods, about 2,557 tons.

had sold £70 of passenger tickets in one day, which he thought was a very great deal. Official statistics give the revenue of the line during the first four months of 1888 at £57,945, or about £57 per verst. This, of course, does not include the new section from the Amu Darya to Samarkand.

I have been sharing the foregoing remarks with the reader on my way from Chardjui to Merv, at which latter place I arrived about nine o'clock at night, after fifteen hours' journey. I had received an invitation to stay with the Governor, Colonel Alikhanoff, and see something of the Tekke Turkomans. Most of the Russians here relieve the monotony of their existence by coming to the station to meet the trains, and it so happened that among their number on this occasion was Colonel Alikhanoff himself. I therefore received an immediate and very cordial reception. He took me home to supper, together with Prince Gagarin, Count Muravieff, and another officer, and then gave me the best bed I had slept in since I left Baku. This was the only place where I was able to get between a couple of clean sheets during the whole time I spent along the Central Asian Railway.

Next day, when I had time to look about me,

Bokhara to Merv. 285

I found the Nachalnik's house splendidly furnished with all the luxury that Turkomania could produce. That is, there were magnificent carpets and rugs covering the entire walls and floors, some of the larger sort being worth £100 or £200 on the spot. There is certainly not much else to be had in this poverty-stricken region, but what there is, at any rate, is good. It really is surprising that these nomads, whose sordid and restless existence has been so long destitute of even the small comforts of the more settled peoples around them, should be able to manufacture such beautiful carpets and tapestry. They are by far the best of all Eastern productions of the same class. There is none of the glaring gaudiness of colour, coarseness of texture, or irregularity of pattern, which are so noticeable in many other Oriental carpets. The colours are pure and well combined, like nature's tints around the smoke-blackened *kibitkas*, and are produced with natural dyes extracted in cold water from various plants and roots. The finer carpets are now rapidly becoming rare, owing to the enormous demand from Russia and Europe, and to the high value set upon them by foreign buyers. The Turkoman women will, of course, work more rapidly and less carefully to supply this great demand, and the finer work will soon be a thing of the past. At present the richest carpets are only found at the houses of the higher Russian officials, who naturally gathered in all the best they could find when they first came into the country, and fixed their own prices. Colonel Alikhanoff's long sitting-room, carpeted and hung with beautiful samples of this Turkoman work, has the bedrooms at one end and the study at the other, while the remaining two sides are flanked by the dining-room on the one hand, and a balcony on the opposite one, formed by a covered colonnade projecting into the garden. At the garden gate, in the position of a lodge, is a small *kibitka*, with a savage-looking Turkoman sentinel carrying a short Berdan rifle. On the opposite side of one of the irrigation *ariks*, which waters the garden, and well within hailing distance, are other Turkomans grouped about their tents, and ready at a moment's notice to mount their fleet horses and escort the Governor to any part of the Afghan frontier. Close by are other whitewashed houses of the commander of the garrison, the post and telegraph offices, &c., all included within the enormous mud enclosure of the Koushid Khan Kali fortress. The new Russian town and railway station are across on

Bokhara to Merv. 287

the other side of the river. The Colonel has a very nice wooden bathhouse in his garden, and a cool dip, murky as the water looked, would have been an agreeable relief from 100 degrees of heat ; but when I saw a snake a yard or two long swimming round the sides, my ardour for a plunge was quickly cooled without the aid of the water. The Murghab and its banks abound in snakes and lizards, and the very name of the river, I was told by the authorities, means snake water, and not white water, as some writers have asserted. Its water at Merv is certainly far from being white. The walls of the Colonel's study are covered with a quantity of Asiatic arms and weapons, chiefly swords, including some splendid specimens of gold and silver mounted sabres. One kept in a case has its scabbard covered with brilliants, and belonged to the Persian General, Sultan Murad Mirza, who headed an unsuccessful expedition against Merv thirty years ago. A few months later this same sword was presented to the Tsar at Baku by Colonel Alikhanoff and a deputation of Turkomans. But among this collection there were two objects which attracted my particular attention. One was a good breech-loading fowling-piece, of London manufacture, which had belonged to one of the members of the Afghan Frontier Commission, and was taken after the disastrous flight of the British representatives at the battle of the Koushk ; and the other, standing in a corner, near the Colonel's writing-table, was the silk banner of the new Turkoman militia, mounted, if you please, upon the tall bamboo spear of a Bengal lancer! The latter, I believe, was a present from the escort of the British Boundary Commission. Altogether the Transcaspian possesses trophies enough of that wretched business at Penjdeh to form a small museum. The Afghan cannon have been placed round the base of the Skobeleff monument at Askabad, and a pair of big boots, an Indian helmet, and several other things are cherished and exhibited by General Komaroff and others as relics of the English retreat. I could not blind myself to the fact, although as an Englishman my national pride would fain have denied it, that these trifles were a perpetual reminder among the Russians and Turkomans of an incident which did as much to lower British prestige as if we ourselves had fought the battle and completely lost it. One day I ventured to draw out Sary Khan, or " Yellow Khan," whom I saw very often while I was at Merv, as to what he thought about us.

Bokhara to Merv. 289

His answer was evidently made up with considerable caution while the question was being put by the interpreter. He simply said, "The English were good and the Russians were good, but the Afghans were unmitigated scoundrels."

The day after my arrival all the four celebrated Khans of Merv came to lunch with Alikhanoff, and I was introduced to Yousouff Khan, Maili Khan, Sary Khan, and Murad Khan. They all wore the Cossack-Circassian uniform, with black lamb's-wool hats a size smaller than the biggest I had seen. Yousouff Khan, the son of the Khansha, or widow of Noor Verdi Khan, who played such an important part in the Russian occupation, is now a tall, handsome youth, strongly devoted to the Russians. His youthful energy and vivacity seemed to carry the older men along with him. Sary Khan is the most influential in point of experience and prowess. I forget how many Persians he had taken dead and alive, and the number of sword-cuts he bears traces of about his body. The scars on his face might rouse the envy of a German student. They all made the mistake of keeping their great hats on at table, except Yousouff, who sometimes committed the military blunder of saluting Alikhanoff with his hand to his forehead without a cap on. Once when he did this Alikhanoff administered a gentle reproof, and Yousouff was ready with the really graceful and typical Eastern excuse that "when the heart was in the right place it did not matter where the hand was." And yet these men are rough, unpolished barbarians! They are the only majors left in the Russian army since that rank was abolished a few years ago. None of them speak Russian, and Alikhanoff seems to be the only Russian who can converse with them fluently. They appear to be fond of him, and follow him about like faithful dogs.

CHAPTER XIII.

MERV AND THE TURKOMANS.

Russian Merv—Chardjui—Mr. Marvin on personal aspect of the situation—Alikhanoff's importance, career, origin, and appearance—His swordsmanship in play and earnest—He reminds me of Skobeleff—Wardenship of the Marches—Reception of Salors—Alielis—Yomuds—Contrast between Alikhanoff and Komaroff—Alikhanoff as magistrate—Turkoman militia—Alikhanoff's satellites—Turkomanland, a place of exile—Exiles and adventurers—Afghans—Circassians banished to the Transcaspian—Banquet by Yellow Khan—Native dining and smoking—The "earth pipe"—The Khan takes strong drink—Mahommedan tricks to save appearances—Tekke women—Female acts of belligerency—Photographing the harem—Alikhanoff's tutelage of Turkomans—Departure from Merv—Extent of territory and population—Foreign elements in the majority—Administration—Elders and greybeards — Justice — Native punishment—Authority of the Khans—Fiscal, commercial, and agricultural figures—Imports and exports—Religion, customs, and immorality—Military importance of Turkomania, and commercial aspect of Bokhara—Former opinions concerning 'the Turkomans—Mr. Veniukoff and Mr. Palgrave—Neglect of Turkomans by England, Turkey, and Persia—Russia's policy towards the Cossacks — Persian Cossacks — The Turkomans became marauders from necessity—Turkoman character—Hardships in the Kara Kum —Water difficulties—Underground reservoirs and water-caverns — Origin and development of the Tekkes—Comparisons with the Cossacks—Turkoman *aul* and Cossack *sietch*—Prisoners—Hadji Baba —Tekkes and Cossacks as slave-owners and raiders —Cossack Ataman and Turkoman Khan—Turkoman *alaman* and Cossack *nabieg*—Dissimilarities—The Cossack link—Reasons for not enrolling the Turkomans as Cossacks—Calmuck Cossacks—Proposed Cossack colonies — Natural Turkoman-Cossack organization—Mahommedan militia in the Caucasus —History of the Tekkes for 300 years—Their conquest of the Akhal oasis—The Jews of Nookhoor—Turkomans as Russian troops—Skobeleff's opinion —Intrigues and denunciations—Askabad—Meeting with General Komaroff—Return to Baku.

THE new Russian city of Merv has already been described, and I will not attempt to add anything to the sketch given in a previous chapter. And indeed the once proud " Queen of the world," as regenerated by the Russians, scarcely affords more scope for description than the Turkoman tents and mud defences, which, only a few years ago, were ignorantly magnified into a native city of vast dimensions. Russian Merv is now composed of eighteen streets, 414 houses, 619 shops, stalls, and caravanserais; four so-called hotels, which would be better designated as lodging-houses of the very commonest kind ; thirteen bakeries, and thirty-four eating-houses and tea-shops. Its mushroom growth reached the limit of these proportions some time ago, and has not since shown any signs of further development. Such an artificial rate of progress as that which distinguished its first appearance could hardly be expected to continue after the extension of the railway into Bokhara. The next Russian town, Chardjui, at the bridge-head of the Amu-Darya, is now rapidly growing in its turn, and seems likely to become the busiest and most important place on the Turkomanian half of the railway.

All my curiosity and interest on this second visit to Merv centred in Colonel Alikhanoff and his obedient Turkomans ; and when I returned to St. Petersburg I was glad to see my estimate of the situation of affairs at Merv confirmed by the accurate insight of Mr. Charles Marvin, who had formed a very correct judgment of the Governor of Merv and of his sphere of activity, which he expressed in a letter to one of the London journals, dealing with the "personal considerations" of the Russian position on the Murghab. Although he had never been on the spot, Mr. Marvin's opinions were almost identical with those which I had formed from personal observation and daily intercourse with the Colonel for nearly a fortnight.

There cannot be the least doubt that, after General Annenkoff, Colonel Alikhanoff is the most prominent and interesting personage in the Transcaspian, and for the safety of English interests on the frontiers, doubtless the most dangerous. He is in many respects a remarkable individual, and so thoroughly the right man in the right place—of course from the Russian, and not the English, point of view—that while Generals Komaroff and Rosenbach may sooner or later be superseded,* there is every reason why Alikhanoff should long continue to be the chief instrument of Russian rule over the Turkomans. His early history as a Circassian officer reduced to the ranks for a duel while attached to the Imperial Lieutenant of the Caucasus,† and subsequently as a journal-

---

* General Rosenbach has in fact been superseded, while these pages were passing through the press, by Lieutenant-General Baron Vrevsky, who is now the new Governor-General of Turkistan.

† Alikhanoff distinguished himself in the Khivan campaign ; returned to the Caucasus as a Major, and fought a duel with Lieutenant B——, the result of which was that both were reduced to the ranks. Alikhanoff went

ist, artist, and explorer, until his daring exploits and diplomatic negotiations at Merv restored him to rank and favour—all this is a more than twice-told tale. One or two gaps in his history, however, I think I am able to fill up. Colonel Alikhanoff, although born at Baku, belongs to a family of Daghestan mountaineers, and claims to be descended from the Avars, who ravaged part of the Eastern Empire in the sixth and seventh centuries. At least, his fellow-tribesmen, the present Avars of the Caucasus, and according to some ethnologists, also the modern Bulgarians, are generally supposed to be the descendants of the fierce people known by that name in early history. Alikhanoff's full name, therefore, such as you will find it in the Russian Army List, is Alikhanoff-Avarsky, which distinguishes him from the crowd of other Mahommedan Ali-khans, who are both Russian and British subjects. He is not dark and swarthy, as might be imagined from the fact of his being a Caucasian-Mahommedan, or, as one might suppose from the bad portraits which the illustrated press has given of him. His thick hair

through the Turkish and first Tekke campaigns as a soldier, and was reinstated in the rank of officer only at the end of 1880, after having received the cross of St. George.

and abundant beard and whiskers, on the contrary, are almost red. In height he measures about five feet ten, with a rather slim and wiry figure; and a severe wound in one of his legs, received during the Khivan expedition, often produces a limp in his gait, and necessitates the use of a walking-stick. On one occasion, when we were together in Samarkand, and Alikhanoff lapsed into a playful mood, I witnessed a bout of fencing between him and a Frenchman, who considered himself an expert; and in this passage-of-arms Alikhanoff's mode of attack showed none of the delicate dexterity of the French school. He swung his broad blade about in such a terrific manner that, had he been in earnest, I do not think the Frenchman's guards would have saved him. Alikhanoff had some serious practice in the use of cold steel among the clever Tekke swordsmen during the disastrous campaign of 1879, in which he took an active part as a subaltern. A Russian narrator of that expedition, Tugan-Mirza-Baranofsky, who was also a participator in the murderous fray, thus refers to him: — "Alikhanoff, leaving the rest, cut his way into the midst of the Tekkes, dealing deadly blows around in every direction. We all thought he would

Merv and the Turkomans. 297

never get back; but fortunately he succeeded in fighting his way out and rejoining the ranks. With a single stroke of his sword he completely cleft in two the head of one of the enemy."

There is something of Skobeleff about Alikhanoff, though much less of polish and education. At times he reminded me strongly of the "White General;" and if he were not a Mahommedan, and could depend upon influential connections in St. Petersburg like those in which Skobeleff was fortunate, his future career might possibly be a very brilliant one. Not long ago he married the daughter of the Khan of Nakhitchevan, whose name occurs in the list of Russian officers who fought under Skobeleff at Geok Tepé.

As Nachalnik, or chief of the Merv oasis and adjoining districts, the whole of the Russo-Afghan frontier is under Colonel Alikhanoff's immediate supervision. He is thus a kind of Lord Warden of the Marches, and the pristavs or military commissioners over the districts of Yolotan, Tedjent, Penjdeh, and Zulficar are subject to his direct orders. If, however, he can possibly help it, he does not imitate our English example, and leave any trouble on the frontiers to be attended to by subordinate officers, but immediately gallops off himself to the spot, accompanied by his convoy of Turkoman border-rangers. When I first met him on our way to Samarkand he had not long returned from the reception of 168 Salor Turkomans in full flight from their Afghan pursuers, and had sent them on to live at Sarakhs. He told me that, fortunately for the Afghans, and perhaps for all concerned, Abdurrahman Khan's troops had succeeded in regaining their own side of the frontier before he had been able to come up with them. They had violated Russian territory, he asserted, for more than ten miles. English information, on the contrary, represented Alikhanoff as having previously trespassed on Afghan territory, in order to prearrange the whole affair, but Alikhanoff assured me that he had done nothing of the kind. I do not pretend to judge between the two accounts. The only thing to my mind demonstrated by that incident, however brought about, is the complete inefficiency of the present frontier to prevent the successful realization of Russia's ethnological or ethnographical claims, against which we argued so strongly during the negotiations in 1885. No secret is made at Merv of the certainty which the Russians feel of eventually securing the allegiance of every single Turkoman who is still left outside the Russian boundaries. The stampede of these Salors from the Afghans over to the Russians is only an example of what may be expected to happen again at any moment. The opinion at Merv was that the next clansmen to gravitate to the Russian camp would be certain of the Alielis Turkomans. Other candidates for Russian nationality are the Yomuds, who not long before my visit had again exposed the utter weakness and helplessness of the Persian authorities, by plundering the Persian inhabitants of the frontier with impunity, and were only restrained by the Russian Consul at Astrabad threatening to send Russian troops against them, and to hang up every tenth man indiscriminately. It is only regarded as a question of time, therefore, when these outsiders on Persian territory will also have to settle peacefully in the Russian Transcaspian.

General Komaroff, who is Colonel Alikhanoff's superior, and may one day be the supreme chief of the Transcaspian, when the province is freed from its present dependence upon the higher authority at Tiflis, would be less likely to distinguish himself in an emergency, if he had not got a man like Alikhanoff at the front. I have no desire to underrate the abilities of General Komaroff, especially as he is presumably an able military administrator; but many persons well acquainted with both officers have asserted that Komaroff's triumph on the Koushk was in a great measure due to Alikhanoff. In any case, Alikhanoff is not only essentially a fighting man, but is at the same time so thoroughly acquainted with the Turkomans, as well as understood by them in return, that General Komaroff must be in no small degree indebted to him for his success in governing the natives. I have met General Komaroff both in St. Petersburg and at Askabad, and I never saw a man in uniform look less like a soldier. He is very short, stout, and squarely built, with bushy beard and gold-rimmed spectacles, which give him a professorial and learned air. He occupies his leisure by studying archæology, and has made a valuable collection of local antiquities during his residence at Askabad. An amusing story is told of his alleged indifference during the engagement on the Koushk, which has, no doubt, been in-

Merv and the Turkomans. 301

vented as characteristic of the man. While Alikhanoff and the Russian troops were attacking the Afghans, General Komaroff is described as chasing a rare butterfly within sight of the battle. I do not think there is much friction or jealousy between the two men. Their different characters suit the situation and supply each other's needs. Alikhanoff is the man of action and resource in a situation where such qualities might be vitally necessary at any moment, while Komaroff, fortunately, perhaps, for the peace of the Transcaspian, is of a more solid and serious type.

Alikhanoff, the Governor of the Merv district, is not only the superintendent of the entire frontiers, which have cost so much to regulate and define, but he is also a justice of the peace and judge of appeal among all the Turkoman clans. His judicial functions are exercised daily in Merv as the presiding magistrate and president of a court composed of delegates from all the auls or groups of kibitkas. When he drives through the dusty unpaved streets of the Russian town, the Armenians and Jews come out of their shops and bow low, as though he were the Emperor. He keeps 300 Turkomans constantly under arms; and he told me that in twenty-four hours he could have ready 6,000 more mounted men of the Turkoman militia fully equipped. It would not be difficult to mobilize on short notice even a greater number, as every Turkoman is a ready-made light trooper of the true Cossack type [of irregular soldier, and requires nothing but firearms and ammunition to enter the field.

Each Turkoman of the three permanent squadrons, or sotnias, receives 25 roubles, or 50 shillings a month, besides a Berdan rifle of the light calibre carried by the Cossacks, which is exceptionally high pay for a Russian cavalry soldier, and equals that of Lieutenants in Russian regiments of the line. All else, including his horse and keep, the Turkoman has to provide at his own expense, like the Cossack. The Turkoman officers are paid about 100 roubles, or ten pounds sterling per mensem, which is as much as the pay, exclusive of extra allowances, of a Russian Major-General. The Government, for evident reasons, has always been more generous to its Asiatic soldiers than to its own Russian troops. Until the present Tsar abolished the Imperial Asiatic escort at St. Petersburg on the score of economy, all the privates of that unique troop received the full pay

Merv and the Turkomans. 303

of officers. Under such comparatively liberal conditions the Turkoman militiamen are naturally proud of their Russian shoulder straps and medals, and would eagerly rush into the jaws of death to win the Cross of St. George.

Not only the Turkoman Khans, but several young officers and civilians, one or two of them bearing well-known names and titles, were hovering round Alikhanoff in the hope of some frontier expedition or disturbance, whereby they might gain distinction and advancement. They were like the satellites that gathered round Skobeleff; and their presence in this part of the Empire was explainable to a great extent by the fact that Turkomanland is now the fashionable place of voluntary and involuntary exile. Formerly Tashkent and Turkistan formed the appointed, or chosen, destination of military duellists, insurbordinate officers, whose position or friends saved them from commoner punishment, and various other privileged offenders. At present these delinquents are banished, like Bokharan criminals a century or two ago, to Merv and the Transcaspian. A few adventurers, seeking to gain or retrieve reputations and fortunes, also find their way into this region, as Turkistan, in respect of chances valuable to individuals of this kind, is considered for the present to be "played out." I often met at Merv a young Baron, who had been reduced to the ranks, and permitted to join one of the Transcaspian rifle battalions, for having committed some serious offence, which did not, however, prevent him from living on such easy and familiar terms with his superiors that he was able to avoid most of the inconveniences of serving as a private soldier. Those who have made a false step, and are not actually sent into the Transcaspian, are often recommended to go there, as the most likely field for opportunities of regaining their footing in society. About a couple of years ago another exile of well-known family was living here by Imperial order, Prince S——, of the Guards, whose crime had been the killing of a brother officer in a duel, and who not long ago died of the effects of a fall from his horse near Askabad. A civilian bearing a celebrated name, who attached himself to Colonel Alikhanoff during my visit, was just as eager as any of his military compatriots to gird on a sword, which he had brought for the purpose, and accompany the colonel on his excursions round the border. And it must not be forgotten that Alikhanoff himself is a successful example of the men who have gone to the Transcaspian to rehabilitate themselves in the eyes of the Government and the world. I told them all in a joke, that I should be very glad if a little Russian *alaman* or foray could be got up while I was in the neighbourhood, like the abduction of the Afghan Salors, and they thought that if I waited long enough some adventure of the kind might be arranged. There were also a couple of Afghans of some note staying at Merv, and in constant communication with Alikhanoff, who no doubt employed them to keep touch with affairs on the Afghan side of the frontiers.

A recent item of intelligence from the Caucasus, which has been published by the *Kafkaz* newspaper of Tiflis, indicates that the Transcaspian is likely to become a second Siberia for law-breakers of a very different description. For some time past the neighbourhood of Koobi in the province of Baku has been infested by a numerous band of desperadoes and highway robbers, chiefly escaped prisoners, who lately robbed the post on its way from Derbent, and carried off 20,000 roubles. The letters were found torn open and strewn over the road, and the postmen and driver had disappeared. The depredators are all Mahommedans, and owe their safety from recapture to the means of concealment offered by their friends and relatives. These aiders and abettors have been all arrested, and condemned by Prince Dondukoff Korsakoff to be transported by " administrative order " to the province of Transcaspia as penal settlers. This is a cheap method of colonizing the Transcaspian deserts, which General Annenkoff, in his paper on the subject, does not appear to have thought of, and it would probably be more successful than holding out inducements to the careless and improvident Russian peasantry. China sends her criminals to settle or serve as soldiers along the Russian Mongolian frontier; and there is no reason why Russia should not do the same on the frontiers of the Transcaspian.

One of the most interesting incidents of my stay at Merv was a Turkoman banquet offered in my honour by Sary or "Yellow" Khan, which took place at the Khan's residence, about twenty minutes' drive outside the town. Yellow Khan, like several of his compeers, has been induced to build a very respectable brick house, well whitewashed, which, however, he does not care to inhabit, but uses for entertaining his

Russian guests. He and his family, with their immediate followers, still prefer to live in a number of felt-covered kibitkas grouped round this new house, the whole being enclosed by a low mud hedge. Colonel Alikhanoff took me with him in his carriage, escorted by a cohort of Turkomans, and followed by another carriage full of other guests. When we got half way the Khan, surrounded by his mounted retinue, rode out to meet and conduct us on to the premises. A common deal table, covered with a rather soiled cloth, was set out on the open carpeted verandah in front of the house, and special Tartar cooks were working hard in a trench close by preparing the eatables, which showed that our Turkoman host had made every effort to give the feast in something like European, or at least, in Russian style. There were plates, knives and forks, a great display of wine, seltzer water, beer, and lemonade, and a medley of curious dishes brought us by Tekkes from across the yard. At the same time we had a sight of the real native way of dining by watching an old man shredding the meat off several entire sheep's ribs with his hands and teeth. This Turkoman being a very respected elder, he was permitted to sit with his big wooden bowl full of boiled mutton bones on the edge of the verandah at our feet, while about a hundred more Tekkes stood round staring at a respectful distance, occasionally enveloping themselves in thick clouds of tobacco smoke by vigorously puffing in turns at the *kalian* or water-pipe, made of a common gourd.

The Tekkes are such inveterate smokers that when on expeditions far away from home, and deprived of their pipe as an unnecessary incumbrance, they resort to an ingenious method of improvising one out of the soil, which they call the *yer-chilin*, literally "earth-pipe." They scratch up a long ridge of earth or clay, make a groove along the top with their fingers, then lay a string or strap in the groove and fill it up with earth, pressed very hard. The cord or strap is then drawn out so as to leave a tube, and a funnel is moulded at one end to contain the tobacco from their pouches. The Tekke then drops on all fours, or lies down flat, and applying his lips to the orifice at the other end of this original smoking apparatus, he draws away until his eyes grow dim, and sometimes converts himself into a *kalian* by holding water in his mouth.

To return to the feast, I noticed that our Mahommedan host, the Khan, drank wine and brandy as freely as the Russians. His religious scruples, if he had ever possessed any, were evidently not proof against this vice, which Western civilization, whether introduced by English or Russians, inevitably brings in its train. He readily responded to the profane Russian toast that a triple libation is loved of the gods, and tossed off his three big glasses of vodka without wincing. The late Khan of Khokand, previous to the Russian annexation of Ferghana, was at one time in the habit of receiving champagne from Tashkent under the name of lemonade; and I heard of Turkoman sirdars, still careful of appearances, who were accustomed to drink lemonade, with which brandy had already been mixed by the accommodating manufacturer. This reminded me of a similar trick sometimes practised by the Moscow merchants, who have been known to transact business over so-called "cold tea," which on close inspection of the contents of the teapot turned out to be sweet champagne. There seemed to be an equal laxity of strict Mahommedan principles in regard to the members of the Khan's harem, who moved about between the kibitkas with their faces quite uncovered, and were not ashamed of indulging in occasional glances at us infidels.

The position of the Tekke woman, I may here remark, is infinitely superior to that of her Bokharan sister, who not only shrouds her face with a long black and almost impenetrable veil of woven horsehair, but considers it her duty to turn towards the wall, or thrust her head into a doorway or any other recess when an unbeliever passes her in the street. The contrast between the women of the two countries is as striking as that between the men. Indeed, throughout the realm of Islam there are probably no women less fettered and secluded than those of the Tekke Turkomans. According to Russians, who have studied their life and customs, there were formerly Tekke Amazonians, who often rode to the border foray, and wielded arms as well as the men; and in exceptional cases like that of Goolijamba-bai, the celebrated *khanim* of Noor Verdi, who helped to decide the fate of Merv, they even rose into great authority among their countrymen. Instead of being mere toys, like the women of the settled Mahommedans in Persia, Bokhara and Turkey, they assisted in cultivating the fields, and generally shared the work of the men both in peace and war. It is related that in 1859, when the Shah of Persia sent an army of 40,000 men with thirty-two guns

Merv and the Turkomans. 311

against Merv, and owing to the strength of the Persian artillery the Tekkes were obliged to confine themselves to the defensive, their women took the lead in deceiving and destroying the besiegers. The Tekkes sent a deputation into the Persian camp to tender their submission, which was immediately despatched by a courier to the Shah at Teheran. Meanwhile the Persian commander, Sultan Murad Mirza, who was suspicious of Turkoman treachery, established a fortified camp outside the walls, and ordered that none of the Tekkes should be allowed to enter, except their women with provisions. Accordingly the Tekke women came into the camp in increasing numbers every day, and at last ceased to attract any particular notice. One evening many of them were sitting with the Persians in their tents, and others were engaging the attention of the Persian officers, when, upon hearing the signal of a gun report they all threw off their veils, and suddenly fell upon the Persians with the greatest ferocity. One-half of the veils, it is true, concealed Tekke men, but the other half of the assailants were real women, who had been necessary for the success of the stratagem. At the same time two strong parties from Merv attacked the

Persian camp on opposite sides, and completed the panic and confusion. Only the Persian commander with a few horsemen succeeded in escaping from the massacre which ensued.

There seems no doubt that Tekke women also fought against the Russians, which may in some measure perhaps account for the killing of so many of them by the Russian soldiery. Mirza-Baranofsky says : " Such was the exasperation and hatred of the Tekkes, that their women and children rushed at our troops, armed with anything they could lay their hands upon. Some of them were in the front ranks of the enemy. One of the company commanders of the Georgian battalion felt a heavy blow upon his back, and turning quickly round, he saw an old virago with a large iron spade uplifted to strike at him again. At another place a boy about nine dashed at an officer of the Erivan battalion with an enormous knife." Some dragoons, while driving a party of Tekkes back into their fortress at Geok Tepé, were fired at three times from the edge of a Tekke canal. Two or three troopers on riding up to the spot found a young girl grasping a long pistol, with two more pistols lying by her side. On being taken before the officers of the staff, she declared

Merv and the Turkomans. 313

that not one Russian Giaour should ever leave the country alive. Another heroine with a gun—this time a grey-haired old woman—fired at the Russians from her hiding-place in one of the canals, and was killed on the spot by the infuriated soldiers. Such acts of female belligerency seem to have been frequent during the Russian campaign, and show that the Tekke women are not the ordinary harmless creatures of the Mussulman harem.

After dinner with Sary Khan, we persuaded several Tekke women to come outside their tent and sit still on the ground while their photographs were being taken by Prince Gagarin, a proceeding which in Bokhara would have probably involved us in some risk from the fanaticism of the men. Before leaving we also got up a scramble for coppers among the youths and children, and were then escorted halfway home to the Governor's house in oriental fashion by the Khan and his attendants.

The way in which Alikhanoff tutors these half savages, while remaining on the easiest and most familiar terms with them, is one of the interesting studies of nascent society in the Transcaspian. Many Englishmen, including those who have had good means of judging, seem to regard the Governor of Merv and his Turkoman pupils in a different light, and can hardly pronounce the name of Alikhanoff without using terms of the strongest reprobation. I can never see the justice of this view, except in so far as it helps to prove the cleverness and success of Alikhanoff. Another English opinion is that the Russian Turkomans all detest Colonel Alikhanoff; and this notion, I was told at Merv, had been spread by the escort of Turkomans hired by the British agent, now the consul at Meshed. The Russian explanation was, that these Turkomans had furnished the British Boundary Commission with camels and other requisites, at something like four times the prices paid by the Russians, and that they therefore naturally abused the Russians and praised the English. What the real feelings of the Turkomans may be, either on the one side or on the other, it would be difficult probably for anybody to discover; but as far as an impartial observer can judge, the chief Khans of the Tekkes in constant intercourse with the Governor of the Merv district have a very wholesome respect for Alikhanoff, and seem devoted to his interests, which are also, of course in the circumstances, their own. As to his intrigues on the Afghan frontier, the simple truth is that the great object which he keeps before him is to collect all the still scattered groups of the Turkoman tribes who have not yet been gathered into the Russian fold, and in pursuing this aim we may be sure that he will suffer no opportunity to escape him.

On the evening I left Merv for good, about an hour before the departure of the train, I took part in another banquet, given by Colonel Alikhanoff as a farewell compliment to his assistant, Captain Taranoff, who was just starting to occupy a new post as Governor of Mangishlak. His place at Merv has since been filled by Captain Kozloff, of the Guards in St. Petersburg. This entertainment took place in the buffet-room of the railway station, and was really as excellent a dinner as one might expect to get in any but the very first-rate restaurants in St. Petersburg. All the Khans were present, and also the two Afghans; and a Cossack band of music played outside during the repast. Colonel Alikhanoff was kind enough to propose to the Khans to drink my health in a few words on friendship between England and Russia, and they emptied their glasses as though they had been champagne drinkers all their lives. On the platform, before parting, the Colonel and I embraced in Russian fashion, and I started off on my return to the Caspian, carrying with me some further interesting information, which I shall here endeavour to impart to the reader.

In the first place, Colonel Alikhanoff was good enough to allow me to take the following notes and statistics from his interesting report in manuscript, compiled in 1887. The figures presumably relate to the year 1886, and are the latest that can be obtained.

For general administrative purposes the whole of the Transcaspian is divided into the districts of Krasnavodsk, Chickishliar, Akhal, or Askabad, Merv, and the Tedjent.

The territorial extent of the Merv administrative region, approximately calculated, is 156,567 square versts.* This includes the districts in charge of pristavs; to wit, Sarakhs 14,000 versts, Yolotan 30,000, and Pende 40,000 versts. The remaining 72,507 square versts belong to the Merv oasis and the deserts thereto pertaining. Strictly accurate no distances can be given, owing to the indefiniteness of the frontiers of Khiva and Bokhara. The Tekke population, composed of the four tribes of Vekil,

* The square verst equals ·43947 of a square mile.

Merv and the Turkomans. 317

Bek, Sitchmaz, and Bakhshee, each possessing a certain number of canals, amounts to 17,632 kibitkas and 105,452 souls. The Saryks are 8,193 kibitkas and 49,158 souls, the Salors 1,798 kibitkas and 10,788 souls, thus making a total of Tekkes, Saryks, and Salors of 27,623 kibitkas and 165,398 souls.

The Tekkes and Saryks are divided into tribes and localities as follows :—

Tekke Tribes.	Kibitkas.	Souls.
Vekil	4,948	29,443
Bek	5,235	31,415
Sitchmaz	3,414	20,384
Bakhshee	4,035	24,210
	17,632	105,452
Saryks in Yolotan	4,109	24,654
„ at Pende	4,084	24,504
	8,193	49,158

One of the most curious items is that which gives the extraneous population attracted into the country in the course of the year, with the districts towards which the new-comers were most and least affected. It will be noticed that three years ago the Russians were in the minority; and there is every reason to believe, that although their numbers may have since increased, yet the proportions remain the same, if they have not grown still more in favour of those extrinsic Russians who are not of Slavonic race. The Slavonic Russians have acquired the Transcaspian, and built a strategical railway in the capacity that best suits their genius, and that of the State organism of the Russian Empire, but the lion's share of advantages offered by the new country, as a field for commerce and enterprise, is falling as usual into the hands of foreigners, not necessarily outside foreigners, but those numerous Armenian, Jewish, German, and other foreign subjects of the Tsar, who live on Russian territory, and far surpass the native Slavs in all the arts of peace. The following table will illustrate these remarks, and it must be borne in mind that while most of the Russians probably visited the Merv districts in their military or official capacity, the great majority of the rest must have gone there for their own private reasons:—

	Russians.	Poles.	Armenians.	Georgians.	Persians & Tartars.
Merv...	2,120	168	3,182	546	3,260
Yolotan	—	—	4	—	3
Sarakhs	12	—	100	—	400
Pende...	27	—	13	1	6

	Khivans and Bokhariots.	Jews.	Afghans.	Germans.	Greeks.
Merv	958	249	2	72	84
Yolotan	95	21	—	1	—
Sarakhs	26	12	—	1	—
Pende	—	16	2	—	—

	Hungarians.	Ossetins.	Lesghiens.	Kirghiz.
Merv	3	240	183	9
Yolotan	—	1	1	—
Sarakhs	—	—	—	—
Pende	—	—	—	—

The total number of strangers who thus entered Merv and its districts during the twelve months were 2,159 Russians, 168 Poles, 3,299 Armenians, 547 Georgians, 3,669 Persians and Tartars, 1,076 Khivans and Bokharans, 298 Jews, 4 Afghans, 74 Germans, 84 Greeks, 3 Hungarians, 241 Ossetins, 184 Lesghians from the Caucasus, and 9 Kirghiz.

There are 40 volosts or sub-districts in the Merv circuit, with 4 to 9 *auls* or groups of kibitkas in each volost. Each volost elects a *starshiná*, or elder, and each *aul* an *aksakaul*, or *ak-sakal*, which is an exact repetition of *starshiná*, and means literally "greybeard." Thus, the simple office of *starshiná* in the patriarchal administration of the Russian peasantry fits in exactly with the ideas of these semi-nomads;

and is probably not the only Russian institution which, to the advantage of Russia's civilizing mission, can be introduced among the natives of Central Asia without requiring the least modification, or causing half the difficulty in training the Turkoman to understand it, that the Russian Government has experienced in educating its own people to appreciate—for instance, the British jury system.

These elders and *aksakals* among the Turkomans all report to their khans, or pristavs (the latter being Russian officers), who in their turn report to the chief of the circuit, Alikhanoff. The *aksakals* and three elders form a court for the trial of small offences, entailing up to five roubles fine, or three days' arrest. The khan has the right of sentencing to 25 roubles fine and seven days' arrest. Delegates from each tribe, under the presidency of the pristav with the assistance of a kazi or religious member, may inflict a fine of fifteen roubles and a punishment of four months' imprisonment. Other and more important cases are decided by Colonel Alikhanoff with representatives from all the sections.

Nominally, the judicial business of the Transcaspian is within the jurisdiction of the courts

Merv and the Turkomans. 321

at Baku, just as litigation between Russians and Bokharans in Transoxiania is supposed to be subordinate to the Russian judicial authorities of Turkistan at Samarkand and Tashkent. As a matter of fact, in both countries justice is independently administered, in Bokhara by M. Charikoff, whose action is, of course, confined to disputes between Russians and the natives, and in the Transcaspian by Alikhanoff and the officers already mentioned. In Bokhara, the diplomatic agent, M. Charikoff, is so careful of the interests of the natives that his own countrymen begin to think him too impartial. At Merv more severity is necessary, and most criminal cases, such as murder and robbery, are tried by a military court, and very often by drum-head court-martial. Although appeals are theoretically supposed to reach the court at Baku, in reality they never get beyond the Governor-General of the province at Askabad. In some cases it would appear that the khans have been allowed to inflict such native punishment as best appeals to the understanding and feelings of their half-savage countrymen. For example, in the summer of 1885, when relations between England and Russia were very much strained, a number of lazy Tekkes, employed

Y

upon the construction of a river dam which was required in great haste, were ordered by Makhmud Kuli Khan to be stripped naked and placed on the banks of the Tedjent, to be bitten by mosquitos. In half an hour the work went on briskly enough.

The authority of the various khans, which was formerly subject to the free consent of all the tribe, and must have been greatly shaken by the squabbles and intrigues preceding the Russian occupation, is at present entirely dependent upon the support of the Russians, who favour its enforcement within certain limits, just as the Russian nobility are now being encouraged to reassume the patronizing position among the peasantry which they lost by the emancipation of the serfs. The Turkoman sirdars probably never enjoyed such certain power over their turbulent people as they now exercise in the capacity of Russian representatives.

The taxes paid by the Turkomans amount to five roubles per kibitka—namely, four roubles 40 kopeks for the exchequer, and half a rouble for local needs of the zemstvo or land commune. In return, all caravans entering or passing through Merv pay one-fortieth of their goods. This was established in 1866, because the Bokhariots and Khivans make the Russian caravans pay. In 1866 this duty produced 30,293 roubles 69 kopeks. The crops for the same year were:—Sown—wheat, 450,000 poods; barley, 150,000 poods; rice, 60,000 poods. Reaped—wheat, 29,700,000 poods; barley, 4,398,000 poods; rice, 2,400,000 poods. The quantity of cotton grown by the Turkomans is very small, and only for their own use. About eighteen miles above Merv the Koushut Khan Bend, or dam on the Murghab, sends an equal flow of water into the two halves of the oasis by means of two principal canals, the Otamuish and the Okhtamuish, named after the two principal divisions of the Tekke tribes. These in their turn supply the many smaller canals of the tribes and families. This water arrangement is looked after by an official called the *mirab*, elected annually. Each district is subdivided into *kelemes*, and each *keleme* consists of twelve proprietors. Two *kelemes* make an *atalyk* or *sarkar*, and enjoys water for twenty-four hours in turn. Yolotan is watered in the same way from the Murghab dam Kazilik Bend. Pende is the worst irrigated district of all, as the Saryks have destroyed many of the canals.

The following are the numbers of horses

cattle, &c., in the whole territory :—Horses, 20,520; camels, 16,758; sheep and goats, 699,734; cattle, 44,164; asses, 21,468.

The household productions of the Turkomans consist of small silver articles worn by the women and horse trappings, which do not exhibit the same taste and sense of beauty as those wrought in the Caucasus and Bokhara; but the Turkoman carpets, made by the women, are of first-rate quality, and superior to any others in the East. Alikhanoff lately persuaded them to copy the Persian patterns, which they are doing successfully, although the enormous demand is now leading to the introduction of aniline dyes, and consequent deterioration. Carpets are made only in the Merv oasis and, to a small extent, at Pende. The prices have lately risen enormously. In the course of the year 4,000 carpets were exported to Russia, Persia, and France, representing a total value of 320,000 roubles. This number has since risen to 6,000 carpets exported in the course of the year. The Yolotan women make very fine cloth of camel and goats' wool, which is much prized by the Persian aristocracy. In Yolotan and Pende the fox is hunted during the winter and the skins sold in Bokhara; 20,000 of these

Merv and the Turkomans. 325

fox skins were sold there by the Saryks in 1886. Camel transport along the line between the Caspian and the Amu Darya has naturally diminished since the opening of the railway. In 1886 about 26,000 camels entered and left Merv.

It is difficult to give exact figures of the import and export trade. Colonel Alikhanoff has only one assistant and a clerk, and they are far too busy to make a proper investigation. During a period of five months they had as many as twenty-six civil and criminal cases to attend to per day, and on an average fifty-three documents every day which required to be dealt with in some way or other. As far, however, as can be ascertained, the year's imports and exports are represented by the following figures:—

			Roubles.
Import from Bokhara...	...	...	585,144
,, ,, Khiva ...	...	...	62,568
,, ,, Dereges...	...	...	60,172
,, ,, Meshed...	...	...	371,690
,, ,, Afghan Turkomania	...		58,879
,, ,, Tashkent and Askabad			740,050
	Total ...	...	1,878,503
Export into Bokhara and Khiva		...	328,632
,, ,, Persia	...	...	280,000
	Total ...		608,632

Russian articles sold in the shops at Merv came to about 719,765 roubles. Bokharan goods now enter free of duty by special favour, and there is no means of judging of their value. There are also no regular statistics of goods entering by railway. Altogether the overturn is reckoned at five millions, which is putting it at its very highest figure. This amount also represents the transitory animation of business caused by the arrival of the railway, with its host of officials and workmen. Since the line passed on into Bokhara the shopkeepers of Merv have complained of the disappearance of customers; so that the above figures must be much above the total of trade in ordinary times.

The semi-nomadic Turkomans are now almost settled. They still live mostly in kibitkas, but the Khans, as I have said, have already begun to build themselves brick houses. Education among them is very rare, and they appear to have no religion worth talking about. They do not observe the Shariat nor the Mahommedan feasts. Their women are still bartered and sold. A wife costs from 250 to 1,500 roubles (£150). The rich have from two to four wives; and the poorer class ruin themselves in getting married. Their manners and customs are rude and coarse,

TURKOMANS DRINKING YELLOW TEA.

and I heard from a competent authority that the race is addicted to excessive immorality, which, I am sorry to say, is not likely to be eradicated by the force of Russian example.

It will thus be seen that the poor region of Turkomania, from a commercial point of view, is not to be compared with the rich land of Bokhara the Noble. It is true that considerable mineral wealth, such as naphtha, salt, alum, saltpetre, and brimstone,* is reported to exist in different parts of the deserts and mountains, which may some day be properly utilized, and that the experiments of cotton-growing on the Emperor's Murghab estate may also increase the bulk of future Russian trade; but these sources are at present practically unavailable, or, at least, only very slightly worked. The actual importance of Turkomania is more of a military character, while that of Bokhara is decidedly commercial. Bokhara, which is already a dependency of Turkistan, is destined to be the great emporium of Russian trade in Central Asia, capable of eventually covering the pecun-

---

* A company of Armenians (not Russians, it will be observed) are now engaged in procuring sulphur about seventy-five miles from Geok Tepé for chemical factories at Baku.

iary deficit incurred in maintaining the unprofitable administration at Tashkent; whereas the chief advantage of Russia's acquisition of Turkomania consists in the addition to the Tsar's armies of a numerous race of high-mettled fighting men, trained by generations of almost constant warfare, whose utility and importance as border Cossacks on the Afghan and Persian frontiers cannot be too highly rated. This high value set upon the Turkomans as military material and future pioneers of Russia's possible advances, may not perhaps be apparent to every one, but will hardly fail to strike those capable of appreciating the quasi-European and semi-Asiatic methods by which Russia ensures her successes in Central Asia. Russia, with her Asiatic aptitudes and tendencies, was the only Eastern Power which ever discerned the importance of subjugating these vagrants of the desert, and is probably the only one now in a position to reap the full benefit of such a conquest. By this I, of course, refer to no other superiority of Russia than that of her Asiatic affinities already mentioned. The Turkomans were so highly esteemed for their fighting qualities in the vanguards of the armies of such great Asiatic conquerors as Tamerlane and Nadir

Shah, that their incorporation in the legions of Russia, and the inevitable, though gradual, expansion amongst them of the Russian military system, are military facts of no small significance.

It was in vain that many years ago public attention was directed to the advantages which would accrue to other Eastern Powers if they forestalled Russia, while there was yet time, in securing possession of the Turkomans. Colonel Veniukoff says the English Press once distinctly declared "that in order to preserve the country north of the Hindoo Kush from the incursions of the Russians, we must do so with the aid of Turkomans well armed, and commanded by skilled officers." It is too late now for any practical purpose to revive all that was formerly written on this part of the subject, but a few notes from an interesting paper read before the British Association in 1868 by Mr. G. Palgrave, may help us to form a notion of what these Turkomans may become in the power of Russia. Mr. Palgrave spoke in favour of Turkoman settlements on the Turkish frontier as a protection against Russian encroachment. During his travels in Asia Minor, he clearly foresaw the merits and importance of the Turkomans, although he alluded more particularly to those dispersed among other races of the Russo-Turkish and Turko-Persian frontiers. Owing to the monopoly of attention enjoyed in recent years by the Tekkes and other Turkomans of the Transcaspian, one is apt to forget that the Turkoman race, which derives its origin, like the Central Asian Uzbeks, from various clans and confederacies of Turkish immigrants, and are the primitive stock of the Osmanli Turks, has spread itself abroad on both sides of the Caspian Sea. Large numbers have intermingled with the other inhabitants of the Asiatic highland, south-east of the Black Sea, and south-west of the Caspian, on the North-Eastern Turkish frontiers; and their more peaceful existence seemed to augur well for the possibility of taming the marauding instincts of their wilder brethren of Akhal Tekke. Mr. Palgrave, in his time, noticed a remarkable fermentation and commingling of races inhabiting the Turkish borders—Kurds, Armenians, Georgians, Circassians, and others, in which the Turkomans played the most prominent part. Turkoman characteristics were nearly always uppermost in the children of mixed marriages, and the other races were tending to become merged in that of the Turkomans; "thus pro-

Merv and the Turkomans. 331

mising at no distant period to crystallize into a new nationality, with a type and destiny of its own." At the same time, thousands of Turkomans fled into Turkey from "Persian anarchy" and "Russian tyranny." As many as 6,000 annually for several consecutive years were stated to have retreated from the Russian Transcaucasus alone. But Turkey seems to have taken no steps to make use of this movement; and the Turkoman refugees were left to shift for themselves. Of the fiercer members of the Turkoman race on the other side of the Caspian and along the frontiers of Afghanistan, England then knew but very little; while she apparently ignored the danger indicated by the attention which Russia, alone of all others at that time, was turning towards them. The Persians, whose reigning dynasty is of Turkoman origin, were just as indifferent to the situation; or, if they tried at all to profit by it, their feeble policy proved miserably unequal to the task of winning the friendliness of the Turkomans, and of inducing or compelling them to become the guardians, instead of being the scourge, of the North Persian frontiers. Persia might have taken a lesson from Russia's policy of mingled force and persuasion, exercised with signal success about the 16th century towards the Cossacks, who were then a similar set of freebooters, and occupied much the same position on the South-Eastern Russian frontiers that the Tekkes down to 1881 held on the frontiers of Khorassan. The Shah has done what he probably thinks a much wiser thing. Having neglected, or driven into Turkey and the deserts, his ready-made Turkoman Cossacks, his Persian Majesty has now started the organization of Persian Cossacks under Russian instructors; but no training in the world will ever convert a Persian into a genuine Cossack. Had not the descendants of the subjects of Darius degenerated into utter impotency, they would have had these Turkomans as friends and allies on their side; and Russia would not now be provided with the best living defence that she has had on her eastern frontiers since the formation of the Cossack communities on the Don and the Dnieper.

As nomads are not necessarily robbers, it is very probable that the Turkomans did not become marauders and manstealers by choice or preference, but were gradually driven to these expedients by dire necessity and stress of circumstances. After the destruction of the great cities of the plain and their principal works of irrigation, the Turkomans found themselves restricted by the ever-spreading sands to the wretched patches of meagre pasture and arable land at the foot of the mountain frontier of Persia, and were led to engage in brigandage and the slave trade as auxiliary means of existence. This may seem a far too charitable explanation of their terrible depredations, but it has a precedent in the history of the Russian Cossacks, who avowed the same reason for resorting to robbery and pillage, as soon as they failed to receive the subsidies which they were accustomed to draw from the Imperial treasury in the early period of their connection with the Muscovite crown.

In the following quotation Mr. Palgrave sums up the character of the Turkomans, in whom, twenty' years ago, he seemed to detect a rejuvenescence of independent nationality, which did not, however, resist the triumphant march of the Russians on Kars and Erzeroum in 1878, and which received a crushing blow in the Akhal Tekke campaign of 1881. His estimate was of course formed from the settled and well-to-do specimens of the race in Asia Minor; but he also refers to those in the Transcaspian.

He says: "These Turkomans are fearless

and lovers of fight; but they possess also the more sterling qualities of a dogged perseverance and a power of working to an end hardly inferior to that claimed by our own Anglo-Saxon race. Their fathers, under the Seljook dynasties, Kara-Koiounlis and Ak-Koiounlis, men of the Black Shepherd clan and the White, long ruled over Western Asia. History, and in the further East the testimony of our own days, show us the Turkoman shepherds and neatherds in the main rarely as fixed cultivators or villagers. But from the pastoral life,—unlike that of the hunter or the savage,—to the agricultural is but a step, and whenever an opportunity occurs this step is readily made: once made, it always tends to become irrevocable. Their skill in agriculture, the wide harvest-covered fields that surround their settlements, the comparative comfort of their dwellings, and the constructive ingenuity of the huge stables in which their sheep and cattle find refuge and provender during the long winter months, all prove *that their nomad condition in Central Asia is more the result of circumstances than of an innate and irrepressible bent;* that under the forms of tribe they have the materials of a nation; and that the city, with all its con-

TEKKE TURKOMAN PLOUGHING.

Merv and the Turkomans. 335

sequences of wealth, culture, and peaceful civilization, is at least as natural to them as the tent and the mountain side."

Considering the ill-conditioned nature and savage aspect of their surroundings, it is not surprising that the Tekkes and other cognate tribes should have developed so very differently from their better favoured kindred on the uplands of Asiatic Turkey. Covered in prehistoric times by the sea, and subsequently supporting flourishing cities and prosperous populations, which lured the conquering hosts of Alexander the Great, and the desolating hordes of Timur the Lame, these great plains have now for centuries past been plagued by a sea of sand as shifting and restless as the Turkoman shepherds, whose sphere of peaceful occupation it must have continually diminished. After flitting from place to place round the ever-widening edges of the Kara Kum, through which their wanderings and efforts to battle with the resistless desolation of nature may still be traced in large numbers of abandoned and sand-choked wells, the wandering Tekkes finally took to the narrow belt of comparatively fertile country along the mountain base of the Persian frontier. It is owing to this mountain barrier, with the aid which it affords in renewing vegetation along the foot of its northern slopes, that Persian Khorassan has not been attacked by the invading sand like the Khanates of Khiva and Bokhara. Along this lengthy but contracted margin, alternating in steppes of sand, salt, and clay—the latter often so hard as to defy all attempts at tillage—and small tracts of more or less fertile country, the Tekkes have carried on a constant struggle against the natural disadvantages of their position.

The hardest part of this struggle has always been the attainment of the chief and most precious of all bounties in these regions—a regular and adequate supply of water. For 115 miles, from the Caspian to Kazandjik, there is not one drop of fresh water, while for 350 miles thence to Merv there are only thirty-six rivulets and small *ariks* of muddy water, most of which are dried up during the great heats. Besides atmospheric evaporation, the Tekkes formerly had to contend with another cause of diminished water supply—the retaliations of the Persians, who, having the sources of a good deal of the water on their side of the mountains, were able to stop its flow into the Turkoman canals. This was a point on which

Merv and the Turkomans. 337

the Russians laid some stress during the negotiations concerning the regulation of the Persian frontier. In order to preserve the water from evaporation, the Tekkes also constructed with immense labour a number of *kariz* or underground aqueducts, often several miles in length, running from the springs and reservoirs in the mountains. The existence of these reservoirs and underground lakes seem to imply that there is more water in the Transcaspian than is generally supposed, and that if it could only be properly conducted over the surface, a much greater area of cultivation might be created than at present exists. There is a very remarkable specimen of these water caverns between the stations of Bakharden and Keliat, which contains a large covered basin of sulphurous water, and the roof of which affords a retreat for great numbers of pigeons.

Such being the unattractive haunts of the Tekke Turkomans, it becomes interesting to trace, as far as the paucity of information will permit, the origin and development of these roving bandits, and the circumstances of their first appearance in the Transcaspian.

In the foregoing pages I have frequently made comparisons between them and the primi-

Z

tive Russian Cossacks, and something more may here be said from this point of view. Without going to the length of agreeing with Mr. P. Vassilieff, that, like the Zaparogian Cossacks of the Dnieper, the Tekkes came into existence as gangs of outlaws and runaways from the surrounding nations, and are not a pure race, there still remains a striking analogy between the two peoples. Even supposing such to have been the case, the original Turkish stock of the Tekkes has certainly assimilated all other concomitants, as the Russian blood of the Cossacks has completely predominated over the admixture of Asiatic elements. But although no data exists to show that the formation of the Tekke tribes was the same as that of the first bands of Cossacks, who originated in an aggregation of fugitives from Russia and the neighbouring peoples, and were constantly recruited from among their discontented elements, there is good reason to believe that the Tekke *aul*, like the Cossack *sietch*, must have often been a refuge for rebels, criminals, and malcontents, flying from the Asiatic despotism of surrounding countries, and willing to seek relief and safety in risking the dangers and privations of the desert. Many prisoners taken by the Tekkes must also have become merged into the Turkomans, as it is evident that the captives were not always sold; and very few probably ever succeeded in escaping like Mr. Morier's Hadji Baba of Ispahan, who regained his liberty while taking part in a Turkoman raid on his native town. In modern Russian literature attempts have been made to elevate the early Cossacks into a kind of chivalrous army of Knights Templars, fighting only for the Russian orthodox faith; but we know that they were border raiders like the Tekkes, and that, like the latter, they enslaved their captives, making the poorer prisoners do the hard work of the community, and demanding heavy ransoms for the richer ones. There is evidence that they sometimes even sold their prisoners into slavery among the Turks; and if they did not carry on such a systematic traffic in human flesh as the Tekkes, it was only probably for the want of regular slave markets like Khiva and Bokhara. Both Cossacks and Turkomans were animated with an intense love of freedom, which sweetened all privations and hardships, and was the mainspring of the organization of both peoples; but nevertheless they both occasionally gravitated to the States which hemmed them in on all sides, the Turkomans placing themselves under the nominal rule of Bokhara, Khiva and Persia, and the Cossacks lending their services to Turkey, Poland, and Russia. The Cossack Ataman and the Turkoman Khan were similar supreme heads of authority, elected by communities of equals for superior wisdom in council, or distinguished courage in strife; and it is needless to explain that the *alaman* of the Asiatic Turkoman and the *nabicg* of the semi-Asiatic Cossack were precisely similar forms of incursion and pillage.

With all these resemblances there was apparently a difference between the two peoples in the fact, that while the first condition of the reception of a new-comer among the Cossacks was that he should confess the orthodox Eastern faith, the Turkomans were more or less indifferent to their religion, and probably made the Persians their favourite victims, not because the latter were Shiite Mahommedans, detested by the Sunnites, but because they were the easiest prey, and utterly incapable of defending or revenging themselves. At the same time there is no proof that the Tekkes did not also exact conformity with their particular tenets in the case of Persians and others coming amongst them as prisoners or otherwise. They certainly pressed Mahommedanism upon their Russian prisoners.

Another dissimilarity is supposed to have been the strict exclusion of women from the Zaparogian republic; whereas the Tekkes were always eager to gain possession of the women of the other peoples around them. Very possibly the celibacy of the Zaparogian Cossacks, like the polygamy of the Turkomans, was a matter of religion, and only a reflex of monasticism in the Russian Church; probably also the prohibition against women may have been in force only within the bounds of the *sietch* as a military camp, and may not have been binding upon its members when outside. The other and later Cossacks had no such regulation. In any case, these details do not affect the broad resemblances, which are remarkable enough; and the Cossacks of to-day, though considerably changed and improved, form a link between Russia and the Turkomans, as, indeed, they do between the whole of European and Asiatic Russia, which is of no small importance.

The best organization that the Russians could have given to the Turkomans, so as to obtain the fullest value of their military services, would have been to incorporate them *en masse* into the Cossacks, like some of the other nomads of Central Asia; but the Turkomans being professed, though not fanatical, Mahommedans,* such a measure would have affected the religious side of Russian policy. Traditional sentiment dictates the necessity of preserving the ideal of the name of Cossack, as designating an ardent champion of orthodoxy, and a deadly enemy of all Mahommedans, The Mongolian Calmucks, whose religion is only a very harmless kind of Lamaism, have long been enrolled among the Cossacks of the Don; but Mahommedans, although perhaps naturally Cossacks in all but name and religion, could not be officially accepted as such, unless they embraced Christianity, as they would have been obliged to do on entering the Cossack community four centuries ago.

* The following anecdote illustrates the religious temperament of the Tekkes :—In 1885 one of the houses at Kizil Arvat, intended for an apothecary's store, was blessed by the Russian clergy in the usual way, and throughout the religious ceremony a number of Tekkes remained kneeling with their hands crossed on their breasts in prayer. Several Russians, surprised at this, asked them why they prayed during a Christian service. They answered ironically with the question, "Have you then got a different god?"

Merv and the Turkomans. 343

A proposition to establish Cossack colonies along the frontiers of the Transcaspian was made by General Arzishefsky soon after the annexation of the province, but the project met with no official support. The Turkoman militia, however, as far as it at present goes, is essentially of a Cossack character; and the fact of it being possible to raise a large body of Turkoman cavalry in a few days, and indeed the entire male population in no longer time than it takes to serve out rifles and ammunition, shows that a Turkoman-Cossack organization, call it what you will, already exists. Military men may scout the idea of calling a horde of Asiatics raised in this way a military organization, but the Tekkes have been trained by years of fighting; they possess their own horses and sidearms, mostly the Persian sabre, and on an Asiatic field of battle would be no despicable adversaries of Afghans or even of native Indian troops. The Mahommedan militia of the Caucasus is now being treated in the same way as the Turkoman levy at Merv; that is, recruited at will by the attraction of good pay as a preliminary measure to the eventual introduction of compulsory service.

As very little of an authentic nature has

hitherto transpired concerning the origin and history of the Tekkes, the following contribution of a Russian resident in the Transcaspian, who gathered the particulars from the Turkomans themselves, will be found to be new and interesting.

According to native tradition (for the Turkomans, like all nomadic peoples, have no written records), the Tekkes and their congeners of Merv are direct descendants of the Seljookian Turks, and the home of their ancestors two hundred years ago was in the vicinity of the town of Marghilan, the ancient Marghinan, in the Russian province of Ferghana, formerly the Khanate of Khokand, and the scene of General Skobeleff's early exploits. Scattered members of the numerous Turkish race are still found throughout this district of Central Asia, from the Syr Daria to the foot of the Alai Mountains. Being harassed and persecuted by the Kiptchaks and other and stronger hordes of nomads, the Tekke Turkomans left this region about two centuries ago with their wives, flocks, and herds, and immigrated into Bokhara. They at first settled near the ruins of Noor-Kara-Baira, whence they subsequently moved to Chardjui, and there separated into two sections. At that

Merv and the Turkomans. 345

time the whole of Turkistan had been conquered by the victorious Nadir Shah, who demanded 200 families of the Tekkes as hostages. One division of the Tekkes, the Mervli, complied with the Shah's request, but the other, and more prosperous, half of the tribe, the Akhals, being anxious to preserve their freedom, quitted Chardjui under the able leadership of their venerable and half-blind chieftain, Kaimoor-Kera, and removed to Mangishlak, on the north-east coast of the Caspian. This Kaimoor-Kera had been much liked and petted by Nadir Shah, who once asked him the name of the chief Tekke fortress, to which the Turkoman leader replied, " Khotan-Kala," or "the Camel's back," meaning that the camel carried all the tribe then possessed. The other division of the Tekkes left at Chardjui, became discontented with the Bokharans, and migrated to Merv, where they accepted Persian nationality, and settled in the outskirts of Bairam-Ali, the residence of the Persian Governor. Five years later the Tekkes who had gone to Mangishlak again decamped, and this time sought a new home close to the Balkan Mountains, where their celebrated Kaimoor-Kera died. This district proving too bare and barren, they soon began to meditate the conquest of the adjacent country, the present Akhal oasis, which at that time was peopled by Persians, and a few Turkomans settled there by Nadir Shah. The Persians dwelt at Dooroon, where Persian inscriptions on ruined mosques 300 years old still attest the fact, at Keshi, Askabad, and Bogir, the ancient Nisa. The Turkoman inhabitants were distributed in the following towns :—The Imrali Turkomans at Bami, Beurma, Ak Tepé, and Yoradji; the Migin Turkomans, numbering 1,000 families, near the ruins of the present Migin, not far from the aul of Keliat and Kariz of Noor-Verdi ; and the Alieli Turkomans near the present Khoormant-Kala and the aul of Shar-Kala. The Persian Governor of the Akhal country, Iskander Khan, appointed by Nadir Shah, then resided in the fortified town of Dooroon, which contained 3,000 families. The strongest of the Turkoman tribes just enumerated were the Imralis ; and these were persuaded by the Tekkes to assist them in ousting the Persians, on condition that the land should be equally divided between them ; but no opportunity for decisive action seems to have arrived until long after the death of the terrible Nadir Shah. Accordingly, about 130 years ago, the Tekkes took the field

Merv and the Turkomans. 347

under the lead of their four tribal chiefs, Anna-Ovez-Bai of the Sitchmaz, Anna-Saat-Vekil of the Bakhshee, Anna-Kurbana of the Tilka (probably a mistake for Vekil), and Sarash-Sultan of the Bek clan. They thus entered the Akhal oasis, effected a junction with their allies the Imrali, and opened war upon the Persians. The first success was the capture of Kizil Arvat, which they fortified and garrisoned with several hundred families in charge of the camel train and heavy baggage. From Kizil Arvat they moved on without unnecessary impediment to old Geok Tepé, where they fortified themselves, and prepared for the worst work of the expedition, the attack on the official capital of Dooroon. Conjointly with the Imralis they soon laid siege to Dooroon, which held out for nearly two years, and was taken at last by storm, the Persian Governor Iskander, or Alexander, Khan, perishing in the defence. Within a year afterwards, the Tekkes and Imralis captured the town of Migin, and became masters of the situation. The remaining Persian inhabitants, seeing their utter inability of contending against the Turkomans, voluntarily abandoned the towns of Askabad, Keshi, and Bagir, and retreated into Persia, thus leaving the entire oasis in possession of the invaders. Having expelled the Persians (115 years ago) the Tekkes next turned against their former allies the Imralis; and after no less than twelve years of constant fighting, succeeded in driving them and the other tribes into Khiva, Gurgen and Mian.

Thus, after a sanguinary struggle of twenty-five years, the Tekkes, 103 years ago, completed their conquest of the Akhal oasis, and established their barbarous republic of robbers and brigands. Occasionally they pretended to recognize the nominal authority of Persia and Khiva, but in general their mode of existence was one of wild independence and a reign of terror to the surrounding nations.

In the process of expelling all the former inhabitants of the Akhal country, the Tekkes seem to have spared one small set of rather mysterious people, who are apparently the only mountain dwellers in the Transcaspian. These are the Nookhoors, inhabiting one or two small settlements in the Kopet Dag, ten miles from the railway station of Archman, east of Bami. They are evidently a distinct race, living independently of both Turkomans and Persians, with a resemblance to the Hebrew mountaineers of the Caucasus. M. Charikoff lately visited their villages, and he told me that he had been unable to identify them with any other race in Central Asia, except the Jews. Mr. P. S. Vasilieff says, "The mountain villages of Nookhoor are inhabited by Mahommedanized Jews, who, owing to their geographical position and peaceful habits, have always maintained their independence. In dress and general appearance they do not differ from the Tekkes, but their features are handsomer. They lead a completely settled life in clay-built houses of two stories, the lower apartment serving as stable and storehouse, with windows covered with bladder skins. Since the advent of the Russians, Nookhoor has become a centre of viniculture."

A writer in *Blackwood's Magazine* for December, 1889, has made some disparaging remarks regarding the usefulness and importance of the Turkoman militia as Russian troops. He says that the enrolled Turkoman horsemen are an insignificant force, which, for political reasons, it is not thought fit to increase. We are perfectly well aware that the 300 or 296 Tekkes kept under arms at Merv are not a formidable body; but, as I have already pointed out, these three squadrons could be easily used as the cadres for thousands of others throughout the Transcaspian, who have been thoroughly habituated to war, and only require fresh arms and very little instruction to appear as a considerable force of Turkoman Cossacks. This is no boast of the Russians, but the simple and unavoidable deduction from an unprejudiced acquaintance with the conditions of the Russians and Turkomans in the Transcaspian. Nor is it true that this opinion arose from the display which was made of the Turkoman militia at the opening of the railway to Samarkand, as none of the Turkoman volunteers took part in that ceremony, which occurred hundreds of versts away from Turkomanland, and, to the best of my belief, not a hundred of the mounted militiamen were seen together at Merv by any of the foreign visitors. Alikhanoff, as I have elsewhere related, took his Turkoman horsemen with him to the inauguration of the railway at the city of Bokhara; but when he went to the opening of the line at Samarkand he was entirely alone. It must also be remembered, that in speaking of the possibility of raising 6,000 Turkoman cavalry, Alikhanoff referred only to his own district of

Merv and the Turkomans.

Merv. The writer in question furthermore makes the following rather rash statements. That at the time of the opening of the Samarkand branch of the railway, the Turkomans generally, whose attitude towards Russia is by no means favourable, were, as a measure of precaution, being forcibly deprived of their horses, and that as the Turkomans have never fought on foot, this would render them perfectly harmless. There is not the least evidence, beyond unfounded rumours, often circulated with a purpose, and which British and other Russophobes are always ready to believe, that the Turkomans have ever been forcibly deprived of their horses, or, if at all, to such an extent as would affect in any appreciable degree the immediate enrolment of large numbers of them in the Turkoman militia. The horses of the Tekke tribes have certainly not been taken away, as some 4,000 of them lately bore their riders into Merv on an occasion to which I shall presently refer. During the whole of my intercourse with Russians on the subject of the Transcaspian, which has probably been as extensive as that of any other Englishman, I have never received the least proof or confirmation of such a proceeding. If a few dozens, or even a few hundreds of horses, were taken away from some of the more restless tribes on the frontiers, in order, possibly, to prevent them from galloping over to the other side, or from constantly migrating from one side to the other, as they have always been accustomed to do, that does not make it impossible to raise thousands of Turkoman cavalry whenever necessity requires it. The attitude of the majority of the Turkoman clans is undoubtedly one of willing submission; and there has not yet been the least attempt at organized insubordination or revolt. As to the Turkomans being harmless on foot, I need only refer to General Skobeleff's instructions to his officers, dated 30th December, 1880, shortly before the storming of Geok Tepé. Skobeleff then wrote: "The enemy is valiant and skilful in single combat; they fire with precision, and possess excellent side-arms. .... In the open field their brave cavalry on fleet horses, and their dexterous use of the sabre, will be a constant danger to long and extended lines. Their infantry masses, though without formation, but enthusiastic and strong, cleverly wielding their weapons, and drawing on a hand-to-hand conflict, must balance the chances of the battle in their favour." In former times the Cossacks were also regarded as utterly useless without their horses; but for some years past a body of Cossack infantry has been successfully maintained under the name of Cossack platoons, or battalions of about 735 men each.

While these pages have been passing through the press a veritable epidemic of intrigue and denunciation has broken out among the military officials of the Transcaspian and Central Asia generally. Two high military functionaries, who exercised authority between the Caucasus and the Chinese frontier, have resigned in disgust, and others are expected soon to follow their example. Some may be compelled to quit their posts by pressure from St. Petersburg; and it will be well if nothing worse results from this extraordinary development of the demoralizing custom of secret denunciation. The worst feature of the evil is, that it seldom arises from motives of purely patriotic concern for the welfare of the State, but is generally traceable to the lowest incentives of envy and malice. The proof of this is, that in the majority of cases those who denounce their colleagues are generally denounced by others in their turn. Colonel Alikhanoff, like the rest, has been denounced, and has retired from the headship of affairs at Merv, pending the result of an inquiry. His many enemies are naturally eager to see his temporary withdrawal made final and permanent; but it is not yet positively certain that Alikhanoff will not resume the important post of Governor on the Murghab. If he is obliged to resign altogether, it will be a great loss to Russia in the management of the Turkomans, as I feel sure that, in spite of his shortcomings, it will be very difficult to find another man as well fitted for the peculiar and exceptional conditions of the post. A Russian orthodox saint as Governor of Merv among the Tekke Turkomans would be quite out of place. The report that Alikhanoff has been suspended, and is about to lose his place for having ordered the flagellation of a few barely reclaimed Turkoman brigands is far too absurd. The real causes of the trouble now agitating official circles in the Transcaspian and St. Petersburg must be traced back to the beginning of a long story of intrigue and opposition, which gives us an exceptionally good insight into the morals, discipline and solidarity of the Russian administration in Central Asia. We hear a good deal about Russian intrigues outside Russia; but for intriguing amongst themselves, and undermining one another with diabolical unscrupulousness, commend me to the Russian officials at home.

Just before I quitted Merv the news arrived of the appointment of Lieutenant Captain Kozloff as Colonel Alikhanoff's assistant. Captain Kozloff had been an officer of the guards in St. Petersburg. He possessed no particular qualifications for service in the Transcaspian ; but was a favourite of the Minister for War, and enjoyed the good fortune of being married to a Princess Souvoroff. It seems pretty evident that no love has been lost between Alikhanoff and his assistant Kozloff. Colonel Alikhanoff soon afterwards married as a Mohammedan the daughter of the Khan of Nakhitchivan. It had been thought at one time that he would probably marry into the Christian family of the commander of the garrison at Merv ; but as a staunch Mussulman this would have been inconsistent with his religious principles. These personal matters often play such a large part in the careers of Russian functionaries that, if altogether omitted, the story of their successes or failures would seldom be complete. While I was in Merv Alikhanoff and the commander of the troops were quite estranged, although they lived next door to each other, and the relatives and friends of the commander were very hostile towards Alikhanoff. Thus a certain amount of Russian opposition to Alikhanoff was already on foot at Merv before the events occurred which led up to the charges at present under official investigation.

One night, at the beginning of 1889, an attempt at murder and robbery was committed in the sleeping-room of the woman who kept the small buffet of the railway station at Merv. The woman was unable to identify the burglar, on account of his mask; but her niece, a girl of nine years of age, who was roused from sleep in an adjoining apartment, said she recognized the man in a certain B——, who was living at Merv, apparently without any very settled occupation, except that he seems to have constituted himself the newspaper chronicler of the opposition to Alikhanoff. The only evidence of the little girl was that the man wore the same kind of grey cherkess uniform as B——, which was, of course, not a very weighty proof. Soon afterwards this girl was secretly murdered, and her dead body found in a hole in the suburbs of Merv. Suspicion fastened itself on B——; and it was suspected that the girl had been made away with in order to destroy her testimony against the perpetrator of the first crime. Another account states that the girl was not really killed. In any case it is certain that B—— was compromised, and that Colonel Alikhanoff had him arrested; but Captain Kozloff ordered the policemaster to let him go; whereupon B—— made good his escape, probably over the Persian frontier. Alikhanoff was naturally very angry at this, and prohibited his assistant, Kozloff, from giving any more orders on his own authority. It is said that Kozloff and the police master subsequently had a fierce altercation on the subject, and even came to blows. The upshot of this incident was that Captain Kozloff denounced Alikhanoff to the Minister of War, accusing him of various irregularities, and of allowing the Turkoman Khans to rob their fellow tribesmen. The War Minister, who gives more heed to these denunciations than is, perhaps, always advisable, instructed General Komaroff, the Governor-General of the Transcaspian at Askabad, to investigate the matter; and General Komaroff accordingly sent his Chief of Staff, Colonel Levashoff, to institute an inquiry. Colonel Levashoff, instead of remaining at Merv, allowed himself to be conducted through the Turkoman villages by Captain Kozloff to find the natives who had cause of complaint against Alikhanoff. This produced a lively commotion among the Turkomans, and Colonel Levashoff discovered, to his cost, that the grievances of the few discontented Turkomans were not so much against Alikhanoff as against their own Khans, who have purposely been retained, and even strengthened, in authority by the Russian Government. The Russian policy has been rather to favour the Khans, and not to interfere with the old organization and native administration any more than was absolutely necessary. Alikhanoff cannot be made responsible for the adoption of this sytem. The Khans possibly use their authority often in an arbitrary and vexatious manner, especially as they now have the power of Russia at their backs, and cannot be deposed or slain by their dissatisfied clansmen as in former times. But this can hardly be anything very new to the Turkomans. As marauders and thieves by profession, it is not likely that they regard a little severity, or gentle plundering on the part of their Khans, as anything very atrocious. It is an accepted principle among Asiatics that their despots, whether big or little, should take what they consider necessary. The Turkoman Khans, for instance, still requisition forage for their horses, and exact other gratuitous services from their tribesmen, to which they consider themselves entitled. They also, I believe, often administer summary punishment according to the primitive code of pains and penalties long in force among the Turkomans. At the same time, it must not be forgotten that the country is still exclusively under military law. Considering, therefore, all the circumstances, it is most improbable that anything would have been heard of this discontent among the Turkomans, had it not been excited by the action of Alikhanoff's enemies.

However this may be, Colonel Levashoff's method of procedure in the district of Merv soon led to very startling consequences. One morning 1,500 Turkoman horsemen rode into Merv and requested the dismissal of Maili Khan, the head of one of the four tribes. In the afternoon 3,000 more mounted Turkomans entered the town, and begged that Maili Khan should be retained in office. This political demonstration and revival of old party quarrels among the Turkomans caused considerable apprehension at Askabad, and General

Komaroff at once started for Merv. On arriving there he dismissed Colonel Levashoff, and appointed Colonel Neftonoff, chief of the district of Askabad, to continue the inquiry within proper bounds. The new commissioner appears to have been unable to find anything seriously incriminating Alikhanoff. Evidence with which to support his impeachment was even sought for by criers calling out for complainants from the tops of the tall wooden platforms on the bazaar ground at Merv, used for making proclamations to the people, like muezzins from the heights of the minarets. The whole country was canvassed for testimony against him. Among others, it seems that the Polish engineer, Poklefsky, engaged in irrigating the Murghab estate of the Emperor, complained of Alikhanoff not allowing him to employ Turkomans as navvies on the work of restoring the great river dam and its irrigation canals without paying them. The honour of working on the Emperor's estate was presumably to be considered as sufficient remuneration.

The next phase of the matter was that Colonel Levashoff, having been dismissed, denounced his former chief, General Komaroff

Merv and the Turkomans. 361

to the War Minister as unjustly defending Alikhanoff, and conniving at his crimes. It is said that in Levashoff's telegram to St. Petersburg he even went so far as to request General Komaroff's re-call. In the meantime, Levashoff himself was denounced by his adjutant on account of the alleged disappearance of a sum of money from the funds of the staff at Askabad, over which Levashoff had had the principal control. In the face of this imbroglio of charges and counter-charges there was nothing for the War Minister to do but to send a special commission to investigate the whole affair. For this purpose General Maximovich and Colonel Baranok have been sent to the Transcaspian, and their report and its consequences are anxiously awaited.

A denunciation has also been laid before the War Minister against General Annenkoff by an individual named Kolontaroff, calling himself a son of an ex-Marshal of Nobility at Rjeff, in the province of Tver. This person complained that he had been employed in the department of the Transcaspian railway; that he had been discharged by Prince Khilkoff, General Annenkoff's traffic manager, because he refused to cook the accounts of the railway, and that when he appealed to General Annenkoff at Kizil Arvat the General had him whipped by Cossacks. General Annenkoff's lawyer was able to prove the falsity of all these assertions, and it was also ascertained that the mysterious denouncer, who is probably of Armenian origin, had never been in any way connected with the nobility of Rjeff. The actual Marshal of the Nobility of Tver certified under his official seal that no such family had ever been known among the nobility of his province.

But this does not exhaust the list of recent denunciations against important personages in Central Asia. General Kolpakofsky, late Governor-General of the Steppe territory, bordering the Chinese frontier, was denounced by two of his subordinates, the Governor of Semiretch at Viernoe, General Ivanhoff, and the Governor of Semipalatinsk, General Protsenko, for certain irregularities and defalcations, which accusations were proved to be unfounded; but General Kolpakofsky was so disgusted that he sent in his resignation. General Protsenko was also obliged to retire. The commander of the troops at Samarkand, General Bibikoff, was denounced by a subordinate officer, in whose sphere of duty Bibikoff had found similar

Merv and the Turkomans. 363

irregularities. The commander of the Turkistan Rifle Brigade at Tashkent, General Levashoff, who is no relation of the Colonel Levashoff already referred to, has also been denounced by a colonel of one of the battalions. An inquiry is being made into similar denunciations among officers in the Caucasus, where Prince Dondonkoff Korsakoff is about to resign the General Governorship ; and last, but not least, General Rosenbach, one of the most honest men in Russia, has had information laid against him for accepting too many presents from the Ameer of Bokhara. This last fact is believed to have greatly influenced General Rosenbach in quitting the General Governorship of Turkistan. The exchange of presents, in spite of Russia's wish to abolish the practice, is still *de rigueur* between high Russian officers and the Bokharan sovereign, and the Ameer's gifts were more than repaid by General Rosenbach's return presents, consisting of a carriage and pair, a massive silver table service, and other valuable articles, worth altogether about £1,000.

The train in which I travelled back to Ozoon Ada was delayed at Askabad for five or six hours, and I had time enough to take a look at the town. It is decidedly the best built place on the railway. There are some very good streets full of Persian and Armenian shops, a fine public garden, and a profusion of wild grape vines growing over the garden walls. On returning to the station I accidentally met General Komaroff, and he asked me what I thought of the railway. I said that I thought it was a very noble enterprise, and reflected great credit on General Annenkoff, but that it required to be finished, and made a little more secure against the floods from the mountains. "*Eto neechevo,*" said the General. "That's nothing, it does not matter." The next day I was back in the wretched harbour of Oozoon Ada, and the day after across the Caspian at Baku.

CHAPTER XIV.

THE RAILWAY AND TRADE.

British alarms at the commercial success of the railway—
Exaggerations and contradictions—Facts overlooked
—Brilliant future—Big talk—Increased traffic not all
increase of trade—Tapping the old land routes—
Falling off of Asiatic business at Nijni—Baku fair—
Mr. Ivanoff's opinion—Political and commercial
centre of gravity—General Tchernaieff's desert track
through the Ust Urt—Inconvenience of military
railway management—Annenkoff's eye to business—
His personal supervision of the line—Mistaken
notion of the recency of Russia's conquest of the
Bokharan market—Reversal of business methods—
Opinions of Messieurs Grigorieff and Petrofsky—
Indian tea trade—Russian and Persian figures—
Indian testimony—Bad effect of Abdurahman's
attitude towards England—Interruption of trade by
Afghan troubles—English muslins—Russian and
British trade in Khorassan—English cottons at
Tabriz—Turban cloths—Former blunders of British
merchants—Russian sugar monopoly—Overturn of
Bokharan trade—Messieurs Petrofsky, Krestofsky
and Heyfelder on—Will the increase last?—Specula-
tion and loss—Bad wares—Mr. F. Law on Russian
speculation in Persia—A German's enterprise in
Afghanistan—Export of sheep's gut for sausages—

366 *Russia's Railway Advance.*

Bokharan sheep in Russia—A *coup* in sugar—Russian statistics—How obtained—Russian and Bokharan trade with Afghanistan—Figures for 1887 and 1888—Apparent superiority of Anglo-Indian trade—Figures for 1889—Deductions from—Balance of trade on the side of Afghanistan—India's participation in the overplus—Latest figures—Exports into Afghanistan conveyed by natives—Decline of Orenburg—Central Asian cotton—Cotton cultivation on the Murghab.

ALTHOUGH unable to extract any information on Bokharan trade from the Ameer's cautious Chancellor of the Exchequer (lately promoted to the higher dignity of Koush Begi), I have since met with a few Russian figures, which have been commented upon as proofs of the enormous increase of Russian business with Bokhara, and of the crushing effect of the railway upon Anglo-Indian trade in Central Asia. We have been told that the Central Asian railway has conquered entirely new markets for Russia, and is completely ousting the productions of England and India from Eastern bazaars, where they formerly enjoyed an undisputed monopoly. By the aid of a few unsatisfactory figures, gathered in quite exceptional circumstances, and of vague, general statements, taken from consular reports and other documents, we

The Railway and Trade. 367

have been treated to a rather alarming picture of Russia's sudden commercial progress over the Transcaspian railway, and of England's inevitable retreat into the background. British panics at Russia's military advances upon Merv and Penjdeh would seem likely to be followed by similar alarms at her commercial successes in the same direction. But if we sift the information adduced in support of these sweeping conclusions, we shall find that they have been somewhat overdrawn. There is, at least, every reason for reserve until we can obtain more convincing evidence of the permanent effects produced by the railway. The little information that exists at present has been published in such contradictory forms by the different Russian channels through which it has reached the public that no positive deductions drawn from it can be safely accepted. Russian journals, with their customary carelessness, publish a set of figures one day as referring to six months of the year, and the next day the very same figures are applied to the whole twelve months. Even officials interested in the matter seem to be sceptical of the accuracy of these Central Asian figures. In any case, the extremely optimist view of Russia's new commercial triumphs by means of the railway requires to be modified by reference to certain facts and considerations which have been hitherto overlooked. It would be idle to deny that trade has increased and expanded since the opening of the railway to Bokhara; and the brilliant future in this respect which it opens up to the Russians, if they are only enterprising enough to take advantage of it, is equally undeniable. But no trustworthy data which have yet been produced can justify the extreme views adopted by some English and Russian writers. The real truth is probably to be found, as usual, in the *juste milieu*. The Russians, like the Americans, are fond of "talking big," and if only half the gigantic trading schemes now under discussion in Russia were realized, Englishmen might well tremble at the probable consequences. Even where a large increase of trade, within the railway radius in Central Asia, can be plainly proved, the profit of it does not seem to be so entirely on the side of Russia as we have been led to suppose.

It may be first pointed out that a corresponding increase of trade is not necessarily implied either by the increase of traffic over the railway, or by the addition of a dozen new Russian commercial agents in Bokhara to the solitary

The Railway and Trade. 369

one whom Schuyler found there in 1873. The railway is shifting the movement of Central Asian commerce, and tapping the old land routes of their camel-borne goods ; while a great deal of business formerly done between Russians and Asiatics at the different Eastern fairs, and in other indirect ways, is now transacted directly through Russian representatives in Bokhara. This may, to some extent, account for the falling off in Central Asian business at Nijni Novgorod during the last two fairs. There were less Asiatic goods and buyers at the fair in 1889 than in the previous year. In 1888 the value of wares from Bokhara, Khiva and Tashkent amounted to 6,953,460 roubles, and in 1889 to only 5,686,625 roubles. Persian goods also showed a similar decline. Possibly the new fair at Baku, which made a wretched beginning in 1888, may have helped, in conjunction with the railway, to cause this diminution. With more moderation than most writers on the subject, Mr. Ivanoff observes in the Russian *Viestnik* that, " The trade of Central Asia and its economical development have received a fresh impulse, which the Transcaspian railway is centralizing towards the south in exchange for the old roads by way of Orenburg and

Siberia." If the political centre of gravity has been moved from Turkistan to the Trans-caspian, as English authorities on the political statics of Central Asia are so anxious to inform us, although in reality Tashkent is now as politically important as Askabad, the main streams of Central Asian trade are also being diverted from their old arteries and concentrated in the same region. This would naturally not be effected all at once. The old trade routes into Russia have not yet been entirely abandoned. Last year Khivan cotton was still being transported with great difficulty through the Ust Urt desert to the Dead Bay on the Caspian, along a route running to the north of, and parallel with, the railway. This was the favourite desert track of General Tchernaieff while Governor-General of Turkistan, and there is still some fantastic project among his admirers for rendering it practically available by the construction of a tramway. The immediate effect of the opening of the railway was to reduce the camel freight *via* Orenburg from several roubles [to half a rouble per pood; and this reduction, combined with the inconveniences and annoyances caused by the military management of the line, had the result at one time of

The Railway and Trade.

driving a good deal of the private traffic back on to the old routes, where the caravan-bashis showed more care for the interests of their employers. An instance may be cited of the way in which trade is sometimes facilitated on a Russian military railway in ordinary circumstances, and with ordinary military officials. Before General Annenkoff was invested with full power over the line, a certain colonel, who was then the Managing Director, refused to forward twelve truck loads of goods to Askabad until the consignors had subscribed 300 roubles towards the erection of a Russian church at Kizil Arvat. As soon as Annenkoff was placed in charge of the working arrangements every possible encouragement was held out to private enterprise, and the caravan trade was again drawn off from the old land routes. With the General's extraordinary energy, and his particular eye for business, the development and animation of trade within the scope of his functions are probably due almost as much to his own personal initiative and activity as to the intrinsic advantages of the railway. Contrary to what could have been expected, judging from most other Russian military officers, his first endeavour was to make the line subservient in every possible way to the interests of trade. He has, indeed, sacrificed his other lucrative posts—the directorship of military transports, and a seat at the board of the Ministry of ways of communication —in order to be able to continue personal supervision over the railway on the spot. His retirement from the Transcaspian would be a great loss to the management of the line, and a risk for the interests of its mercantile traffic.

It is very astonishing to find students of Central Asia writing that Russia has only now acquired absolute command over the Bokharan market, with new outlets in this part of the world, just as if Russian trade had never before penetrated as far, and was only now making its way into regions hitherto closed against it. It seems more certain, considering the superior total value of the Indo-Afghan imports into Bokhara over the return imports of Russia and Bokhara into Afghanistan, that the command of the Bokharan market is on the Indian side of the Afghan frontiers. Russian trade in these parts has always been pretty large, but has only begun to attract European, and even Russian, attention since the opening of the railway. Russia has for years past virtually held the monopoly of foreign trade with Bokhara, and

The Railway and Trade. 373

through Bokhara with the other nearest Khanates; while the disposal of British goods has nearly always been on a much inferior scale. Only occasionally, perhaps, has English enterprise flooded the Bokharan bazaars with low-priced goods and undersold the Russians. One of the changes undoubtedly effected by the railway, and one which has its advantages, is that whereas the natives formerly came to the Russians to make their bargains, the Russians, no longer deterred by dangers and difficulties of the desert, now go to the natives. The late Professor Grigorieff, the well-known Russian orientalist, said that, " In the first quarter of the nineteenth century the Bokharan, Khivan, Tashkent and Khokandian traders went about through the whole broad extent of Russia in perfect safety, bought Russian wares from the manufacturers at the place of production, and for their own goods which they had imported they were able, in the absence of competition, to fix most advantageous prices."

In 1872, Mr. Petrofsky, formerly commercial agent of the Trade Department of the Ministry of Finance, and now Russian Consul in Kashgar, reported from Bokhara that, "At present I think we can say that trade in Russian wares has here the first place, and the dependence of Bokhara on the Nijni Novgorod fair is felt at every step. Bokhara is literally filled from top to bottom with Russian cotton goods, and there seems to me to be at least six times as much of them as of English goods." It is true that Mr. Petrofsky expressed a fear, that with the carelessness of the Russians in regard to the Bokharan market, the trade of Central Asia might pass entirely out of their hands into those of the English and the Afghans, but that fear was never realized, except in the case of imported green teas and white muslin for turbans, which at that time were already a monopoly of the Anglo-Indian and Afghan traders, and which still figure as the principal items of Anglo-Indian imports. Bokhara has always served as the depôt and agency for distributing Indian teas as well as Russian wares throughout the surrounding countries. The natives will not drink Russian Kiakhta teas at any price, and the Russian tea is only used by Russians and other Europeans living in the Khanate. When I visited the Bokharan Minister he offered me Russian tea in a tumbler, but he and his attendants sipped Indian or " white tea " (*ak-chai*) as they call it, out of small Chinese cups. The Russian prohibitory tariff may succeed in shutting out Indian teas from Turkistan, but it cannot yet supplant them in Bokhara. In spite of Russian duties, the total import of Indian teas, which can hardly be all consumed in Bokhara itself, promises in perfectly tranquil times to equal, if not to exceed, the totals of several years ago. This may seem inexplicable in view of reported complaints of Indian tea planters, who find a diminution in their northern frontier trade; but such data as can be obtained in Russia seems to point to no other conclusion. It has apparently escaped attention in India that during the last two or three years a great deal of tea has reached Bokhara by way of Persia. Eighteen years ago Mr. Petrofsky gave the highest annual amount of Indian tea imported into Bokhara as 5,000 camel loads, of an average of sixteen poods each, thus making about 80,000 poods.* The same total was given by Prince Wittgenstein's Embassy to Bokhara in 1883. In 1887 and 1888 Doctor Heyfelder, on the strength of the best official information, both Russian and Bokharan, stated that 70,000

* A pood contains thirty-six pounds English, and forty pounds Russian.

poods were imported direct from India, which excluded the quantity then being received *viâ* Persia and Meshed—a route which has been much used since the beginning of troubles in Afghanistan. During the first half of 1889, according to a notice in the official *Russki Invalide*, the quantity of Indian tea imported into Bokhara direct through Afghanistan was 23,880 poods, and during the second half of the year 22,680 poods. A correspondent, writing to the *Times*, on "Persia and the Persian Question," states that in 1888–9 the import of Indian tea to Meshed, half at least of which, if not more, went on further into Bokhara, paid 18,000 tomans of duty at 5½ per cent. By a calculation, based on 3½ tomans to the pound sterling, and the cost of the above Russian weight of 22,680 poods, which represents 216,360 roubles, we arrive at the total of about 45,000 poods more of tea introduced into Bokhara *viâ* Meshed, thus making a total of over 90,000 poods. Therefore, if we take into account the tea now imported into Bokhara by the roundabout way of Meshed, in order to avoid the exorbitant dues levied by the Afghans, and also the fact that in the early part of 1889 the Afghan transit trade was completely stopped for a time by the renewal of intestine troubles, and also again suspended in the months of July and August on account of rumours of the outbreak of cholera in Bokhara, as attested by the *Russki Invalide*, we may reasonably conclude that the total import of Indian teas into Bokhara is now larger on the average than it was before the opening of the railway. The figures cannot, of course, in the circumstances be absolutely accurate ; but taking them as only approximately correct, I fail to see any cause for alarm even in the alleged decrease of the Indian tea trade in this part of Central Asia. It may be said that information from India is sufficiently conclusive of the ruin which is said to be overtaking Anglo - Indian commerce wherever Russian rivalry and the Central Asian Railway have penetrated. Here is a specimen of official Indian testimony to this effect, lately brought forward by a distinguished English politician : " The trade beyond Quetta is as yet not large ; the trade with Cabul is not progressing as it might do ; there is certainly no indication of material increase." These are the vague official phrases of our Indian authorities, accompanied by the equally indefinite explanation that the

Indian Government does not know "whether this stagnation (why stagnation ?) of trade is to be attributed to Russian customs, restrictions on the border of Northern Afghanistan, impeding the transit trade between India and Central Asia, or to the illiberal fiscal *régime* of the Amir, or to tribal disturbances." Our Indian officials do not make bold, positive statements like the Russians in the Transcaspian, but frankly avow their ignorance, and confess to a notion that the trade has not increased as they think it ought to have done. We allow Abdurahman Khan to keep us at arm's length, and to enforce a fiscal *régime* by which our Indian trade suffers as much as from the high duties of the Russians; and then we are surprised at not being able to compete with rivals who impose the most favourable conditions for their own trade up to the very limits of their political influence. The effects of the railway are not half as detrimental to our commerce in the long run as the awkward and unprofitable position in which England has placed herself towards the Ameer of Cabul. Not wishing to have a conterminous frontier with Russia for fear of her protective duties, we calmly tolerate all kinds of extra exactions

The Railway and Trade. 379

from an intervening Asiatic despot, nominally under our sole and exclusive influence, which impose a double burden upon Anglo-Indian trade, and do more harm than would be likely to result from the establishment of contiguous frontiers.

All the figures obtainable up to the present are open to the strong objection that they relate to periods of political disturbance and rebellion, which have undoubtedly had a most depressing and paralyzing effect upon Afghan and Anglo-Indian commerce. Ever since 1881, when Skobeleff took Geok Tepé, down to 1889 the border territories of Afghanistan and adjacent lands have been plagued by constant revolts, panics and perturbations, to the hindrance and obstruction of Central Asian trade. In 1884 the Russian advance to Merv and Sarakhs spread the fear of further Russian movements in the direction of Herat; in 1885 occurred the battle on the Koushk and other disquieting incidents; in 1887 the rising of the Ghilzai and Shinwarri tribes; in 1888 the rebellion of Ishak Khan; in the beginning of 1889 the rigorous suppression of the same, when, as the Russians assert, the Afghan trade with Bokhara was entirely suspended for a month; and in July and August last trade was again completely interrupted (*vide Russki Invalide*), by rumours of cholera in Bokhara, consequent upon the outbreak of an epidemic, which preceded the appearance of influenza in Russia and Europe. It would be manifestly unfair, therefore, to accept the Russian figures, which I shall presently give for what they are worth, as a fair test of the settled changes wrought in Central Asian trade by the railway to Samarkand.

Against the pessimist view of Indo-British trade and its prospects in this region of Central Asia it is interesting to note the opinions on the trade in English muslins, which the French Consul at Tabriz, probably under the influence of the fashionable Russophile tendencies of his countrymen, declared in July, 1888, were far inferior in quality to those of Russia, and doomed to complete expulsion from the Persian markets. In contradiction of this, an able writer in the *Times* of December 21 last, in a letter from Tcheran, says: "English muslins, which the Russians have not yet learnt to make of equal quality, come both from Bombay and Tabriz." The same correspondent gives quite a favourable account of British trade in North

The Railway and Trade. 381

Eastern Khorassan—the very district which hasty English authors had just previously declared to be completely under the commercial domination of the Central Asian Railway. The writer in question says that "Meshed still does a larger trade with Bombay than with the whole of Russia." The British Consul at Tabriz reports just the opposite of his French colleague already mentioned, and asserts that, "Russian competition with English cottons in the Tabreez market, and therefore in the Azerbaijan province generally, has almost completely ceased, the Manchester cotton goods retaining their superiority." Doctor Heyfelder wrote in 1888 (*Russische Revue*) that the white turbans of the Bokhariots were still made exclusively of Manchester muslins. The Russians have always flattered themselves, especially in the supply of stuff for coloured turbans, that they understand native requirements better than any other Europeans, but we may confidently hope that English merchants are no longer liable to commit blunders like the one referred to by Khanikoff, and which is still remembered in Bokhara, although it took place fifty years ago. A quantity of English shawl turbans and sashes, said to have been made in

Glasgow, arrived in Bokhara from Peshawur *viâ* Meshed, and could not be sold, in spite of their very fine quality, while the Russian check turbans were all disposed of at very good prices.

The secret was that the English shawls bore a bird pattern, which could not be worn by strict Mohammedans during prayers. This attention to the peculiar wants of the natives aided the Russians in gaining a monopoly of the sugar supply, in which they were also assisted by the drawbacks on sugar exports over the Asiatic frontiers granted by the government. Having noticed that the natives were in the habit of making presents of sugar, and did not like to give pieces broken off from the ordinary large loaves, the Russian manufacturers produced very small loaves, from two pounds and upwards, which were soon highly appreciated. Of the two great articles of import into Bokhara—tea and sugar—the latter is just as bound to enter from Russia as the first is certain to come from the side of India. Four years ago a pood of Russian sugar over the Orenburg route cost forty tengas, or about ten roubles, and now the railway has reduced the price to twenty-seven or thirty tengas.

The Railway and Trade. 383

The Bokharans consume a great quantity of sweetmeats, and are now beginning to use sand sugar for sweetening instead of fruit syrups.

It will be interesting to inquire how far Bokhara's trade with Russia and other countries can be shown to have increased during the last few years by the estimates of its entire overturn, as contained in the only figures at present available. Sixteen years ago Mr. Petrofsky, probably the greatest expert on the subject in Russia, paid an official visit to Bokhara, and estimated the total value of all its trade at not less than 40,000,000 of roubles. In 1883, Captain Krestofsky, a member of General Tchernaieff's embassy to the late Ameer of Bokhara, Muzzafar Khan, was informed by Mohamed Sherif Inak, the Ameer's Minister of Trade and Finance, that the overturn of Bokhara trade was from 35,000,000 to 40,000,000 roubles. After these figures no more are procurable until we come to those of Doctor Heyfelder, obtained from the Russian and Bokharan officials and merchants about the middle of 1888, when the railway had just entered the country. At that time most of the Russian firms in Bokhara were already established, while some of them had sent their representatives into the country several years before. These latest figures, representing the total trade of 1887, are 31,715,000 roubles, made up of 16,675,000 imports, and 15,040,000 exports. It therefore appears that Bokhara had to pay a balance of 1,635,000 roubles over and above the return value of her exports, or else this sum was defrayed by other countries like Russia, for which she acts as the intermediary. It is to be regretted that there are no later figures of the aggregate of Bokharan trade. Up to the time of the extension of the railway into the country the Russians never gave the matter any particular attention. Since then they have frequently published the results of their increasing trade with Afghanistan, as though determined to show to the world that that particular sphere of British influence—which, however, does not seem to be much influenced by any consideration for English interests—is now falling completely under the commercial supremacy of Russia. In asserting this they cannot be contradicted, as nobody knows what the extent of this trade was before, and therefore it is impossible to guage the extent of its alleged, and presumably inevitable, increase in Russia's favour during the last two or three years. In

The Railway and Trade. 385

any case, we see that the sum total of all Bokhara's trade, including Russia's trade with Afghanistan, and Bokhara's trade with all the surrounding countries, was in 1887 8,000,000 of roubles less—taking it at the very lowest computation, without calculating the difference in the value of the rouble—than its average yearly totals of sixteen and six years ago respectively.

Consequently it must be shown that during the last two years the railway has produced an increase in the total trade of Bokhara of more than 8,000,000 of roubles.

Granting that there has been an enormous increase, such as many persons assert, is it likely to be a lasting one? It is well-known that the novelty of the opportunity, and the attractive prospects held out by General Annenkoff and his friends, at first produced a great deal of speculation at all the principal places along the railway. If some were enriched, others must have been half ruined by the competition. Doctor Heyfelder in the *Russische Revue* states that one of the largest Russian firms doing business in Central Asia had given up trade in Bokhara altogether, retaining it only in the Transcaspian and Persia; and while I write, the news arrives of another Moscow house having closed its business in Bokhara. The Bokharan bazaars were overstocked with Russian wares of the commonest and cheapest description. On this point Doctor Heyfelder writes in the *Russische Revue* for September, 1888:—"A proper spirit of enterprise is not being shown by the Russian mercantile community. The inundation of the east with specially bad wares (see the circular of Koudrin's Central Asian Trading Company, 6th January, 1886), which is partly the fault of Asiatic, and partly of Russian importers, cannot contribute towards a lasting and solid development of Russian trade in Central Asia." After describing the wretched quality of many Russian articles, he states that the Russian cotton goods are so bad that they will probably force the Bokhariots to return to the use of their own more durable homespun material. Mr. Fitzgerald Law in his official report on trade in Persia, February, 1889, gives a similar account of the spasmodic efforts and unsound speculation of Russian merchants in Northern Persia. What the Russians themselves confess as to the forced trade of Merv, described in a previous chapter, has no doubt been to some extent repeated in the case of Bokhara. I

The Railway and Trade. 387

hear of one merchant in Bokhara who has made a great deal of money during the last few years, and he happens to be a German. Other Germans, in spite of Russian Teutonophobia, have established business concerns in different parts of Central Asia, where English traders would probably be hardly tolerated. The enterprising German is now found everywhere, even on the borders of Afghanistan. This German "merchant adventurer" was at first struck by the great numbers and excellent quality of the Bokharan sheep—the famous fat-tailed sheep—whose enormous caudal appendages, roasted nicely brown, are exposed to view on the show-boards of the cook-shops in the native bazaars. Next to sugar, one of the principal articles of consumption is mutton fat; and both enter far too much into the native food to be conducive to health in a climate like that of Bokhara. Our German friend discovered that the offal of the sheep when killed was generally thrown away, and could be bought for next to nothing; and in the course of a few years he originated a large export trade in sheeps' entrails, which are now sent in considerable quantities to Hamburg and Vienna, to be used in making sausages and strings for musical instruments. While on the subject of sheep, I may mention that five years ago, before the arrival of the railway, large numbers of Bokharan sheep were introduced into Southern Russia, for the purpose of crossing with the Russian breeds. They soon became acclimatized, and now produce the curly Kara Kul lamb-skins in such perfection that they can hardly be distinguished from the native article, while they can be sold at very much lower prices. This success induced other landowners and stock-breeders to try the experiment, and a few months ago 1,000 more Bokharan sheep were sent to Poltava over the railway. Many competitors arrived on the scene with the appearance of the railway, and then the successful German turned his attention to another important Eastern commodity—sugar. In consequence of Ishak Khan's rebellion in Afghan Turkistan the Ameer Abdurahman came within easy reach of the Russo-Bokharan frontier at Mazar-i-Sheriff, attended by a numerous retinue, for whom the sugar supply of the district proved to be insufficient. The German at once bought up all the sugar in Bokhara, and sold it, per caravan, to the Afghans at a very high price. A corresponding influx of Russian sugar into Bokhara was the necessary

The Railway and Trade. 389

result. This German *coup* reminds me of a remark made by a very high official in St. Petersburg, to the effect that the Transcaspian Railway would prove as profitable to foreigners who knew how to use it as to the Russians themselves.

The circumstances in which the latest figures of trade have been obtained must also be taken into consideration. As soon as foreign visitors and delegates of foreign Governments began to crave for trade statistics of Bokhara a supply was speedily forthcoming to supply the demand. The foreigners who visited Bokhara at the time of the opening of the railway drove the staff of the Russian Diplomatic Agency nearly mad with questions on every conceivable subject, particularly concerning trade. For their own peace and quiet the Russian officials were obliged to procure statistics in the best and only way they could, by inquiring of the principal Russian and Bokharan merchants and native officials. Considering the primitive native method of collecting the two and a-half per cent. *ziaket*, or duty, on Russian, and four per cent. on native imports, we cannot expect any great accuracy in the figures thus obtained. Such as they are, they at least represent all the information which the Russian Government has been able to obtain since the abolition of the Orenburg customs line in 1876. Sooner or later we shall doubtless be supplied with more detailed and trustworthy particulars, as the railway must gradually spread Russian control over everything in the Khanate. It was only on the 13th of November, 1889, that proper custom offices were established at Oozoon Ada, and various other places along the railway, with a cordon round the Persian and Afghan frontiers, but no Russian custom officials have yet been appointed in Bokhara.

The trade of Bokhara with Afghanistan, in which Russia has always indirectly taken part, is exhibited in the following figures for 1887, cited from the Hon. George Curzon's book, "The Russians in Central Asia," in order to show the disposal of the total of 31,715,000 roubles already referred to :—

Exports from Bokhara.

			Roubles.
Bokharan trade with Russia	.	.	12,500,000
,, ,, Persia	.	.	2,120,000
,, ,, Afghanistan and India	.	.	420,000
			15,040,000

Imports into Bokhara.

	Roubles.
Bokharan trade with Russia	10,600,000
,, ,, Persia	5,475,000
,, ,, Afghanistan and India.	600,000
	16,675,000

The relatively small place occupied in the above statement by the Afghan and Indian trade in 1887 is to be accounted for by the Ghilzai rising, and other troubles during that year. This fact was attested at the time by the Indian intelligence of the London newspapers. The next figures for the last half of 1888 are official, and show the effect of Ishak Khan's rebellion in a gradual decline on both sides of the account, until during the last two months of the year the transit trade with Cabul ceased altogether.

Imports into Bokhara from Afghanistan.

	Roubles.
June, 1888 (before the rebellion)	2,153,902
July	807,200
August	554,147
September	459,242
October	386,115
November	438,122
December	35,116
	4,833,844

392 *Russia's Railway Advance.*

Exports from Bokhara into Afghanistan.

	Roubles.
June, 1888	1,235,815
July	545,585
August	532,412
September	336,699
October (in consequence of rumoured preparations for war).	
November	553,642
December	54,172
	3,258,325

The following figures for the first six months of 1889 are from the same official source, the Russian Agency in Bokhara. The Russian Official Telegram Agency first published them as distinctly relating to the longer period between the 1st of January and the 1st of November, 1889; whereas the military gazette, the *Russki Invalide*, reproduces them as representing the trade of only half the year. The same paper explains them in such a way as to prove that the Anglo-Indian goods imported into Bokhara through Afghanistan during this period reached a sum twice as large as the value of the whole of Russian and Bokharan exports into Afghanistan put together; but this, I imagine, must be an error, or else the superiority of the Anglo-Indian trade over that of Russia would

The Railway and Trade. 393

be at once established. The carelessness of the Russians in dealing with facts and figures is proverbial. The value of exports from Bokhara into Afghanistan indicated in the undermentioned items includes both Bokharan and Russian wares, and a note in the *Invalide* explains that in the month of March the trade of Afghanistan with Bokhara was again interrupted, probably by the commotion and dislocation consequent upon Abdurahman's arrival at Mazar-i-Sheriff, and the flight of Ishak Khan into Russia.

	Roubles.
Imports into Bokhara from Afghanistan during the first half of 1889	2,533,040
Exports from Bokhara into Afghanistan during the same period	1,218,389

The foregoing groups of figures seem to show the low ebb reached by the trade in 1889 on account of political and warlike disturbances; the high water mark to which it was temporarily forced in 1888 by the opening of the railway, and in spite of the Afghan rebellion; and the way in which it is beginning to subside in 1889, notwithstanding many months of comparative calm. Unfortunately, there are no figures of the trade previous to 1887, and none for the first six months of 1888. It is possible that further statistics, if they could be obtained, might modify the present aspect of the matter; but the information thus far at our disposal shows no cause for alarm at Russia's latest commercial successes in Central Asia.

The *Russki Invalide* details three items of the above total exports from Afghanistan during the first half of 1889, which are unmistakably of Anglo-Indian origin, namely, tea, 894,840 roubles, indigo, 412,800 roubles, and English muslin, 228,800 roubles, altogether, 1,536,440 roubles, without counting smaller Indian products not specified. On the other side the total of Russian and Bokharan exports lumped together is only 1,218,389; so that we get a clear excess in value of Anglo-Indian trade over that of Russia and Bokhara combined. Another fact plainly evinced by the above data is that the value of exports from India and Afghanistan is twice as great as that of the corresponding exports from Russia and Bokhara; so that from this point of view the advantage of trade is on the side of Afghanistan, even if it cannot be shown that India participates in the overplus. Such an advantage would infallibly be shared in by India, if Abdurahman's relations

The Railway and Trade. 395

with the Indian Empire were regulated by a more reciprocal and rational basis of intercourse. In view of the desirability of such an improvement it ought at least to be gratifying to see that the balance of trade is already on the side of the country which is entirely within the sphere of England's influence, and under her immediate patronage and protection.

The very latest figures fully confirm the conclusions drawn from the previous data. The official statement of trade during the last half of 1889 is as follows:—

	Roubles.
Imports into Bokhara from India and Cabul	1,475,080
Imports into Bokhara from the five Afghan districts of Akcha, Shiburgan, Andkhoi, Maimene and Saripoul	876,152
	2,351,232
Russian and local exports from Bokhara into Afghanistan	1,954,839

According to an official explanation accompanying these figures, the rumours of cholera in Bokhara caused a complete cessation in the arrival of trade caravans from India and Afghanistan during the months of July and August, although there was no interruption of the Russo-

Bokharan export trade into Afghanistan, which must account for the less remarkable excess of value in the Indo-Afghan imports over the Bokharan exports as compared with the previous half yearly statements. It is stated that the export trade into Afghan-Turkistan is still carried on entirely by native merchants, and that no Russians as a rule pass over the frontier. This may lessen the danger of Russian political influence by means of commercial contact.

While the Central Asian Railway has given new life and being to the barren plains of the Transcaspian, it has brought nothing but ruin to the once flourishing region of Orenburg.

A resident in a letter to the *Grajdanin* furnishes a deplorable account of the effect of General Annenkoff's great work upon the former "threshold of Central Asia." Since 1881 the prosperity of Orenburg has gradually, but surely, declined. All the benefits and advantages conferred upon the district by the Orenburg Railway have been destroyed by the rival railway in the Transcaspian. The construction of the almost useless and unprofitable branch line from Samara to Oufa, opened in 1881, instead of extending the main line from Orenburg along its naturally destined path into Turkistan,

The Railway and Trade. 397

was the first blow struck at the financial success of the Orenburg railway; and the opening of General Annenkoff's railway to Samarkand was the final knell of Orenburg's fate. The Orenburg Railway has lost the greater part of its goods traffic from Central Asia, and all of it from the opposite direction. The Kirghiz of the Orenburg Steppes, whose vast herds of camels once performed all the carrying work between the railway terminus and Central Asia, have been deprived of their greatest source of income. The city population has diminished; house property has declined in value; local trade has dwindled down to almost nothing; shops and factories have been closed, and bankruptcy is overtaking the soundest business firms. Social life has changed from a busy, noisy and gay existence like that of a capital city into the dull, dreary monotony of a small country town.

The goods traffic on the Transcaspian Railway is being fed principally, and on a rapidly increasing scale, by the transport of Central Asian cotton. This is now the one great article of export from Central Asia, in comparison with which all other goods carried by the railway sink into relative insignificance. Every visitor to Oozoon Ada is struck by the enormous number of cotton bales heaped up on all sides awaiting shipment across the Caspian—an accumulation and delay chiefly caused by the freezing of the Volga and the want of available vessels. During the last few years, while hundreds of fine new boats have appeared on the Volga, the fleet of the Caspian has made no progress to meet the new demands of the Transcaspian Railway, though I am told that the Kavkaz and ·Mercury Company have at last ordered several new steamers.

As soon as the railway port of Petrofsk is ready on the west coast of the Caspian there will no longer be any necessity to use the Volga route, except on the score of cheapness of water carriage, and it will then be possible to use larger vessels. The quantity of cotton conveyed over the railway in 1889 was 2,200,000 poods, or 35,483 tons, which is nearly all that Central Asia at present produces for the Russian market. Active preparations are being made to bring the quantity up to four or five millions of poods, and General Annenkoff expects to be able to transport next season about 4,000,000 poods. Central Asian cotton is no longer a chimera. Russian enterprise in the Transcaspian is enthusiastically devoted to the increase of its cultivation; and if we may trust all the reports of successful experiments, and the introduction of the newest English and American machinery, its defects of dirtiness and short staple, hitherto so much complained of, may very soon disappear. From Ferghana alone the cotton exports into Russia have increased from 645 poods in 1884 to 735,000 poods in 1888. There is in fact quite a mania in Russia on the subject of the future of Central Asian cotton; and General Annenkoff, having caught the contagion, is talking of exporting it abroad in a few years to compete with cotton from America and Egypt.

For many years past American "upland" has been assiduously cultivated in different parts of Central Asia, and in spite of foreign opinion to the contrary, Russians assert that its quality is not much inferior to that of the original article from the States. The bulk of Russian cotton goods not being required of the finest quality, there is no reason why Central Asian cotton should not in time exclude its foreign rival from the Moscow markets. The best growth is south of latitude 40, while farther north in the district of Tashkent one bad yield is always expected out of every four years of good crops. It is proposed to augment the supply from Central Asia as fast as possible, and to exclude foreign cotton by a gradual increase of prohibitive duty. At present Russia receives about 150,000 tons of foreign cotton at an annual cost of about eighty millions of roubles. The general adoption of Central Asian cotton by Russian manufacturers would effect a considerable saving to the country, though not to the government, which derives a large amount of revenue from foreign cotton in the shape of import duty. This is now such a considerable item that its complete disappearance would be felt at first by a Government whose interest in high protective duties is quite as much for the purpose of filling the State coffers as for encouraging home production; and therefore, to the consternation of Russian cotton growers, who make large profits as things are at present, it has already been rumoured that an excise duty will probably be levied on Central Asian cotton.

If the new irrigation work on the Murghab, under the direction of Mr. Poklefsky and the Department of Imperial Appanages, turns out successful, the largest cotton planter will probably be the Tzar himself.

The Railway and Trade. 401

The immediate prospects of this work, however, have been greatly exaggerated, as usual, in Russia. Instead of 300,000 desiatines, not more than 6,000, or possibly 11,000, desiatines will be placed under cultivation, and the complete success of the plan of fertilizing by means of the Murghab, without injuring the native irrigation in existence before, remains to be seen.

The chequered career of the Polish engineer who has charge of this work may be illustrated by a few more facts, in addition to those already given.

Mr. Poklefsky, formerly a Lieutenant Captain of Engineers, was head of the National Government in Warsaw, under another name, about 1863, at the time of the Polish insurrection. He escaped from the Russians over the Prussian frontier; subsequently took part in the campaign of Garibaldi as chief of the staff of a body of 800 Italians and Poles; and also, it is said, played a certain rôle in the Paris commune. In return for denunciations made against the advanced Polish party, with whom he quarrelled, he received a pardon from Alexander the Second, and was permitted to go to the Seven River province on the Chinese frontier as a

D D

Cossack. Here he interested himself in irrigation and in the navigation of the river Ili, on which he constructed a small steamboat for several Russian merchants. Finding that fortune did not favour him on the Ili, he obtained access to Prince Dondonkoff Korsakoff in the Caucasus, and proposed his seductive scheme for reviving the fertility of Merv, on which about £70,000 have already been expended.

CHAPTER XV.

CONCLUSION.

History of the railway—Technical details—General Annenkoff, Prince Khilkoff, and Colonel Shebanoff—Cost of Construction—Traffic receipts—Financial success—Proposed extension to Tashkent and Omsk—Effect of more direct extension to Orenburg—Isolation of Transcaspian line—Proposed lines to the Caspian and the Transcaucasus—Vladikavkaz—Petrofsk—Necessity of direct railway communication with the Caspian—Inconveniences of the Volga and Georgian Road—Proposals for joining the railways of the Cis and Transcaucasus—Projected lines of Vladikavkaz, Petrofsk and Tsaritsin — Petrofsk — General Annenkoff on the strategical importance of his railway against India—Incorrect notion of the centre of gravity having been shifted—Importance of Turkistan in Afghan frontier affairs—New independent administration in the Transcaspian — Personal changes—Retirement of General Komaroff Alikhanoff—General Kouropatkin—Appointment of M. Sessar to Bokhara—His opinion of Abdurahman—Military train service—Strategical position of Merv station—Proposal to refill old bed of Oxus from Chardjui—Station of Bokhara—Steam navigation on the Amu Daria—Projected canal—Kara Koul wine—Dismissal of the Khans of Merv.

Russia's Railway Advance.

THE military transport service, owing to the inefficiency of the camel train, has always been one of the weakest points in Russian expeditions into Central Asia. The success of an expedition always depended upon the numbers and health of the camels preserved until the end of the campaign, and proper treatment of these animals was almost impossible during rapid marches through the desert. Even the drivers were of no use unless they belonged to the district where the camels under their care had been born and trained. Khivans could not look after Turkoman camels, nor Turkomans after Khivan camels; and the greatest difficulty was experienced in replacing weak and dead camels by fresh ones, which had to be bought at ever-increasing prices. It was in view of these difficulties that the question of a railway in the Transcaspian was first raised in a practical form by General Skobeleff during the Akhal Tekke Expedition of 1880, and that General Annenkoff, director of the military transports of the Empire, was summoned to the spot to give his advice and assistance. The earlier projectors of a Central Asiatic railway, Lesseps, Beznosikoff, Bogdanovich, and others, who proposed the construction of lines from

Conclusion. 405

Orenburg, or thereabouts, would never have dreamt of their plans being put into execution on the Eastern coast of the Caspian ; and the idea of a railway in this region, although entertained somewhat earlier, did not assume any definite shape until Skobeleff undertook to retrieve the disastrous failures of Lomakin and Tergoukasoff.

At first, it was determined to construct sixty-seven miles of Decauville tramway from Michael's Bay on the Caspian, where soundings proved that with very little labour a sufficient depth of water could be obtained for landing heavy war material ; but the shifting sands along fifteen miles from the coast to Molla Kari would not allow of the Decauville rails being laid down without the expensive work of first clearing a track ; and unfortunately the camels required for transporting the necessary 396 tons of rails could not be spared by the troops of the Expedition. A council was therefore held under General Skobeleff at Chikishliar, at which it was decided to construct seventeen miles of ordinary steam railway over the first and worst part of the way as a temporary expedient for conveying the Decauville rails to Molla Kari, whence the tramway was to be made for about seventy miles farther in the direction of Geok Tepé. At the end of the tramway line the transport service was to be continued by means of camels, whose employment over that part of the road would be facilitated by the copious water supply at Kazandjik. The rails and fastenings were sent from the stock remaining over from the material of the Bender-Galatz Railway after the Bulgarian campaign, at Reni and Ungeni, and four locomotives, twenty-five covered goods vans, and seventy-five platform trucks were also furnished from the Government stores. The estimated cost of the work, about £36,236, was to be taken out of the sum assigned for the expenses of the Expedition. Accordingly, the first seventeen miles of railway ever made in Central Asia were laid down from Michael's Bay to Molla Kari in the short space of ten days, from the 25th of August to the 4th of September, 1880. Only twenty-three miles instead of seventy of the tramway rails were afterwards added to the end of the railway, as the Decauville line was difficult to keep in order. The trucks went off the rails, and caused great delays. The railway, however, was proceeded with along the track of the light narrow-gauge tramway, which it gradually

Conclusion. 407

superseded, and eventually pushed out of use altogether. Thus, at the end of 1880, when Skobeleff was preparing to storm the fortress of Geok Tepé, the triple means of transport from the Caspian consisted of a steam railway, horse tramway (a number of Kirghiz horses having been bought for the same), and camel caravans. The railway was completed as far as Atch-Kuima, about half way to Kizil Arvat, before the end of the campaign, and proved of great service to the Expedition, both in the transport of men and material to the front, and in the evacuation of the sick and wounded.

In principle it had already been decided to continue the railway to Kizil Arvat, at the estimated cost of £289,890, provided the experience of the first twenty-six versts turned out satisfactory. The Grand Duke Michael, then Imperial Lieutenant of the Caucasus, and supreme in authority over the Transcaspian, was greatly in favour of the projected extension; and finally an Imperial decree ordered the supply of all necessary materials for prolonging the line with an allotted sum of £270,100.

In September, 1880, the plant sent *viâ* Astrakhan consisted of 869,000 poods of rails, 34,000 poods of fastenings, six passenger cars, of mixed 2nd and 3rd classes, fifteen goods' locomotives, 275 covered vans, and 225 open trucks. The factories of Pootiloff and Briansk also received orders for 72,172 poods of fastenings, and fifty complete sets of points and crossings. These materials were sent by rail from Nijni Novgorod to the lower Volga for shipment from Tsaritsin and Astrakhan to Michael's Bay by the Kavkaz and Mercury and the Droojina Steamship Companies, and had to be loaded on sailing boats in default of available steamers. Unfortunately, before the cargoes could be all got out into the Caspian they were caught by the freezing of the Volga, and 325,000 poods of rails, 28,000 poods of fastenings, 116 platforms, and 23 waggons had to remain at Astrakhan all through the winter until the spring of 1881.

In addition to these materials, 303,000 sleepers were required for immediate use, but as they could not be all prepared in 1880, it was necessary to purchase all that could be found ready at the Volga saw-mills, to the number of 130,246. Of this quantity the Kavkaz Company succeeded in shipping only 52,568 before the close of the Volga navigation, and consequently 60,667 more had to be obtained with

Conclusion. 409

great difficulty on the Caucasian shore of the Black Sea, and at Baku and Lenkoran. An unsuccessful attempt was made to borrow more from the Transcaucasus Railway Company. Everything possible was done to avoid delay. A couple of coasting steamers, the *Bekctoff* and *Karamzine*, were chartered from the Kavkaz Company for transporting certain building materials from Krasnovodsk to Michael's Bay; and the two unfinished landing-stages at the latter port were lighted with electricity to enable the vessels to discharge at night.

The digging of the track towards Kizil Arvat was begun at once on the completion of the section to Molla Kari, as the Grand Duke Michael had resolved upon proceeding with the line before the receipt of the Imperial sanction, in order to keep the workmen employed. The navvies on the first section were hired and provisioned by a special contractor; but owing to complaints from the men, General Annenkoff afterwards took them under his own charge. They were chiefly Persians, the Russian labourers being only 3 per cent. of the whole number. The average rate of wages paid to the Russians was one rouble, or about two shillings per working day, and to the

Persians, who were engaged at Baku and Astrakhan for terms of three to six months, from seventeen to twenty-two roubles each for every thirty working days. Although naturally lazy and indolent, the Persians did the work very well, thanks to their powers of endurance, the unexacting nature of their requirements in the matter of food, and their capacity for supporting the heat of the climate. On the other hand, their ignorance of the Russian language made it very difficult for the Russian gangers.

The ground work was partly undertaken directly by the managers of the construction, and partly by contractors, at the rate of six roubles, or about twelve shillings per cubic sajene, or 343 cubic feet. This high price was paid in consideration of ignorance of local conditions, absence of water, distance from any population, danger from marauders, etc.

The technical character of the work varied in different localities. Among the sand hills and dunes it was much easier; but the wind often sanded over and destroyed the track before it was half finished, or else blew away the ballast from underneath the rails. This last freak of the wind on one occasion caused

Conclusion. 411

a couple of trains to run off the road. On the hard argillaceous plain pickaxes had to be used ; and when it rained on this kind of ground work became quite impossible. The soil completely dissolved and liquefied to a depth of several feet. One, or, at most, two days afterwards, the surface had again hardened to such a degree that it could not be turned with the spade.

At first there was a good deal of disease among the workmen. Deaths occurred from sunstroke and thirst. The engineers declared it would be their grave, and many of them resigned. It was fully believed that the railway would have to be abandoned; but General Annenkoff stuck to the work, and pushed it on with unflagging energy and determination.

Soon after the capture of Geok Tepé General Annenkoff had to leave the Transcaspian in consequence of a wound received during one of the reconnaissances which preceded the final attack on the fortress, and Prince Khilkoff, who possessed a thorough knowledge of American railways, was left in charge of the work. In October, 1882, Prince Khilkoff became Chief Director, and at once began to give a permanent character to the temporary construction of the first section to Kizil Arvat. He also entered into relations with Khivan and Bokharan merchants for the transport of their cotton into Russia, and with the large manufacturing and trading firms of Moscow, Morozoff and Kanshin, for the introduction of their goods into the Transcaspian. By his initiative caravans were sent to Bokhara through Merv before the latter district was annexed ; a commercial agency was opened at Michael's Bay ; shipping arrangements on the Caspian and Volga were made for the convenience of trade ; petroleum borings were begun in the hills thirty-two versts from Rala Ishem, and a light tramway was laid down to bring the naphtha fuel on to the railway. The Prince also tried the experiment of cotton growing from American and Bokharan seed on a few acres of land at Eedjeri, near the station of Kazandjik. Before carrying out all his plans Prince Khilkoff also left the Transcaspian to occupy the post of Minister of Public Works in Bulgaria, and to draw up a project for the Sistovo-Sofia-Kustendil Railway. A certain Colonel Shebanoff was appointed in his place, and according to General Annenkoff the railway then began to go to rack and ruin. On the 26th July, 1884, an Imperial order went

Conclusion. 413

forth for the further construction of the railway from Kizil Arvat to Askabad, 205 versts, in two years, under the direction of Colonel Shebanoff; but in 1885, after the battle on the Koushk, and in view of probable complications with England, it was decided to extend the line right away to the Amu Daria with all possible haste. General Annenkoff was again called upon to conduct the work, and Colonel Shebanoff became his assistant. Instead of laying down 205 versts to Askabad in twelve months, an Order in Council, dated 1st of June, 1885, commanded the construction of 755 versts, or 503 miles of railroad to the Oxus in the course of a single year. In prosecuting this rapid undertaking General Annenkoff and Colonel Shebanoff were quite unable to get on together. Shebanoff lodged complaints against Annenkoff, which resulted in the appointment of a Commission of Inquiry and the retirement of Colonel Shebanoff. General Annenkoff then got back Prince Khilkoff as his assistant, and succeeded in opening the terminus of the railway at Chardjui, on the Oxus, on the 14th December, 1886. A year and a-half later, in May, 1888, the final section through Bokhara to Samarkand was completed and opened for traffic with a flourish of trumpets throughout Europe.

Up to the present the cost of the railway has been variously estimated. The official figures for the Transcaspian line, that is for the line as far as the Oxus, which is distinct from the Bokharan-Samarkand Railway, have now been printed. The accounts for the 237 miles through Transoxiana to Samarkand have not yet been made up. The following is the account of the first half of the Central Asian Railway as far as the Amu Daria, 782½ versts :—

	Roubles.	kopeks.	per verst.	
Cost of the entire construction, exclusive of rails, fastenings and rolling stock furnished from the Government stores, but including the expense of transporting the same	14,593,887	35	18,649	62
Rails and fastenings—without cost of transport	7,626,366	17	9,745	78
Rolling stock, without cost of transport .	2,563,733	35	3,276	21
Total . . .	24,783,986	87	31,671	61

Conclusion. 415

But the above total includes several items which have nothing to do with the actual construction of the railway, as, for instance :—

	Roubles.	kopeks.
Two river steamers for the Amu Daria	391,486	58
Deepening Michael's Bay, and construction of landing stages	103,461	45
Work on the roads from Askabad to Meshed and Herat	150,000	0
Loss incurred by the overflow of the rivers Zedjent and Murghab in 1886	61,798	7
Total	706,746	10

This sum of 706,746 roubles being deducted from the first total, the actual cost of making the railway to the Amu Daria is 24,077,240 roubles, at 30,768 roubles per verst. The following items included in this total, and expressed in roubles, may be interesting: Expropriations and damage to crops, 42,537; preparation of track, 2,169,881; small bridges, culverts, pipes, etc., of which there are now 396 between Kizil Arvat and the Amu Daria, 663,378; surface construction, 13,154,740; telegraph, 137,819; station buildings, 532,110; water supply for the stations, 321,526; and rolling stock, 3,853,554 roubles. The total cost of the entire railway from the Caspian to

Samarkand, calculating the expenses of making the remaining 237 miles through Bokhara at the rate of the official cost of the Transcaspian half, as set forth in the above statement, would be about 36,000,000 roubles; but owing to the much larger amount paid for expropriation in Bokhara and other extras, the complete total will probably be well over forty millions, or £400,000, to which must be added 300,000 roubles for the cost of bridging across the Amu Daria. Other railways in European Russia have cost from 28,000 to 45,000 roubles per verst. Only the Jabinsk-Pinsk line, also made by General Annenkoff for the Minister of War, cost as low as 16,000 roubles per verst. But no comparison can, of course, be made between these lines and the Central Asian Railway, for which everything, even wood and cement, and workmen had to be brought from places thousands of versts away.

General Annenkoff states that the railway is not only covering its working expenses, but already producing a surplus, which he calculates will represent at the end of 1890 as much as 3 per cent. on the cost of construction. In 1888 the surplus of receipts over 2,500,000 roubles, expended on working the entire line,

Conclusion. 417

was stated to be 109,000 roubles, and in 1889 the surplus over 2,417,317 roubles expenses was given as 300,243 roubles. The weight of the entire traffic in goods during 1889 was 350,674 tons. According to another statement about 100,000 tons more of raw produce from Central Asia should be added to this, although I am inclined to think that the total already includes it. A calculation made by a correspondent of the Russian News Agency shows that during 1889 Central Asian imports into Russia, such as cotton, wool, silk, lamb-skins, dried fruits and corn, had increased 127 per cent. as compared with the imports of 1888, and that the import of Russian sugar and manufactures into the whole of Central Asia, as indicated by the advance in the returns of the railway, had increased 94 per cent. If these figures are correct, and one cannot be too cautious about Russian figures, there can be no doubt that the railway is already a financial success, which, for a Russian military and strategical line, is a very remarkable fact. It has been suggested that the cost of the railway battalions, of the higher military officials, General Annenkoff's salary, etc., are not included in the accounts; but the General assures me that they are; in which case it is evident that Russia's trade with Central Asia, struggling in obsolete fashion along the old caravan roads, was fully ripe for the railway, and in urgent need of the changes now taking place. It remains to be proved by those who assert it, that the demands of trade in Siberia are not also extensive enough to warrant the extension of the Central Asian Railway, as proposed by General Annenkoff, through Tashkent and Semipalatinsk to Omsk, where it would join the projected line from the Urals to Vladivostok on the Pacific. The construction of the Tashkent branch from Samarkand seems to have been indefinitely postponed, like the important line from Vladikavkaz to Petrofsk; but the Central Asian line cannot be considered complete until it reaches Tashkent, which it is bound to do sooner or later. Once it arrives at the official capital of Turkistan, the direction of its further extension would naturally seem to be north-west in a straight line to join the other Russian railways at Orenburg, and thus form a double line of railway communication with Moscow; but it seems that this junction would not be altogether to the advantage of the railway in the Transcaspian. On this account, and probably also

Conclusion. 419

for strategical reasons, which it would serve much better, it is proposed to continue the Central Asian Railway from Tashkent towards the Chinese frontiers, and from Semipalatinsk to Omsk, thus making a wider railway loop from European into Asiatic Russia than would be produced by the direct extension to Orenburg. The latter extension would certainly draw off a good deal of traffic from the Transcaspian line, and deprive it of the complete monopoly of the carrying trade from all parts of Central Asia, which it is now rapidly acquiring. A part of the traffic from Bokhara and Tashkent would almost certainly go over Orenburg in preference to the Transcaspian route, in spite of the much greater distance, simply because direct and uninterrupted railway communication would then be established with Moscow, and the cost and inconvenience of shipment and transhipment on the Caspian and the Volga, as well as the uncertainty of the wooden bridge across the Amu Daria, could be entirely avoided. I may here observe that the small half-wooden bridge on iron pillars across the Tedjent is about to be turned into an entirely iron bridge, but the long wooden bridges across the wide and treacherous current of the Amu Daria are not likely to be superseded by anything more solid and permanent for some time to come. In any case, the construction of a direct railway from Samarkand to Orenburg would create serious competition with the line in the Transcaspian, and soon make a difference in its traffic receipts.

Apart from such competition, the Transcaspian Railway will continue to be isolated and hampered by defective and uncertain communication with the centre of the Empire as long as the Russian railway system is not extended to the west coast of the Caspian. It is very strange that the proposed Vladikavkaz-Petrofsk line, which would accomplish this desired extension, has not yet been taken in hand. Nothing has yet been done beyond repeating surveys and altering plans. The port of Petrofsk rarely freezes, except for a few weeks in very severe winters, and as the terminus of the proposed railway it would be of great importance for military purposes. According to the latest plan, this line is not to start from the terminus at Vladikavkaz, but from the station of Prokladnaia, about sixty miles farther north, which meets with much opposition from the inhabitants of Vladikavkaz, and also from the Chechentsi tribesmen living along the foot of the mountains.

Conclusion. 421

These Chechentsi lately petitioned to have the railway built through their chief town of Grozni, on the main road to Petrofsk. Plans of several other new railways running into the Caucasus from the North are now under discussion. The Central Asian Railway is forcing on the necessity of direct railway communication between Moscow and the Caspian, and between the Russian system of railways and those of the Transcaucasus. The lower Volga route into the Caspian and the Georgian Military Road across the mountains are two inconvenient breaks between the railways of the Transcaspian and the Southern Caucasus which no longer satisfy the necessities of an altered situation. Sooner or later they will have to be discarded in favour of new railways. The inconveniences connected with the Volga will have to be obviated by a railway debouching upon the Caspian in the same way that the winter delays and difficulties which formerly affected the grain trade at the mouth of the river Don have been surmounted by the new railway outlet in the opposite direction at the port of Novorosisk. Besides the projected railway from Vladikavkaz to Petrofsk, which is fully decided upon in principle, and is estimated to cost about eleven millions of roubles, and also the line to be cut some day through the centre of the mountains to Tiflis, with about twenty-seven miles of difficult tunnelling, it has been proposed to join the railways of the Transcaucasus to those of the rest of the Empire by lines at both ends of the range skirting the Black and Caspian Seas. Projects are being discussed for a line to branch off from the Vladikavkaz-Novorosisk Railway below Stavropol and run through the mountain valleys to join the Batoum-Tiflis Railway at Gori or thereabouts, also for a branch from the Batoum line to Soukhoum Kale on the Black Sea, and thence to join the line to Novorosisk. But these proposed railways on the West are comparatively unnecessary, and in view of the existing railway *débouché* at Novorosisk would hardly be profitable undertakings; while quite the contrary would be the case with the proposed lines to the Caspian basin on the Eastern flank of the Caucasus. In regard to these, the *Kavkaz* newspaper of Tiflis, which is a great authority on the subject, advocates the two lines of Tsaritsin-Petrofsk and Vladikavkaz-Petrofsk. From the junction of these two railways on the coast of the Caspian an extension could be

Conclusion. 423

easily made to Derbent and Baku, and eventually on to the Persian frontier to meet the contemplated Persian railway from Teheran. In winter, when the mouth of the Volga is frozen, goods landed at Petrofsk and conveyed by rail to Tsaritsin, which is already connected with the entire railway system of Russia, would gain 220 miles over the route up the Volga. Similar and pretty equal advantages in this respect would be afforded by the other line from Petrofsk to Vladikavkaz. As to possible competition between these two lines in the carrying trade between Moscow and the Caspian—a form of progress which the Russian Government tries to prevent among railways as in everything else—this would be counteracted by both lines running through, and tapping fertile, grain-producing territories as large as one or two of the countries of Europe.

It must not be supposed that General Annenkoff, with all his concern for the commercial success of his famous railway, has forgotten the connexion of its military and strategical importance with Russia's power of threatening India. The General is actuated by the friendliest feelings towards England and Englishmen, and would gladly see a junction of railways and frontiers, and an alliance between England and Russia all the world over, but not to the detriment of the political and military advantages gained by Russia's railway advance towards India. No Russian authority can afford to ignore this important element in the situation without laying himself open to the suspicion of being indifferent to the vital interests of the Empire. The use of the Central Asian position as a means of menacing and disturbing India, if not of actually attacking or conquering it, has now become a traditional and fixed principle of Russian policy, and Russian official writers on Central Asia can no more omit the subject of India from their reports to headquarters than Mr. Dick in "David Copperfield" could keep Charles the First out of his petitions to the Lord Chancellor. The idea of Central Asian pressure upon India having been introduced as an auxiliary factor in a Russian solution of the Eastern Question, the subject has thus been brought nearer home to Russians as well as Englishmen. Attempts are often made to palliate the real danger of an invasion of India by the consideration that a conquest of India is a mere chimera, but a successful invasion would very soon change the chimera into a feasible possibility.

Conclusion. 425

In one of his reports General Annenkoff thus refers to this sword of Damocles, which his railway is to help in suspending over the British in India in order to keep them on their good behaviour towards Russia in Europe : " Henceforth the Transcaspian region—the theatre of future events of universal importance, —will be a reliable forepost, whence Russia may successfully counteract the hostile designs of England. Russian troops from the bases of Kazan or the Caucasus have only 360 versts from the Tedjent station to Herat, 430 versts from Herat to Kandahar, 200 from Kandahar to Quetta, and 320 from Quetta to the valley of the Indus, altogether 1,310 versts or 816 mile . (This distance has been somewhat reduced by the further extension of the Indian railways.) The troops of Turkistan, in order to reach the same destination, have only 1,290 versts to go from the station of Merv. At the same time, from the Russian outpost of Kelif on the Amu Daria, which is now directly united with the railway by regular steam navigation, there are only 400 versts to Cabul, and thence less than 300 versts to Peshawur, from which point the Indian railways would convey a conquering army into the very heart of India."

It will thus be seen that the troops of Turkistan, who would have a shorter distance to traverse on their way to India than those of the neighbouring province, are called upon to play as important a part on the Afghan frontiers as the troops of the Transcaspian. The Governor-General at Tashkent is therefore not less concerned in the matter than his colleague, the Governor-General at Askabad. The notion so much harped upon by verbose politicians, as to the centre of gravity having been shifted from Tashkent to Askabad, is by no means correct. Before the railway reached Samarkand there was perhaps some reason for this view, but since Turkistan and the Transcaspian have been united by the railway through Bokhara, and especially since the detachment of the Transcaspian from the administration of the Caucasus, there are in reality two centres, both exercising pretty equal control over affairs on the Afghan frontiers. When the railway is extended to Tashkent this will become still more evident. At present the troops from Tashkent can be put upon the railway at Samarkand, a distance of about 190 miles, in a day or two. Both sides of the Amu Daria as far as the frontiers of Khiva, with the whole of Bokhara, are under the authority of

Conclusion. 427

Tashkent, and the Rifle Battalions of Turkistan, and not those of the Transcaspian, form the garrisons at Chardjui and the important outpost of Kerki and Kelif on the Afghan frontier.

The independent administration now established in the Transcaspian places that province on the same footing as Turkistan, but does not introduce any essential alteration in the methods of government hitherto pursued. There will be changes only in minor details, increased numbers of officials, increase of expenses, of salaries, —the latter being very much needed—and so forth. The conduct of diplomatic affairs, which consists in gathering information about Afghanistan and other border territories, and in holding direct communication with the Foreign Office in St. Petersburg, will be nothing new. Mr. Lessar, before he became Russian Consul at Liverpool, assisted General Komaroff as Diplomatic Agent, and did exactly what is required in this respect by the new regulations. The allowance for life of 1,200 roubles a year to each of the four Khans of Merv is simply a confirmation of the 100 roubles per month hitherto paid to the Khans as officers in the Russian service. The separate organization of the Transcaspian is a *voyenno-narodnaia* administration, or a combination of military and popular government, consisting of exclusive military control over native laws and customs accepted and upheld within the bounds of Russian interests. This is exactly what it was before while subordinate to a similar kind of rule in the Caucasus. Such form of government is peculiar to all the Asiatic confines of the Empire during their first experience of Russian authority. Therefore the change effected by the new regulations simply resolves itself into the administrative separation of the Transcaspian from the Caucasus. Russian Justices of the Peace have been appointed at Chardjui for the trial of Russian cases, but disputes between Russians and Bokharans will continue to go before the Russian Diplomatic Agent accredited to the Ameer.

Far more personal changes have taken place, for reasons already referred to, in the higher posts of the administration. General Komaroff has retired in the midst of a storm of accusations and counter-charges among his subordinates, and intends to reside at Samarkand or Tiflis pending the report of the Special Commission, which, it is believed, will exonerate him from all blame. Russians have forgotten for the time his great services in annexing Merv

Conclusion. 429

and raising Russian prestige by the battle on the Koushk, but there is every reason to suppose that his only crime is the amiable one of having been too good natured towards less scrupulous officials under him. Colonel Alikhanoff has also retired to the Caucasus during the investigation of the Commission. It is reported that his reputation has already been virtually cleared by the discovery of an order of his assistant and denouncer, Captain Kozloff, awarding the same corporal punishment which he accused his chief, Alikhanoff, of meting out to the Turkomans. The whole affair is a striking and scandalous repetition of the state of things which Mr. Schuyler disclosed in Turkistan fifteen years ago.

The new Governor-General of the Transcaspian, Lieutenant-General Kooropatkin, is already well known in England as having been the right-hand man of Skobeleff, and as the principal candidate for the chief command of a possible Russian army against India. His reputation as an authority on Central Asia is deservedly high. In 1874 he followed the French Expedition in Algeria; subsequently took part in the conquest of Khokand under Skobeleff; was sent in charge of an embassy to Yakub Bek at Kashgar; acted as Skobeleff's chief of staff during the campaign in Bulgaria; afterwards took charge of the Asiatic section of the Grand Staff, and was despatched in 1880 to fortify part of the frontier against China, whence he marched his detachment 466 miles through the deserts to join the Akhal Tekke Expedition. He has been several times wounded in battle. In personal appearance he is not much taller than General Komaroff, and hardly presents a more soldierly figure. His talents and experience are beyond question, and his presence in the Transcaspian as Governor-General and Commander-in-Chief is of great importance. It is stated that he holds a very high opinion of Alikhanoff, and provided the latter's reputation survives the Commission, he hopes to be able to induce him to return to Merv.

The next important change is the appointment of Mr. Lessar in the place of Mr. Charikoff as Diplomatic Agent in Bokhara. Mr. Lessar, who is an indefatigable worker, and does not let the grass grow under his feet, is in the habit of keeping a sharp look-out on all that goes on in Afghanistan and India. On the eve of starting for his new post he professes to be perfectly well aware of the doings and private views of the Indian Government regarding Afghanistan.

Conclusion. 431

Abdurahman's position is considered exceedngly precarious, as proved by three attempts made upon his life, and by his long stay at Mazar-i-Sherif for fear of returning to Cabul. It appears also that he and the Indian authorities are at variance on the subject of further conquests, and the disagreement may at some time or other become serious. The Ameer's ambition is to conquer several small territories on the North East, which are claimed as directly dependent upon India. Among the alleged preconcerted plans of the Indian authorities in the event of serious trouble with Russia, Mr. Lessar, like other Russian authorities, seems to believe in the existence of one for working upon the religious fanaticism of the anti-Russian faction in Bokhara.

It would be a fair proposition to make to the Russian Government that one or two British Consuls should be allowed to reside in the Transcaspian and Bokhara in return for compliance with Russia's expressed wish to maintain Consuls in India. Russia could hardly ask to have her Consuls in Afghanistan in exchange for a British Consul in Bokhara, seeing that the Afghan Ameer refuses to receive a single representative Englishman.

A few notes omitted from previous chapters may here be inserted.

It has been stated somewhere that General Annenkoff has calculated for twelve pairs of military trains every twenty-four hours. The real number is six pairs, or twelve trains, and one pair of service trains.

I find the following official explanation of locating the station of Merv on the left bank of the Murghab, where there is risk of inundation. This station was built on the left and lower side of the river for strategical reasons; principally because being the only large station between the Tedjent and the Murghab, with rolling stock kept ready, it could always be used by troops moving on to the Afghan frontier when both bridges across the Tedjent and the Murghab might be destroyed or out of repair. Had it been placed on the Eastern bank of the Murghab, in case of the bridge being rendered unavailable, the troops of the Transcaspian would be unable to make use of it.

A gradual fall in the level of the country from the Amu Daria to the Caspian, as shown by the gradients of the railway, is a new argument for more learned discussion in the possibility of deflecting the waters of the Oxus,

Conclusion. 433

especially through the old channel from Chardjui. All the railway stations from Merv to Askabad are lower than the Murghab, which is unfortunate for the railway in case of inundation. On the other hand, it favours the latest project of turning the waters of the Oxus into the Caspian, which a number of scientific theorists seem determined at all cost to advocate, if only in order to have a waterway to compete with Annenkoff's railroad. Probably the new irrigation work of Mr. Poklefsky will render this more than ever impracticable.

The damage caused to the railway in 1886 by the great flood at Merv was partly due to the Alikhanoff canal, which runs for some distance parallel with the line. The average depth of water in the Murghab is about four feet, but sometimes reaches fourteen. The station of Dort Kuyu, about thirty-two miles west of Merv, is 100 feet lower. An official report apologizes for the disaster of 1886 in a way that reminds one of the favourite pretexts for Russian claims on next-door neighbours who hold possession of the sources of rivers running into Russian territory.

"We cannot be reproached," writes a local official in his report to St. Petersburg, "with the inundation and damage caused by the Murghab, which was only annexed in 1884, and which cannot be properly explored or regulated, because it runs for the most part through the territory of hostile Afghans."

Complaints are made by travellers over the Transcaspian Railway of the inconvenient distance (ten miles) of the Bokharan station from the native capital. The nucleus of a future Russian town round the station has made less progress than was at first expected. Some of the Russian merchants have even sold out land on which they intended to build, because business has to be transacted in the city itself, and a daily ride of thirty versts from the station and back over a wretchedly bad road, as long as any kind of accommodation can be had in the Bokharan metropolis, is not appreciated. Ten versts farther eastward the railway runs within five versts of the city, which can be seen from the train. Annenkoff and other officials find it more convenient to take horses from this point; and yet the half station here has been abolished, and the principal one built fifteen versts off from the town. The Dragoman of the Russian Agency in Bokhara prefers to drive twenty

Conclusion. 435

versts to meet the train at the station of Yakatut in the direction of Chardjui.

There is now a regular service of the two steamboats on the Amu Daria between Chardjui and Kerki, the trip being made in three days one way and four days the other, steaming only in the daytime. Nocturnal navigation of the river is too dangerous. A report has appeared of a proposed steamboat company for the Amu Daria, to be called " The Orient," with a capital of five millions of roubles.

Many other brilliant projects as well as airy castles for increasing the prosperity of the region are constantly kept before the public. General Annenkoff, for instance, proposes a new canal to Kara Koul between the Zarafshau and the Oxus, which he has endeavoured to get the Bokharans to construct at their own expense under his direction. Failing the attraction of this proposal, he has begun to produce excellent native wine at Kara Koul, and has just sent samples of it to his friends in India.

The latest consequence of the investigation at present proceeding in the Transcaspian is the dismissal of the four celebrated Khans of Merv from their posts as chief administrators of the four tribes, and the appointment of Russian officers in their stead. This confirms the account of Turkoman discontent with these native leaders. In all other respects the native administration remains as before. Turkoman Khans still command in the militia, and the four Khans of Merv will continue to receive their pay. Hitherto they have administered with the aid of Russian officers as assistants; henceforth they themselves will probably have to perform the part of assistants, unless set aside altogether. I asked a well-known authority what these four chieftains would now do, and whether they might not become troublesome; and the answer was that they would most likely spend the rest of their lives in card-playing and drinking.

APPENDIX.

For the use of intending travellers to Samarkand I subjoin a few particulars from the time-tables, compiled by order of General Annenkoff, in connexion with the principal railway centres of Europe.

The shortest possible time has of course been put down for the journey over each route, and implies the exact meeting between trains and steamboats, which, as far as Russia is concerned, is not always to be absolutely depended upon. In one case the traveller from Paris has been allowed only five minutes to go several miles through the streets of St. Petersburg from the Warsaw Railway terminus to catch the night train to Moscow, which is of course an impossibility. Allowances must therefore be made for little extravagances of this kind; and it would be advisable for the sake of convenience to reckon a day or two more than the time given in the tables.

The following are the main railway routes, with the time occupied in travelling over each :—

1. St. Petersburg, Moscow, Tsaritsin, Baku, Samarkand, 10 days, 23 hours, 30 minutes. This is the

Appendix.

Volga route. The steamer starts from Tsaritsin on Thursdays and Saturdays, and touches at Baku on the way to Oozoon Ada.

2. Paris, Cologne, Berlin, St. Petersburg, Moscow, Rostoff, Novorosisk, Batoum, Baku, Samarkand, 12 days, 22 hours, 34 minutes. By this route the main chain of the Caucasus is avoided in a rather roundabout way, which includes a short sea voyage from Novorosisk to Batoum. Steamers start from Novorosisk on Mondays and Thursdays.

3. St. Petersburg, Moscow, Orel, Sevastopol, Batoum, Baku, Samarkand, 12 days, 10 hours, 30 minutes. Over this route the traveller goes through the Crimea and the Black Sea. The steamers start from Sevastopol on Tuesdays, Fridays and Sundays.

4. St. Petersburg, Moscow, Rostoff, Vladikavkaz, Tiflis, Baku, Samarkand, 10 days, 1 hour, 20 minutes. This includes a trip by post horses across the mountains over the Georgian Military Road to join the railway between Tiflis and Baku.

5. Paris, Vienna, Warsaw, Moscow, Rostoff, Novorosisk, Batoum, Baku, Samarkand, 12 days, 23 hours. By this road Poland is traversed and St. Petersburg avoided.

6. Paris, Vienna, Odessa, Batoum, Baku, Samarkand, 10 days, 10 hours, 9 minutes. This is the shortest and quickest route from Paris. Steamboats start from Odessa on Mondays, Thursdays, and Saturdays.

The journey over the Transcaspian Railway from the Caspian to Samarkand occupies by the post train,

Appendix.

which runs twice a week (Tuesdays and Saturdays), 63 hours, 15 minutes—10 hours 33 minutes of which are lost in stoppages. The mixed goods and passenger train which runs every day takes 87 hours, 55 minutes, including stoppages of altogether 20 hours 19 minutes.

Woodfall & Kinder, Printers, 70 to 76, Long Acre, London, W.C.